Contesting Post-Racialism

Contesting Post-Racialism

Conflicted Churches in the United States and South Africa

Edited by R. Drew Smith, William Ackah,
Anthony G. Reddie, and Rothney S. Tshaka

University Press of Mississippi / Jackson

www.upress.state.ms.us

The University Press of Mississippi is a member
of the Association of American University Presses.

First printing 2015

∞

Library of Congress Cataloging-in-Publication Data

Contesting post-racialism : conflicted churches in the United States and South Africa /
edited by R. Drew Smith, William Ackah, Anthony G. Reddie, Rothney S. Tshaka.
pages cm
Includes index.
ISBN 978-1-62846-200-5 (cloth : alk. paper) — ISBN 978-1-62674-505-6 (ebook) 1. Race
relations—Religious aspects—Christianity. 2. South Africa—Race relations. 3. United
States—Race relations. 4. Church and social problems—South Africa. 5. Church and social
problems—United States. 6. Post-racialism. I. Smith, R. Drew, 1956– editor of compilation.
II. Ackah, William, editor of compilation. III. Reddie, Anthony, editor of compilation. IV.
Tshaka, Rothney S. (Rothney Stok), editor of compilation.
BT734.2.T74 2015

261.8328496—dc23   2014031673

British Library Cataloging-in-Publication Data available

Contents

IV. Theology and (Re)Vitalized Race Consciousness

V. Concluding Thoughts

Acknowledgments

Many persons have contributed to the production of this volume, and we are deeply gratefully for each contribution. Our thanks goes especially to those who contributed chapters to the volume, but also to all the conference participants who served as interlocutors when these chapters were presented at the 2011 Transatlantic Roundtable on Religion and Race (TRRR) conference at University of South Africa, and at the 2012 TRRR conference at University of London, Birkbeck College. We also want to acknowledge the generous support provided for these conferences by the University of South Africa's College of Human Sciences and Department of Philosophy, Practical and Systematic Theology, and by Birkbeck College's Department of Geography, Environment, and Development Studies. We are also indebted to Craig Gill at University Press of Mississippi for his interest in the research we assembled in this volume and for shepherding the volume through to publication. We are most indebted to the persons and groups discussed in these chapters whose grapplings with intersections of religion and race have provided cautions, critiques, and crosswalks for those caught at the crossings.

Contesting Post-Racialism

Introduction

R. Drew Smith

Against the backdrop of the 2008 election and 2012 re-election of Barack Obama as president of the United States, and the 1994 election of Nelson Mandela as the first of several blacks to serve as South Africa's president, many within the two countries have declared race to be an irrelevant social distinction within their societies. The formal narrative has shifted, some say, and while there are still those proceeding slowly—or not at all—into this new day, there can be no doubt as to its dawning. Witness not only historic black political and other professional achievements within the two countries, but also the new interactions of people of all colors easily and confidently working together, sharing neighborhoods, and intermarrying. As some argue, these kinds of indicators point to the arrival of a post-racial maturing of historically racialized countries, with the United States and South Africa (the leading purveyors of racial hierarchy) taking great strides to distance themselves from their respective tortured racial histories.

The presumed demise of race may be a premature conclusion. So long as blacks are disproportionately subject to high levels of poverty, homelessness, incarceration, school incompletion, unemployment, and medically preventable deaths, race remains relevant as a category of social explanation—especially given the historical role racial distinctions played in establishing social trajectories contributing to these outcomes. Blacks in the United States and South Africa do indeed continue to fare significantly worse than whites along almost all quality-of-life indices. In the United States, the 2010 poverty rate for blacks was 27 percent, compared to 9 percent for whites; black unemployment was almost 16 percent, compared with 8 percent for whites; and the secondary school four-year graduation rate was 52 percent for black males, compared with 78 percent for white males. In South Africa, black household income was 16 percent of white household income in 2011; the 2013 black unemployment rate was almost 29 percent, compared with 7 percent for whites; and in ninety-five of the nation's poorest (primarily black) schools, only 20 percent of students passed the secondary school graduation exam, whereas only five of the nation's wealthiest schools produced such low rates. Despite these grim realities, it has become more difficult to articulate race-related dimensions of these problems due. Increasingly, "race" has been deemed unacceptable as a social distinction and explanatory category within self-consciously "post-racial" contexts. Although attempts to move beyond artificial racial constructs may be laudable, the legacy of hundreds of years of race-based social policies and structures persists. While not completely explaining present-day black social realities, this legacy cannot be ignored in accounting for these realities.

The United States and South Africa have quite some distance to travel to move beyond their respective pasts, which included racial distinctions written into formal policies and the popular consciousness for much of their history as nations. In the United States, that history included centuries of black enslavement, which was not abolished until the 1863 Emancipation Proclamation declared slavery illegal in the slaveholding states of the South—and ultimately did not become the law of the land until the 1865 surrender of the Confederacy. It would be another one hundred years before the Civil Rights Act of 1964 and the Voting Rights Act of 1965 officially ended most of the overt forms of formalized racial segregation put into place after slavery to prolong systematic black oppression and marginalization. The South African context was characterized by a somewhat shorter period of slavery and a longer period of systematic racial oppression and pauperization. The Dutch began selling persons mainly from south Asia and east Africa into slavery in the Cape region of South Africa in 1653, and slavery was not formally abolished in the Cape until the Slavery Abolition Act of 1833. A series of laws and practices were enacted after slavery ended and into the early-1900s imposed indentured servitude and other forms of economic servitude on blacks, Asians, and coloureds, also severely constricting their residential patterns, freedom of movement, and general social mobility. These forms of oppression became more systematic and severe with the enactment in 1948 of the apartheid policies that accompanied the Afrikaner rise to national political power, lasting until South Africa's democratic transformation in 1994.

Perverse and inverse racial patterns of social development were clearly in operation throughout the racial histories of both countries. As whites became wealthier, blacks became poorer; as whites were empowered, blacks grew more disempowered; as whites became structurally and institutionally entrenched, blacks became increasingly marginalized; as whiteness became the standard for superiority, blackness became the standard for inferiority. Although black existential prospects were never fully determined by white actions, blacks paid a steep price in lost life, brutalization, and dehumanization, and in opportunities diminished, discouraged, and denied. Within both countries, during these long, tragic periods, many whites eagerly embraced race as a rationalization for the unequal social treatment of blacks—though not as an explanation for the unequal social performance of blacks vis-à-vis whites.

In the US context, white racial rationalizations and sociological explanations encountered formal setbacks owing to policy decisions made during the civil rights movement, including the Supreme Court's 1954 ruling in *Brown v. Board of Education*, which rejected the notion that there could be equality of resources and opportunity between segregated white and black school systems. And the 1964 Civil Rights Act addressed as an inherent contradiction the fact that rights and privileges that had not been made available to all of American society were nonetheless enjoyed by some. This formal acknowledgment of racial bias in public policy as a causative factor in race-specific social development constituted a brief moment of mental clarity in America's public narrative—one that clouded over by the early 1970s, as affirmative action and other racial preference policies, intended to correct America's history of racial discrimination, came under systematic attack. The public narrative shifted back to denials of American racial policy and history as causative in race-specific social development—even as black progress was slowed by subtle forms of "institutionalized racism" and by occasional forms of overt racism. In the later years of the twentieth century, cumulative and residual effects of racism exacted what historian Roger Wilkins referred to as a "fierce psychic (and I would add, social) black tax." Among middle-class blacks, post-civil rights movement vacillations on race engendered a creeping cynicism about the American social project, while producing a thorough rejection of that social project among the burgeoning black poor.

Barack Obama's emergence in 2008 as a wildly popular presidential candidate shifts the script for many reasons—the most obvious being the enthusiasm Obama's candidacy generated among diverse constituencies representing various sides of America's public narrative and counter-narratives. On the one hand, with his African roots, his proudly African American wife, and his subtle black church and black hip-hop affectations, Obama was unmistakably black. On the other hand, Obama's mixed-race heritage, together with his campaign rhetoric submerging social differences beneath a goal of becoming "one America," conferred a racial transcendency on Obama and his candidacy. These "post-racial" aspects of Obama's candidacy resonated for many Americans and helped pave a path to Obama's nomination and election, which some believed might finally put to rest the issue of race in American life.

For the most part, race-conscious African American leaders winked at post-racial characterizations, accepting them as strategies for solidifying a broad base for Obama's candidacy and post-election presidency. Not all black leaders, though, accommodated post-racial talk, as evidenced by the clash between Obama and Rev. Jeremiah Wright during the presidential primaries, and in pointed criticisms leveled more recently at Obama's policies by Princeton University religion scholars Cornel West and Eddie Glaude. Owing to his Afrocentric—and, according to some, anti-American—views, Wright, the long-serving pastor of Trinity United Church of Christ in Chicago (where the Obamas had been members for several years), became a target of conservative critics during the presidential primaries. These critics hoped to use Obama's Trinity Church affiliation and close relationship with Wright as a basis for undermining Obama's post-racial, all-American image. Owing to the intense focus on a series of potentially inflammatory sound bites culled from Wright's public pronouncements, Obama eventually disassociated himself from the pastor and from Trinity Church. The clash between Obama and Wright brought into view some prominent African American race leaders' strong objections to efforts to gloss over the significance of race in contemporary American life.

Cornel West harshly criticized Obama's perceived failures in advancing urgent black policy interests or a policy agenda generally premised on social justice. West, who endorsed and actively campaigned for Obama during the campaign season, stated in 2011 that Obama had turned out to be "a black puppet of corporate plutocrats," someone "who wanted to reassure the establishment," rather than pursue progressive politics on behalf of the poor. Eddie Glaude shared concerns about an Obama policy agenda that seemed unwilling to grapple seriously with racial factors owing to what Glaude said was fear that "any effort to address the suffering of black communities directly would trigger deep-seated prejudices that still animate American life" and shift America "even farther to the right." Acting upon this premise, Obama and Congress, said Glaude, "don't have to deliver 'the goods' because any race-specific policies are rejected out of hand as holdovers from a time long gone." Meanwhile, Glaude concluded, "black suffering [is banished] from public view."[1] Glaude's remark that post-racial framings of the public space banish black suffering from view seems on point, but in a broader sense it can be said that post-racial framings limit our ability even to discuss social implications and public policy ramifications of race.

As a result of the 1996 constitutional encodings of post-racialism, and the high-profile articulations and embodiments of post-racialism by luminaries such as Nelson Mandela and Desmond Tutu, in South African post-racialism has achieved a greater level of formalization and mainstreaming than in the United States. In this context, some of the harshest criticisms of post-racialism within South Africa have come not from persons panning it as overblown, but rather from persons accusing the ruling African National Congress (ANC) government of being insufficiently committed to the idea. For example, in a recent publication by George Devenish, a white South African professor of law who assisted in drafting the 1994 interim constitution, champions post-racialism as "a golden thread . . . woven into [the South African] constitution" and a "fundamental principle . . . of a true humanity," which he suggests is being violated by certain leaders of the ANC. He warns against a "racial nationalism" he sees as "gaining support in the ANC," and argues that "racial nationalism, by its very nature, is the antithesis of non-racialism."[2] Similarly, spokespersons for South Africa's leading opposition party, a predominantly white party called the Democratic Alliance (DA), charges the ANC with reverting to "narrow racial nationalism", in contrast to the DA's efforts at creating a "rainbow nation."[3] Meanwhile, the DA has been promoting a younger generation black South African woman, Lindiwe Mazibuku, as an "Obama-style, post-racial" standard bearer for the party in the hope that Mazibuku will be able to mount "a serious challenge" to the ANC in the 2014 election.[4]

A prime target of proponents of post-racialism has been the now suspended ANC Youth League president, Julius Malema, whose fondness for singing the former struggle song "Shoot the Boer," calls for nationalization of South Africa's mining industry and land redistribution, and racial mocking of ANC opponents has made him a darling of younger generation blacks and a nemesis of the political and corporate establishment. Malema seems especially contemptuous of post-racial ideals, referring to Mazibuku as a "tea girl" of white opposition politicians and countering the forgiveness ideal Mandela bequeathed to the country with a new call to black South Africans to never forget what was done to them. Malema is not alone in questioning South Africa's post-racial standard. Even Desmond Tutu, one of the persons most associated with the rainbow nation concept, has been outspoken in criticizing not the post-racial ideal, but its application within a context where overwhelming numbers of blacks continue to be afflicted with grinding poverty. South African theologian Barney Pityana quite explicitly questioned post-racial characterizations of South African society, stating, "We talk all the time about how we are a multi-racial, multi-cultural, multi-lingual and multi-religious society, but how do we take these facts seriously? In reality all other cultures are subservient, or what the African-Americans call 'subaltern', to the dominant hegemonic cultures in our society."[5]

Just as there are competing American and South African assessments about the continued relevance of race, there are competing assessments of the issue within both countries' church sectors. A study summarizing survey data on Christian racial tolerance in the United States, for example, showed that roughly two-thirds of churchgoers expressed strong racial prejudice, as compared with roughly half of non-churchgoing respondents. The study also showed that liberal Christians were only slightly less racially prejudiced than conservative Christians, with liberals professing racial tolerance while practicing intolerance.[6] The gap between principle and practice is an important inconsistency, but there are also major inconsistencies among Christians in both countries as to fundamental understanding of social functions and institutional embodiments of race.

This volume engages post-racial ideas in both their limitations and their promise, while looking specifically at the extent to which contemporary church responses to race consciousness and post-racial consciousness enable churches to advance an accurate public accounting of the social implications of race. Contributors examine Christian institutional and intellectual frameworks in the United States and in South Africa, focusing mainly on post-movement contexts within the two countries—meaning essentially since 1968 in the United States, and since 1994 in South Africa.

Central to the inquiry is whether churches operate from analytical frameworks, leadership approaches, and programmatic emphases that realistically and usefully grapple with race. The contributors to this volume are largely in agreement about the persistence of racially-conditioned social landscapes within their respective American and South African contexts—despite the emergence of any "official" narratives to the contrary within those contexts. Variances between the chapters are evident mainly with respect to whether acknowledgments of race in the situations under examination are sufficiently far-reaching, well-aimed, and critically examined to overcome the more distorted, injurious, and manipulative ways race has often functioned. The volume opens with a chapter by Allan Boesak, followed by another written by Walter Fluker, both of which track evolving ideological permutations of racial thought over several decades within their respective South African and American socio-religious contexts. Both examine ways that race endures as a social currency in ongoing negotiations over identity and social and religious purpose within those contexts. The second section of the volume examines church responses to institutionalized racism and racial injustices—in some instances faulting churches for racially or sometimes ecclesiastically self-interested approaches that have perpetuated racial antagonisms, and in others applauding churches for helpful and sometimes courageous racial correctives.

Chapters in section three explore ways religious cultures of the socially empowered have dulled rather than sharpened the sensitivities of the empowered to the injuries and indignities of race (in segregationist twentieth-century America and contemporary South Africa), and of class (with regard to contemporary South African youth demands for economic justice). These concerns with religious and racial "perspectivism" are also central to chapters in the fourth and the concluding sections, with several of these chapters making a case for race-consciousness as a social resource—at least to the extent that race-consciousness aligns with progressive traditions premised on social justice.

Overall, the volume provides little support for the idea that a post-racial era has dawned—or soon will—in the United States and South Africa. The volume does lend support, however, to calls for liberating persons and institutions from imprisoning racial constructions, whether imposed from outside one's group or from inside, while wrestling with the tensions between racially-grounded approaches that account for black suffering and racially-transcending approaches that point (theologically and anthropologically) beyond the socially-constructed self.[7]

Notes

1. Eddie Glaude Jr., "Black Critics and President Obama," *Root* (May 23, 2011).

2. George Devenish, "South Africa Must Embrace Non-Racialism," *Herald* (June 24, 2011).

3. Carien du Plessis, "Put Racial Politics Behind You—Zille," *Cape Time* (March 29, 2011).

4. South African Civil Society Information Service, "Mazibuku and Malema—New Profiles, Re-Shuffling Social Forces," *Africa News* (November 4, 2011).

5. Barney Pityana, "What is Racism?," seminar on What is Racism? (Johannesburg, July 25, 2001).

6. Deborah Hall et al., "Why Don't We Practice What We Preach? A Meta-Analytic View of Religious Racism," *Personality and Social Psychology Review* 14, no. 1 (2010): 126–39.

7. As comparison, see analysis by Willie James Jennings, *The Christian Imagination: Theology and the Origins of Race* (New Haven: Yale University Press, 2010).

I. Periodizing the Discourse on Black Christianity and Race

A Restless Presence: Church Activism and "Post-Apartheid," "Post-Racial" Challenges

Allan Boesak

Church Activism?

In this essay I propose to discuss my understanding of "church activism," visiting historical contexts of such activism before discussing church activism in post-apartheid times. Throughout I shall argue that the "church activism" we are speaking of is not the institutional church, but what Martin Luther King Jr. called "the church within the church, a true ecclesia and the hope of the world,"[1] driven by a radical gospel of justice, hope, and liberation.

Colonial conquest of South Africa in the middle of the seventeenth century brought with it racism, dispossession of the land, exploitation, dehumanization, oppression, slavery, and genocide. With conquest came western Christianity, which was central to the colonialist project and the global outreach of western imperialism. But simultaneous with colonialization was the birth of the first signs of church activism, by which is meant the prophetic engagement of Christians in public witnessing and action on the basis of their faith, and on behalf of dispossessed, enslaved, and oppressed communities imagining an alternative future.[2]

Three observations must be made. First, the recognized church was the established church, deeply rooted in Europe, and its ecclesial, cultural and political traditions were those of the white settler and slave owner. Alternatively, there was the church as represented by the oppressed and colonized, and by those seeking identification with the colonized, who saw in the gospel a call to recognize the situation of oppression, to heed the voice of the oppressed, and to seek justice for the oppressed. Second, from the beginning there were two manifestations of the church, two readings and understandings of the gospel, and two applications of the gospel to public life. Thus two hermeneutical constructs became clear: a hermeneutic of oppression and possession, and a hermeneutic of protest and liberation. Third, two understandings of the role of the church and of Christians in public affairs arose. These understandings were underpinned on the one hand by a theology of conquest, appropriation and justification, and on the other by a theology of prophetic challenge and resistance.

This distinction has persisted throughout South Africa's history, and it has found expression in every era, sometimes in movements, and sometimes in courageous, faithful individuals who carried the torch for prophetic Christian witness in South Africa.[3] There was the church that lived in the center, benefitting from conquest and enslavement, and there was the church on the margins, seeking to resist both the enslavement of people and the appropriation of the gospel for that enslavement. In both, the church was actively involved—on one side for the establishment, maintenance, and justification of imperial and colonial designs, and on the other for the sake of justice and rights of the colonized.

The one church saw itself as a "church" because it was recognized as such by the state, clothing itself with ecclesial power, and more often than not allied with political power and with the power of tradition. The other church, representing the powerless and destitute, did not claim any alliance with or protection from earthly power. In fact, this church almost always found itself resisting political power, including ecclesial power structures. It found its strength precisely in its powerlessness, recognizing in that powerlessness more of the church which first presented itself to the world in the followers of Jesus of Nazareth, arrayed against the realities and pressures of the Roman Empire. It is the ecclesial tradition of the first-century church that the contemporary Christianity of the destitute and powerless seeks to emulate, rather than the tradition of throne and alter that became the hallmark of Christianity during the Constantinian era. The Christianity of the destitute and powerless glorified the holiness of God in the sanctuary as well as in the streets of protest, discerning the signs of the times through the eyes of the suffering children of God.

Charles Villa-Vicencio spoke of these last-mentioned Christians within as "a restless presence that has disturbed the church."[4] The "restless presence" we are speaking of here is not the institutional church as a whole, but the prophetic church—an alternative to the Christianity of the established church, a church in tension with and in resistance to both society with its systematic injustices, and the dominant church with its embedded, privileged complacency. This alternative Christian approach is the difference between those who always seek ways to negotiate with the hegemonic powers that rule society and those drawn to and gathered around Jesus of Nazareth, the defender of the poor and powerless, the revolutionary teacher who exposed and resisted the established powers of the palace and the temple, who was rejected and crucified by those powers on the cross of an occupying power. Like him, they live in resistance on the margins of the institutional church and of society, representing a radical rather than an accommodationist Christianity.[5]

There is still much debate on the role of the missionaries of the early colonial years, and some are extremely critical of that role, convinced that in the final analysis missionaries were at times tacit, at times conscious agents of the imperial powers, justifiers of the colonialist project who, despite good intentions, identified Christianity too much with western civilization and allegiances.[6] For the majority of missionaries, by far, that characterization is unquestionably true.

Other observers distinguish between this kind of missionary (of the Dutch Reformed or Lutheran churches for example) and the missionaries of the London Missionary Society (LMS) who, they argue, championed the cause of the indigenous people against the racial exclusivism of the settlers.[7] I do not hold the view that all LMS missionaries had "pure motives," or that all of them made the choice to stand with the indigenous peoples in their struggle for justice and rights. But I do believe *some* of them did. Even a critical observer such as Villa-Vicencio must admit that Johannes van der Kemp, for example, saw the "needs" of the indigenous people differently than did some other missionaries, who saw only the need for these people to be Christianized, that is, westernized. "The need van der Kemp witnessed was socio-economic, not evangelical, and he committed himself to strive for the political and economic rights of the oppressed."[8]

As a descendant of the Khoi, the first peoples of this land and the first to bear the brunt of conquest, dispossession, annihilation, and slavery in South Africa, I cannot simply write off these efforts as if they do not matter. They did matter to the indigenous people during their imbalanced struggles with the conquerors, and they matter to this generation now. Van der Kemp and the few who made the choice for justice became the bane of settler society and its churches. The hostility was visceral. Because they married indigenous women, these individuals were called "immoral"; because they took up the cause of the oppressed and exploited native peoples they were accused of "meddling in politics." Because they enlisted public opinion overseas and sought to influence government decision-making processes, they were called "traitors." Because they were passionate about justice and unflinching in exposing injustice, they were called "one-sided."[9] Van der Kemp's public witness to the Dutch governor of the Cape, Janssens, is as clear now as it was then: "I could not forbear to warn him of the displeasure of god who most certainly would hear the cries of the oppressed."[10] When all is said and done, "the church's struggle against racism and injustice in South Africa really begins in earnest with their witness in the nineteenth century," says John de Gruchy—and he is right.[11] No wonder Janssens would report, "If the harm that missionaries have done in the Colony . . . is weighted against the good they have done, it will be found that the harm is very serious and the good amounts to nil. Most of these missionaries (rogues) should be sent away with the greatest possible haste . . . ."[12]

Still, Villa-Vicencio's point is well taken. Caught in historical processes fraught with ambiguity, suffering from the "unintentional collusion" between the humanitarian desire of the missionaries and the selfish, exploitative motives of others,[13] indigenous people would continue to search for the meaning of the gospel for themselves. The more indigenous people would come to understand and interpret the gospel for themselves—and the more they sought their own indigenous, contextual understanding of the gospel as it pertained to their own lives—the more they understood the shortcomings of the missionaries' interpretation, however well meant, and the more they understood the need for an interpretation of the gospel applicable to the world of political, economic, and human subjugation and alienation in which they had to live. That indigenous interpretation would, in time, take on a different form, shaped by what Gayraud Wilmore would call a "radicalized Black Christianity."[14]

Some of the first signs of this "radicalized Black Christianity" could be seen in the "Ethiopian movement," those first black independent churches that broke away from established "mission" churches and aligned themselves with the African Methodist Episcopal Church, powerfully drawn to it by the radical theology and teachings of Bishop Henry McNeal Turner, who visited South Africa in 1896.[15] Their grounds for breaking away were not so much doctrinal or cultural as political, at first raising deep fears among the white population, including missionary circles. Perceptions of "Ethiopianism" later changed, and these breakaway churches were seen as less of a political threat. Nonetheless, Richard Elphick maintains, much modern scholarship has tended to conclude that the movement was deeply political. Zimbabwean historian J. Mutero Chirenje, writing in the 1980s, provocatively concludes that "if the activities of the Ethiopian movement and allied organizations . . . are viewed in the context of their time, they will be seen to be no less acts of self-determination than are armed struggles for national liberation now taking place throughout southern Africa."[16]

That radicalized black Christianity would infuse a spirit of resistance. It would give birth to the anti-colonial Christian millenarianism of Jan Paerl after the failed KhoiKhoi uprising of 1788,[17] and to the rise of black theological critique in the work of Khoi evangelists Cupido Kakkerlak, Hendrik Boezak, and Klaas Stuurman. It would also find expression in the poignant, poetic protest of John Ntsikana's 1884 reference to "gospel as fabulous ghost."[18] From this historic stream would also come the prophetic Christian leadership in African nationalist politics in the nineteenth and twentieth century with leaders such as Dr. John Dube, Rev. James Calata, Pixley ka Isaka Seme, Sol Plaatjie, and Albert Luthuli. In this regard Gayraud Wilmore's observation is correct:

> What we may call "White Christianity" in Europe and North America has made a deep impression upon blacks everywhere, including Africa. But blacks have used Christianity not so much as it was delivered to them in racist white churches, but as its truth was authenticated to them in their experience of suffering and struggle, to reinforce an enculturated religious orientation and to produce an indigenous faith that emphasized dignity, freedom and human welfare.[19]

Decades of Decision

The 1950s were a decade of tumult, with political activism reaching its height in the historic Defiance Campaign, a nationwide campaign of sustained, non-violent resistance, with massive civil disobedience, strikes, and demonstrations manifesting in response to the victory of the National Party at the polls in 1948 and the establishment of apartheid as official policy. The campaign was a watershed in the history of black resistance against oppression in South Africa.

The strong Christian tone set by leaders and followers alike was characteristic of the Defiance Campaign. "A mood of religious fervour infused the resistance," writes South African historian Tom Lodge.[20] During days of prayer volunteers pledged themselves to "a code of love, discipline and cleanliness", and to prayer and fasting. Even though there were speeches "in the strident tone of Africanism," Lodge tells us, "more typically the verbal imagery involved ideas of sacrifice, martyrdom, the triumph of justice and truth."[21] These "ideas," as Lodge calls them, were the lived experience of people who took their faith into the struggle for justice. They understood and experienced the truth of Luthuli's testimony: "The road to freedom is via the Cross."[22]

These black Christians were members of churches with white leadership, even though where blacks were in the majority, and they suffered from the dilemmas of the English-speaking churches. The English-speaking churches in turn shared the dilemmas of apartheid entrapment with the black, so-called mission churches of the DRC: ambivalence towards the struggle for political and human rights of the oppressed majority; paternalism; self-imposed white guardianship; a Euro-centric pietistic theology that separated the spiritual from the secular; and, above all, the fact that the interests of the white leadership ultimately coincided with the interests of white South Africa and its white minority government. This church could not wholeheartedly stand up for justice, because it had "rationalized the demands of the gospel, heeding the demand of the rich and powerful rather than the cries of the poor and oppressed."[23] In this era it was not the institutional church, but the prophetic witness of someone like Father Trevor Huddleston that kept the flame alive.

Ultimately, it was left to black Christians themselves to join the struggle. They could not wait for their hesitant churches to show the way. Instead, they followed Albert Luthuli's theological convictions and charismatic Christian leadership. Luthuli states:

> It became clear to me that the Christian faith was not a private affair without relevance to society. It was, rather, a belief which equipped us in a unique way to meet the challenges of our society. It was a belief which had to be applied to the conditions of our lives; and our many works—they ranged from Sunday School teaching to road building—became meaningful as outflow of Christian belief.[24]

Working together with those who were not Christian would not deter them, either. Luthuli affirmed the foundations of inclusivity, interreligious and human solidarity that were to characterize the anti-apartheid struggle in the years to come:

> For myself, I am in Congress precisely because I am Christian. My Christian belief about human society must find expression here and now, and Congress is the spearhead of the real struggle. Some would have the Communists excluded, others would have all non-Communists withdraw from Congress. My own urge, because *I am a Christian*, is to enter into the thick of the struggle, with other Christians, taking my Christianity with me and praying that it may be used to influence for good the character of the resistance.[25] (emphasis added)

Luthuli, and the growing number of Christians who joined the struggle on the basis of their faith, were the prophetic church, the restless presence disturbing both church and society, giving witness through prophetic speech and action, shaping an alternative imagination.

If the fifties were a decade of hopeful, activist tumult, the sixties brought a tumult of another, far more sinister kind. On March 21, the Pan Africanist

Congress, engaging in a peaceful demonstration against the so-called pass laws, marched toward Sharpeville police station near Johannesburg, where the struggle would take a historic, fateful turn. Police opened fire with live ammunition, killing sixty-nine persons and wounding at least 186 others, most of them shot in the back.[26] Sharpeville, more so than the Defiance Campaign, would become the iconic turning point of the struggle in South Africa. Government reaction was immediate, much harsher and more oppressive than before. Liberation movements and activists were banned, and political leaders and hundreds of activists were imprisoned, exiled, or driven underground. It was the decade of the treason and Rivonia trials and the emergence of Nelson Mandela. Draconian "security legislation" multiplied, and political activity was severely suppressed—a harbinger of worse to come. Albert Luthuli was awarded the Nobel Peace Prize in 1960, and the world began to take serious notice of the struggle for freedom in South Africa. This was also the year the African National Congress decided to form its military wing, Umkhonto we Sizwe, and to make violence part of the strategy of struggle. In his statement at his trial, Nelson Mandela explains why:

> We of the ANC had always stood for a non-racial democracy, and we shrank from any action which might drive the races further apart. But the hard facts were that 50 years of nonviolence had brought the African people nothing but more and more repressive legislation, and fewer and fewer rights. . . . I came to the conclusion that as violence in this country was inevitable, it would be unrealistic to continue preaching peace and nonviolence.[27]

For the churches, too, Sharpeville was a turning point. At the urging of the World Council of Churches (WCC) the Cottesloe conference was called. The situation was discussed by the WCC and its South African member churches, and the Cottesloe Declaration was issued. The Rev. C. F. Beyers Naudé of the Dutch Reformed Church challenged his church on the issue of its moral and theological justification of apartheid, finally breaking with the Dutch Reformed Church to become the head of the Christian Institute of South Africa. The South African Council of Churches and the Christian Institute published the "Message to the People of South Africa" in 1968. Father Cosmas Desmond would be the courageous witness from inside the Catholic Church who worked in the then Ciskei, and would later stir the conscience of the church and the world with his book about the "discarded people" of South Africa's homeland system.[28] The World Council of Churches held its assembly in 1968, instituted its program to combat racism a year later, and in 1970 inaugurated the so-called special fund—the most controversial action in its whole history, and a huge, probably permanent affront to the churches of the North—to provide financial support (for humanitarian purposes) to southern African liberation movements.

Albert Luthuli died in 1967. Among the leadership of the ANC-in-exile, the strong, prophetic Christian influence would—but for the voice of Oliver Tambo—all but disappear. But in South Africa, after a hiatus of almost ten years, black liberation politics would rise again in defiance of both an increasingly militarized and despotic state, and its minions in the black communities—and at its center would be a revived, radicalized black Christianity.

The Boundaries of White Leadership

Charismatic, black Christian leadership in the struggle was always aware of the limitations of the churches under white leadership. Already, Albert Luthuli had uttered a harsh critique of the lack of prophetic witness from the church in the midst of growing crisis. He acknowledged, apart from the oppressive security apparatus, the hold government had on churches in terms of things such as building sites, yearly leases, permits, and the like, but grew far more concerned about churches' responses to such pressures. He decried "white, paternalist Christianity,"[29] but his critique was not just aimed at the white leadership of the church; he accused the black pastors of a lack of prophetic courage as well. "I am extreme on this point," he warned, invoking echoes of Martin Luther King Jr.'s "extremism for justice,"[30] and went on to explain why:

> The threat is that, if a sermon or a congregation or a bishop displeases the Department, the site will cease to be available. Parsons must not talk politics— yet much orthodox Christian teaching can be called "politics" . . . . This threat has many Christian ministers and organizations virtually cowering, as of course the government intends. What is becoming of Christian witness? . . . Let us lose church sites and keep Christian integrity. I disagree with those who want to "save something from the wreck" because what I see happening is the wreck of Christian witness . . . .[31]

It agitated Luthuli that some leaders in the church sought to "save something" from the wreck of church-state relations, as if salvaging church-state relations were the most important thing. Luthuli, however, was concerned about the wreck the church was making of its prophetic faithfulness. The ordained leadership thinks pragmatically. The lay public theologian thinks theologically, and it is his prophetic insight that shames, challenges, and saves the church. He is the faithful one, the restless presence consistent with his commitment from the beginning, calling for a "spirit of defiance." Luthuli remarks, "Laws and conditions that tend to debase human personality—a God-given force—be they brought by the State or other individuals, must be relentlessly opposed in the spirit of defiance shown by St. Peter when he said to the rulers of his day, 'Shall we obey God or man?'"[32]

Scott Couper gallantly defends the institutional church against Luthuli's claim that the church "did almost nothing" in the wake of closure of Luthuli's beloved educational institution, Adams College.[33] But I think that for Luthuli there was more at stake. Luthuli's concern was not simply the church's reaction to the closure of Adams College, but the church's overall lack of courage and prophetic clarity vis-à-vis the whole liberation struggle. What Luthuli saw, and the church did not, was that its virtual silence—the "wreck of Christian witness" regarding liberation for all in South Africa—rendered it almost helpless, even when it came to defending its own institution. One cannot fight with integrity for one's own issues when one is not wholeheartedly in the fight for *all* matters. Adams College's enforced closure was not an isolated incident, but the logical outcome of an evil policy and a corrupt system Luthuli had been praying the church would wholeheartedly struggle against, though it could not. It may be this failure, on top of deep disappointment over the fact that he did not have the unqualified support of the African leadership of his church in the struggle against injustice in South Africa, that prompted Luthuli's "strange" silence on the closure of the college in his autobiography.[34]

For the new generation, too, the boundaries of white, liberal church politics became increasingly clear. Without discarding the value of white Christian support, one must realize the limitation of the extent to which the majority of white Christians wanted to commit themselves. In truth, they did offer protest, but it was constrained by their caution, their desire to compromise, and the pressures of white solidarity. The Trevor Huddlestons, Beyers Naudés, and Cosmas Desmonds were few and far between, and they were not among church leadership. Analysis of the two major church statements after Sharpeville will bear this observation out.

The Cottesloe Declaration[35] was a statement written in the wake of Sharpeville, with the blood still visible on the ground. Crucially, the statement recognizes that "all racial groups who permanently inhabit our country are a part of the total population, and we regard them as indigenous." These groups have an "equal right to make their contributions . . . and share in the ensuing responsibilities, rewards and privileges." But what does this mean if there is no clear condemnation of apartheid, the Bantustan policy, or of the 1913 and 1936 Land Acts? Since the declaration contains no clear vision of non-racial, democratic society or of a radical shift of power relations in politics and society, one is entitled to ask what kind of society and government black people are expected to contribute to.

And what does "groups who permanently inhabit our country" mean when the declaration states that it has "no objection in principle to the direct representation of coloured people in parliament"? Is this the "white parliament" in "white South Africa" they are speaking of? Does this mean tacit approval of Bantustans? What about the black majority who, according to the apartheid dispensation, did not permanently reside in "white South Africa," and therefore has no right to be represented "in parliament"? It is exactly this kind of enlightened apartheid logic that would eventually lead to P. W. Botha's 1983 constitution with its tri-cameral parliament, which was roundly rejected by so-called coloured and Indian people in the formation of the United Democratic Front and to the boycott of those apartheid elections on both political and moral grounds.[36] It also shows just how out of touch with black aspirations white church leadership was, despite good intentions.

There is another serious matter to consider. Cottesloe declares that "present tension [after Sharpeville] is the result of a long historical development and all groups bear responsibility for it." On whose behalf, one wonders, does the declaration speak? How is such ahistorical analysis possible? Exactly how is this "historical development" understood? Even a superficial glance at history shows the long, and amazingly patient engagement by black people in their struggle to make white South Africa understand "the things that make for peace," and the contempt with which this aspiration was treated by white power. Why put the blame for the apartheid regime's violent response to the nonviolent protest of March 21 on the black protesters instead of on the government, its police and its army? Why such a lack of understanding for the root causes of the conflict? The Sharpeville massacre, and its immediate aftermath, do not constitute something black people should take responsibility for.[37] Why could the white representatives of the churches—at least as direct beneficiaries of apartheid, if not its direct perpetrators—not take responsibility for the intransigence of the white government, with its resolute resistance to calls for peaceful change, and for the utter failure of the church to unequivocally stand up for justice? Why force the victims to share responsibility for their oppression, the denial of their rights, and their deaths, with the authors, perpetrators, and beneficiaries of their oppression? Why must the protesters be made to feel guilt about their protest, about the audacity of their hope, about the display of their courage to demand rights, justice, and equality in the land of their birth?

Likewise, the "Message to the People of South Africa" is a strong theological statement, emphasizing the unity of humankind and the sinfulness of separation and apartheid. It introduces the terms "false faith" and "a novel gospel" in reference to apartheid and its (implied) moral and theological justification, and calls for reconciliation. But it is, alas, a theological statement devoid of contextual understanding. Nowhere is there mention of social and political justice, articulation of black aspirations, or sign of recognition that there was a struggle going on—despite the campaigns, trials and deaths— nor was there mention that God was calling the church to take sides in that struggle. Nowhere is there a specific challenge to the white community to define what reconciliation in our socio-political context might mean—be it justice, restitution, or restoration.

We must be careful not to judge with the flawless wisdom of hindsight. It is better to measure such statements within their own contexts—that is, by the known demands of the oppressed at the time, in whose name these white church leaders took it upon themselves to speak. So we compare these statements against the light of Trevor Huddleston's *Naught for Your Comfort*, a scathing attack on white oppression and white complacency coming from a priest who took the people's demands seriously; against the light of Albert Luthuli's autobiography, as clear a Christian witness for justice as this country has ever seen; and, from a purely political point of view, Mandela's statement at his trial, his almost scientific analysis of the reasons for the ANC's opting for violence "after fifty years" of nonviolent resistance. On the specific point we raised, the church leaders also had in their midst Luthuli, a fellow Christian who believed that in these matters black voices should be heard.[38] He made his conviction clear:

> *Africans Should Categorically Reject the Bantustans Because*: they purport to meet our demand for direct participation in the government of the country by some pseudo plan of self-government which is falsely acclaimed by the government as conforming to the traditional form of government in African society. . . . *The progress of Bantustans will not be judged on the affluence of a few: chiefs, traders, civil servants and professional people who are hardly 12 percent of the people.* What will matter more is the raising of the general standard of living of the masses of the people to progressively approach a civilized standard of living.[39] (emphasis in original)

There could have been no doubt whatsoever about the aspirations of black South Africans at the time, the demands they were making, the sacrifices they were called to perform, or the grim determination of the government to

uphold and defend white supremacy. Equally clear were the noble aspirations
they articulated on behalf of all South Africans, as the Freedom Charter of
1955 testifies.[40] White leadership simply found it too hard to speak propheti-
cally—or failing that, to stand aside and let black leadership speak for the
people. Even the best of white leadership failed to grasp this truth. Dr. Frits
Gaum, one-time leader of the DRC and, in his context, also one of the most
open-minded persons, unwittingly still found himself defending the motiva-
tions for apartheid, even though he himself had long since abandoned any
attempt to defend the policy itself.[41]

As a partial explanation of this defense, Gaum quotes Roman Catholic
Archbishop Denis Hurley of Natal, who at the time served also as chair of
the Institute for Race Relations. Gaum reports Hurley as having stated in
1966,

> My personal view is that separate development as a Christian solution for the
> race question could be acceptable if it meets four conditions. One, the policy
> must be implementable. Two, it must have the consent of all concerned. Three,
> there must be a proportional sharing of sacrifices, and four, the rights of all
> people must be safeguarded in the period of transition. *In principle there can be no
> objection to an honest and just sharing of South Africa amongst all its racial groups.*
> But nobody can convince me that what is happening at the moment is either just
> or "sharing."[42]

It is not clear to me what the statement "the rights of all people should be
guarded in the period of transition" means. But the point is not what could
convince the archbishop. The point is that the struggle leadership never spoke
of accepting Bantustans under certain "conditions." They spoke of freedom in
the land of their birth.

Radical Black Christianity

The decade of the seventies brought Steve Biko and black consciousness,
renewed black political activity, the concept of black power, the unequivocal
rejection of white paternalism, and the Soweto Uprising. All this came with
a challenge to black people never experienced before. Steve Biko confronted
black people with what he called the "first truth, bitter as it may seem, that
we have to acknowledge," the fact that black persons have lost their person-
hood, that we were "reduced to an obliging shell," and that, all in all, the black
person had become "a shadow of a man completely defeated, drowning in

his own misery, a slave, an ox bearing the yolk of oppression with sheepish timidity."[43]

Biko accused the black church of not just complacency, but of "conniving" with an oppressive ideology and an interpretation of the scriptures that had become a depressingly efficient instrument for subjugation. We did not just accept, we "connived: at an appalling irrelevance of the scriptures . . . a colonist-trained version of Christianity" that has nothing liberating, comforting, or humanizing to say in an country "teeming with injustice and fanatically committed to the practice of oppression, intolerance and blatant cruelty because of racial bigotry . . . where all black people are made to feel the unwanted step-child of a God whose presence they cannot feel . . . ."[44]

Those words, and the actions of the children of Soweto and across the country, reinventing and redefining the struggle for liberation in myriad ways, constituted the challenge the black church had to meet. It was a challenge to the church's preaching, teaching, and understanding of its role in public affairs.[45] But it could not be the church that perpetuated a colonized theology, conniving with the oppressor and standing sheepishly by the wayside while children were being slaughtered. As a result the seventies saw a fundamental renewal of the black church, a prophetic church, a restless, disturbing presence. It was a church defined not by doctrinal affiliation or ecclesiastical sanction or denominational understanding, but rather by obedience to Christ, by faithfulness to the prophetic call of the gospel, by receptiveness to the spirit of the ancestors—Jan Paerl, Sol Plaatjie, Albert Luthuli—and the compelling, sacrificial presence of the children.

In 1979, at a South African Council of Churches (SACC) conference, I tried to spell out what such a black church should be:

- This is a church that embraces a black understanding of the gospel as a gospel of hope, liberation and justice. It is a gospel that speaks directly to our situations of oppression and subjugation. It is the result of a painful, soul-searching struggle of black Christians with God and with the meaning of God's Word for their lives today.
- This church has wrestled with black history—a history of suffering and degradation and humiliation caused by white racism. They refuse to believe that the gospel could corroborate the narrow, racist ideology white churches were preaching and that white theologians were giving respectability through their teaching.
- This church knows that the God of the exodus and the covenant, the God of Jesus of Nazareth, was different from the God white Christianity was proclaiming.

- This church believed that the gospel of Jesus Christ does not deny the struggle for black humanity, and it is with this light from God's Word that they went into the struggle, both within the church and outside of it.
- Out of this struggle emerged the black church, a broad movement of black Christians, joined in a black solidarity that transcends all barriers of denomination and ethnicity. It shares the black experience, the same understanding of suffering, oppression and the same struggle for liberation from all forms of oppression, firmly rooted in the belief that the gospel of Jesus Christ proclaims the total liberation of all people and that the God of Jesus Christ is the God of the oppressed.
- Moreover, we must remember that in a situation such as ours blackness (a state of oppression) is not only a colour; it is a *condition*. And it is within this perspective that the role of white Christians should be understood. I do not speak of those who happen to be leaders in the black churches. Nor do I refer to those who happen to be in control of churches where blacks are the majority. I speak of those white Christians who have understood their own guilt in the oppression of blacks in terms of corporate responsibility, who have genuinely repented and genuinely converted; those who have committed themselves to the struggle for liberation and who, through their commitment, have taken upon themselves the condition of blackness in South Africa. In a real sense, they bear the "marks of Christ." They are part of the black church not as lords and masters, but as servants, not as "liberals," but as brothers and sisters, for they have learned not so much how to do for blacks, but to identify with what blacks are doing to secure their liberation. . . . this is the black church . . . .[46]

The black church rejected the anemic, inadequate theology of accommodation and acquiescence, of individualistic, otherworldly spirituality foisted upon us by western Christianity that taught us to accept the existing unjust order as God-ordained. We embraced, rather, what we called a "theology of refusal," a theology that refused to accept God as a god of oppression, but rather as a god of liberation who calls people to participate actively in the struggle for justice and liberation.[47] Very much like the black church in the United States, Lewis Baldwin argues, "There was a consensus of beliefs, attitudes, values, and expectations that bound them together despite the incidentals that distinguished them from one another. Thus they were able to establish a broad, interdenominational tradition of shared involvement in the struggle for a just and inclusive society . . . ."[48]

It is important to note two things at this point. One, this black church included those whites who made the choice for justice and liberation, thereby within the context of the times taking upon themselves the "condition of blackness." Two, the apartheid establishment against which we set ourselves was the white minority government and its collaborators in the black communities, its apartheid institutions in the so-called coloured and Indian communities and in the Bantustans, none of which would have existed without the willing cooperation of black people making *their* choice for apartheid and its rewards. This was a huge step away from the racial separatism of pure apartheid, the disengaging paternalism of white liberalism and the multiracialism of modified apartheid, toward the non-racialism South Africa cannot do without.

Four theological documents from the 1980s best demonstrate this phase of the struggle and the character of the prophetic, activist church as described above. The first such document is the Charter of Alliance of Black Reformed Christians of Southern Africa.[49] In this charter, black Reformed Christians, who were hopelessly divided by a history of missionary domination in Southern Africa, deliberately attempt to rescue the reformed tradition from the perversion of the ideologically driven theology of apartheid. This step gave reformed theology a new identity in Africa, and played a decisive role in the ultimate decision of the World Alliance of Reformed Churches to declare apartheid a sin and its theological justification a heresy.

A second document is the *Belhar Confession*, written and proposed in 1982 and finally adopted by the Dutch Reformed Mission Church in 1986. The confession is the church's stand against the heresy of the theology of apartheid and the church's theological understanding of and guidance in its prophetic participation in the continuing struggles for justice ever since. It consists of four articles centered on unity, compassionate justice, and reconciliation.[50]

The third document is the well-known *Kairos Document*, produced by the so-called Kairos theologians and published by the South African Council of Churches and the Institute of Contextual Theology. It was the first of a series of "Kairos documents" that saw the light in many countries across the world. It was a powerful exposure of "state theology" versus "prophetic theology," always recognizing the urgency of the times and the moment of truth (*kairos*) and knowing that the stakes are immeasurably high and a matter of life and death. In these situations neutrality is no longer possible; the church must make choices, since God is a god that takes sides. The confession exposed injustice and oppression, violence and exploitation, exclusion and class struggles, offering a severely critical analysis of the role of the church in these struggles. It also contains deep self-critical awareness of our own complicity and hence a call for conversion, prophetic action, and participation in struggles for justice.[51]

Fourthly, in 1986 a call for the day of prayer for the "Fall of Unjust Rule" was issued. The language of the "Theological Rationale" accompanying this call speaks for itself:

> Now, on 16th June, and twenty-five years after the dawning of this phase of resistance, it is right to remember those whose blood has been shed in resistance and protest against an unjust system. It is also right that we as Christians reassess out response to a system that all right-thinking people identify as unjust. We have prayed for our rulers, as is demanded of us in the scriptures. We have entered into consultation with them, as required by our faith. We have taken the reluctant and drastic step of declaring apartheid to be contrary to the declared will of God, and some churches have declared its theological justification to be a heresy. We now pray that God will replace the present structures of oppression with ones that are just, and remove from power those who persist in defying his laws, installing in their place leaders who will govern with justice and mercy.[52]

These documents, demonstrating the difference between hesitant, paternalistic white leadership and radicalized black leadership, provoked severe oppressive responses from government and the white establishment and caused deep division within the churches, even "anti-apartheid" churches. But the documents established simultaneously a radical theological departure and a new grammar for the churches, redefining the role of the churches in public affairs and in struggles for justice. They brought together a new kind of church, committed to the justice called for by the gospel, across boundaries of denomination and race and doctrine.

We realized that the banning of liberation movements also meant "the church has become more important than ever before as a vehicle for expressing the legitimate aspirations of black people."[53] Rejecting false notions of love, reconciliation and peace without justice and restoration, shunning the "cheap grace" of political accommodation to apartheid, we called for full and meaningful participation in the struggle. We called for the church to "initiate and support meaningful pressure to the entrenched system as a nonviolent way of bringing about change ... to initiate and support programmes of civil disobedience on a massive scale and challenge white Christians especially on this issue,"[54] and worked for divestment and sanctions on the apartheid regime. We called for support for the WCC's program to combat racism, including its special fund, which provided humanistic support for liberation movements.

We challenged the white church and establishment on its hypocrisy regarding the issue of violence: Why was the violence of the oppressed in response to tyranny and in service of their freedom condemned, while the violence of the state in defense of an evil system was not challenged? We called the church from white guardianship to black leadership, from sympathy to engagement, from a theology of protest to a theology of resistance and struggle. The role of this church in the struggle during the 1980s and in the non-racial United Democratic Front is now a matter of record, and the dawn of democracy in South Africa is not conceivable without the role of the prophetic church, a conscientized black leadership, and the infusion of radical black Christianity. In response to the challenge of Biko and the children of Soweto, the prophetic church arose, claimed its historic responsibility, and honored the ancestor-prophets on whose shoulders we stood.

Activism in Post-Apartheid South Africa

After 1994, it was as if the voice of the prophetic church in South Africa had died. Reasons for this silence have been advanced, and most of them are probably valid,[55] but assessments of the church's prophetic positioning depend on where one stands when such arguments are made. The issue for prophetic faithfulness is never who is in power, but whether those in power are using their status in the service of compassionate justice and dignity, especially for those who are most vulnerable. For the small elite who have hugely benefited from change in South Africa in the last fifteen years or so, the quality of our liberation is decidedly different than it is for the vast majority of our people, who remain crushed under the heavy burden of chronic poverty, deepening hopelessness, and angry disillusionment. The true measurement of good government, John Calvin stressed, is whether it does justice and defends and maintains the rights of the poor.[56] Calvin is not speaking of charity, goodwill, or trickle-down capitalism, but of justice and *rights*.

South Africa is a country of vast and unsustainable inequalities.[57] Unemployment is unacceptably high, especially among the youth. Delivery of services to the poor is such that we have had five years of unending, increasingly violent protests on the streets of our townships. The anger is deep and abiding. We have seen reckless militarization of our police force, and almost as a matter of course, instances of police brutality have become alarmingly high. Police have orders to "shoot to kill," and so they do—from toddlers in cars parked in driveways, to teenagers at a party, to protesters against government corruption, to a young woman who accidentally backed her car into a stationary police vehicle.

Our children will be presented with the utter foolishness of our having bought arms worth sixty billion South African rands in a deal fraught with suspicion of corruption, when there is no discernible threat to the country and while we know the greatest threats to our security to be poverty, inequality, and our lack of social cohesion. These are the issues crying out to the activist church in post-apartheid South Africa. Colonialism, slavery, and apartheid were not historical phases. One was the logical consequence of the other, built upon the foundation of the other. Nor were these states just a matter of attitude; they were solidified in political, social, economic, religious, and judicial structures of oppression and exploitation. Racism was at the heart of it for over 350 years. Racism is still a controlling aspect of South African society, and perhaps we should remember at least three things here: a) the way racism, as a system of oppression, creates both victims and beneficiaries; b) racism's enormity and its all-encompassing reality; and c) its effects, for both victims and beneficiaries, are trans-generational.

We have removed all the racist, apartheid legislation from our books, but we are still a deeply racialized society. When one thinks of it (and this is perhaps a fourth factor), one is struck by the permanence of separation in the spatial, physical, psychological, economic, and social legacy of apartheid, and one wonders how we shall ever overcome it. Racist incidents still abound, racist talk comes from both sides of the color line—our political discourse is replete with it—and the ANC has, to the distress of millions, brought back apartheid's official racial categorization. In South Africa, what Emerson and Yancey call "the three dimension of whiteness"[58] is a present reality. White South Africans call every effort to rectify the wrongs of the past "racism-in-reverse," and by the same token resist the process of genuine transformation. Every decision to put a black person in a position of responsibility—whether in sports, business, or the academy—has to be justified; a white appointment guarantees automatic meritorious virtue.[59] We are beset still with racial inequality, racial alienation, and racial division. The activist church must manifest the genuine nonracial community South Africans and the world desperately need.

Genuine non-racialism is fundamentally different from the shallow "color-blindness" that comes from a denial of racism and its pernicious effects. The insistence on South Africa as a now "color-blind" society blinds us to the permanence of separation, as well as to ongoing racial micro-aggression, which is the "brief commonplace daily verbal, behavioural or environmental indignation, whether intentional or unintentional, that communicates hostile, derogatory or negative racial slights and insults toward people of colour."[60] For the vast majority of our people, we are not a post-apartheid, post-racial society. I would suggest that the measure for whether this is so lies not with those few who have become collaborators and beneficiaries of the global neo-liberal capitalist empire, but as Albert Luthuli once suggested, with the masses of those whose hunger and thirst for justice have not been satisfied, the most vulnerable and woundable in our society, those forced to stare at life from the bottom of the well. For them, as the fiery Henry Highland Garnet put it—much more truthfully—so long ago, "There are Pharaohs on both sides of the blood-red waters."[61] The activist church is called to discern this fundamental truth and act upon it.

The activist church will have to learn to see these realities, like the Accra Confession says, "through the eyes of those who suffer." Then we too will "discern the signs of the times," and see a "scandalous world that denies God's call to life for all." We too will hear that "creation continues to groan in bondage", as the "plundering of the earth" continues. We too will see the "dramatic convergence of political and military might", and understand that economic systems are "a matter of life and death."[62] Then we too shall experience the righteous anger that comes from suffering injustice and indignity. We need much more than our current heretical embrace of free-market, neo-liberal capitalist prosperity. We need Robert Franklin's prophetic radicalism, with social justice as the goal,[63] just as we need Martin Luther King's early insight that "the roots [of economic injustice] are in the system rather than in men or faulty operations," that "something is wrong . . . with capitalism . . . [that] there must be a better distribution of wealth and maybe America needs to move toward democratic socialism."[64] The challenges are at once local and global: poverty and wealth, socio-economic justice and the domination and salvific claims of neo-liberal capitalism; gratuitous violence, state and private terror, and global war; gender justice and patriarchal domination; justice and the dignity of human sexuality; environmental justice and the security of the earth and its resources for all.

Finally, the activist church shall have to be inclusive in the broadest sense—not just on the matter of race, but responsive to the urgent call of interreligious solidarity in the ongoing struggles against oppression.[65] This inclusiveness is required not just because the anti-apartheid and civil rights struggles have already shown the way. The threat to world peace in all its manifestations is often carried by multi-religious fundamentalism. The struggle for world peace and justice must be carried by interreligious solidarity. Besides, the thrust of peaceful revolution towards justice, democracy, and a new, meaningful, humane way of life in the world today at present comes from North Africa and the Middle East where, in the midst of momentous events, vital decisions are being made, determinative not just for them, but for the future of our world. In the twentieth century it was the civil rights struggle in the United States and the anti-apartheid struggle in South Africa that presented the international community with a moral choice between justice and injustice, dehumanization and humaneness, right or wrong. Right now that decision is presented by the Arab Spring and the Palestinian question. This is what Martin Luther King called "the right side of the world revolution."[66]

In this way radical, activist Christianity can continue to make a valuable contribution to worldwide activism on the part of the people of the world and the earth itself, remaining a restless presence in the church and in the world.

Notes

1. In his *Letter from Birmingham Jail*, in James M. Washington, *A Testimony of Hope: The Essential Writings of Martin Luther King, Jr.* (San Francisco: Harper & Row, 1986), 300.

2. What Richard Lischer says about prophetic preaching is helpful here": Prophetic preaching consists in speech and symbolic actions that follow the implications of God's holiness and revealed acts to their concrete, vivid and public conclusions. What is whispered in closeted places of fear and suffering, the prophet proclaims form the rooftops. Prophecy begins in dissatisfaction with the present state of things . . . and ends in the imagination of an alternative future." Lischer, "Anointed With Fire: The Structure of Prophecy in the Sermons of Martin Luther King, Jr.," in Timothy George, James Earl Massey, and Robert Smith Jr., eds., *Our Sufficiency Is of God: Essays in Honour of Gardner C. Taylor* (Macon, GA: Mercer University Press, 2010), 231.

3. Apart from examples such as the committed Christian leadership of the African National Congress from its beginnings to the 1960s, one thinks of Christians such as Anglican priests Trevor Huddleston in the 1950s and Bernie Wrankmore in the early '70s; Rev. Beyers Naudé and the Christian Institute in the 1960s and '70s; Revs. George Plaatjies and Izak Theron of the Dutch Reformed Mission Church in the 1960s; the black student and youth Christian movements in the 1970s and '80s; and the Alliance of Black Reformed Christians in the 1980s; as a matter of interest, but today surely as important as the role of Beyers Naudé in the white Dutch Reformed Church in his time, is the persistent prophetic faithfulness of the five theologians in the Netherdutch Reformed Church of Africa (the second white South African church suspended from membership in 1982 in the World Alliance of Reformed Churches for its theological and moral justification of apartheid); Andries van Aarde, Johan Buitendag, Yolanda Dreyer, Ernest van Eck, and James Loader, with regard to their witness to the church in their efforts to move the church towards an unequivocal, and remorseful condemnation of apartheid as sin and heresy and a commitment to justice.

4. Charles Villa-Vicencio, *Trapped in Apartheid: A Socio-Theological History of the English-Speaking Churches* (Maryknoll, NY: Orbis Books, 1988), 5.

5. This church is sometimes referred to as the "prophetic minority," but by the mid-1980s this church, which Frank Chikane has called "the church of the streets," had decidedly become—albeit not for long—the "prophetic majority."

6. See Villa-Vicencio, *Trapped in Apartheid*, 43ff.

7. See John W. Gruchy, *The Church Struggle in South Africa* (Grand Rapids, MI: Eerdmans, 1979), 12ff.

8. Villa-Vicencio, *Trapped in Apartheid*, 58. See also Ido J. Inklaar, *Life and Work of Dr. J. T. van der Kemp 1747–1811: Missionary Pioneer and Protagonist of Racial Equality in South Africa* (Cape Town/Rotterdam: A. A. Balkema, 1988).

9. See Allan Boesak, *The Tenderness of Conscience: African Renaissance and the Spirituality of Politics* (Stellenbosch: Sun Press, 2005), 135. See also Jane Sales, *The Planting of the Churches in South Africa* (Grand Rapids, MI: Eerdmans, 1971), 51.

10. Villa-Vicencio, *Trapped in Apartheid*, 58.

11. Gruchy, *Church Struggle*, 13.

12. See Sales, *Planting*, 51. Villa-Vicencio writes that these missionaries regularly found themselves in conflict not only with the colonial authorities, but also with other missionaries who were differently inclined, as well as with the authorities of the established church. John Phillip argued that it was the task of the missionary to "defend the weak against the strong," provoking Wesleyan missionaries to object strongly, 58. See also the tensions between Bishop John Colenso and the authorities in Natal and Governor Theophilus Shepstone, 62, and with his own Bishop in Cape Town, 16, 61.

13. Villa-Vicencio, *Trapped in Apartheid*, 48, quoting historian C. W. de Klewiet, *The Imperial Factor in South Africa* (Cambridge: Cambridge University Press, 1937), 159.

14. See Gayraud S. Wilmore, *Black Religion and Black Radicalism: An Interpretation of the Religious History of African Americans* (Maryknoll, NY: Orbis Books, 1973, 2006).

15. See Richard Elphick, "Evangelical Missions and Racial 'Equalization' in South Africa," in Dana L. Robert, ed., *Converting Colonialism, Visions and Realities in Mission History, 1706–1914: Studies in the History of Christian Missions* (Grand Rapids, MI: Eerdmans, 2008), 119. The first important independent church in South Africa, the Thembu Church, was founded by Nehemiah Tile, a Wesleyan preacher, who broke with the mission in 1883 because of his political views and activities. Over the next generation, African churches seceded from a great variety of missions, with noted leadership by such individuals as Mangena Mokone and James Dwane. See Elphick, 118–19

16. Cited in Elphick, in Dana L. Robert, ed., *Converting Colonialism*, 121.

17. See Russel Viljoen, *Jan Paerl: A Khoikhoi Cape Colonial Society, 1761–1851* (Leiden/Boston: Brill, 2006).

18. See Es'kia Mphahlele, *ES'KIA: Education, African Humanism & Culture, Social Consciousness, Literary Appreciation* (Johannesburg: Kwela Books, 2002), 298. See also Boesak, *Tenderness of Conscience*, 136–37.

19. Wilmore, *Black Religion*, 25.

20. Tom Lodge, *Black Politics in South Africa Since 1945* (Johannesburg: Ravan Press, 1990), 43.

21. Lodge, *Black Politics*, 44.

22. Albert Luthuli, *Let My People Go* (Cape Town: Tafelberg and Sandton: Mafube, 2006), 232–36.

23. Villa-Vicencio, *Trapped in Apartheid*, 6. See also de Gruchy, *Church Struggle*, 37ff., and Boesak, *Tenderness*, 137–40.

24. Albert Luthuli, *Let My People Go*, 147–48.

25. Luthuli, *Let My People Go*, 146–47. Scott Couper, in his excellent historical study, makes the point that in this, as in so many other things, Luthuli's leadership was decades ahead of the church: "Prior to the formation of the United Democratic Front in 1983, the wider church would not work with and alongside communists, Muslims and black nationalists in a broad-based movement and formed by the congresses as Luthuli did, and did well. During the 1950s and 1960s, whites and insularity dominated the Christian churches . . . ." Scott Couper, *Albert Luthuli: Bound by Faith* (Scottsville: University of Natal Press, 2010), 64–65.

26. In Evaton, also close to Johannesburg, the protest was broken up by low-flying fighter jets, and in Langa, near Cape Town, three people were killed and twenty-seven injured in a baton charge by police. See Couper, *Albert Luthuli*, 86.

27. Nelson Mandela, "An Ideal for Which I Am Prepared to Die," in Tom Clark, ed., *Great Speeches of the Twentieth Century* (London: Preface Books, 2008), 232–33.

28. See Cosmas Desmond, *The Discarded People: An Account of African Settlement* (Johannesburg: Christian Institute of South Africa, 1971).

29. Luthuli, *Let My People Go*, 125.

30. See his *Letter from Birmingham Jail*.

31. *Let My People Go*, 131–32.

32. See Tom Karis and Gwendolyn Carter, *From Protest to Challenge: A Documentary History of South African Politics, 1882–1964*, vol. 2 (Stanford: Stanford University Press, 1973), 486.

33. Couper, *Albert Luthuli*, 64.

34. Couper, *Albert Luthuli*, 63: "Many African Congregationalists proved even more wary of Luthuli's increasing involvement in politics that their former white American ecclesial paternalists who harboured concerns with the ANC's, and hence Luthuli's links with communists."

35. For the text of the Cottesloe Declaration see Piet J. Naude, *Neither Calendar nor Clock: Perspectives on the Belhar Confession* (Grand Rapids, MI: Eerdmans, 2011), 226–29. For the text of the "message," see 233–36.

36. See Allan Boesak, *Running With Horses: Reflections of an Accidental Politician* (Cape Town: JoHo! Publishers, 2009), part 2, 77ff.

37. "And now, as never before the government is responsible for the civil violence that takes place . . . ." Luthuli, *Let My People Go*, 228.

38. "I see no clever strategy in leaving [whites] to attribute fictitious attitudes to us when in fact we have *real* attitudes of our own." His aim was "to ensure that if the whites are ignorant of the realities, the fault does not lie with us," Luthuli, *Let My People Go*, 176–77.

39. In Couper, *Albert Luthuli*, 80.

40. "We the People of South Africa, black and white together . . . declare . . . South Africa belongs to all who live in it. . . . We the People . . . equals, countrymen and brothers . . . ." Cf. Luthuli, *Let My People Go*, 237.

41. See Laurie Gaum and Frits Gaum, *Praat Verby Grense* (Cape Town: Umuzi, 2010), 46

42. See Laurie Gaum and Frits Gaum, *Praat Verby Grense*, 46.

43. Steve Biko, *I Write What I Like* (San Francisco: Harper & Row, 1986), 28.

44. Biko, *I Write What I Like*, 28, 29.

45. See for example Allan Boesak, "Introduction: Relevant Preaching in a Black Context," in *The Finger of God: Sermons on Faith and Responsibility* (Maryknoll, NY: Orbis Books, 1982), 1–17.

46. See Allan Boesak, "The Black Church and the Future," in *Black and Reformed: Apartheid, Liberation and the Calvinist Tradition* (Maryknoll, NY: Orbis Books, 1984), 21–22. See also Boesak, *Running With Horses*, 48–62.

47. Boesak, *Black and Reformed*, 26.

48. Lewis Baldwin, "Revisiting the 'All-Comprehending Institution': Historical Reflections on the Public Roles of Black Churches," in R. Drew Smith, ed., *New Day Begun: African American Churches and Civic Culture in Post-Civil Rights America: The Public Influences of African American Churches*, vol. 1 (Durham, NC: Duke University Press, 2003), 18.

49. The Charter of the Alliance of Reformed Christians in Southern Africa, in Charles Villa-Vicencio and John de Gruchy, eds., *Apartheid Is a Heresy* (Grand Rapids, MI: Eerdmans, 1983), 161–68. The charter was adopted by the Alliance at its conference in Hammanskraal, South Africa, October 26–30, 1981.

50. The text of the confession can be found as an appendix in Allan Boesak, "To Stand Where God Stands: Reflections on the Confession of Belhar," *Studio Historiae Ecclesiasticae* 34, no. 1 (July 2008): 163–67.

51. See for example Dirk J. Smit, *Essays in Public Theology: Collected Essays 1*, Study Guides in Religion and Theology 12, Publications of the University of the Western Cape (Stellenbosch: Sun Press, 2007), 251–54.

52. Allan Boesak and Charles Villa-Vicencio, eds., *When Prayer Makes News* (Philadelphia: Westminster Press, 1986), 26.

53. Boesak, *Black and Reformed*, 27.

54. Boesak, *Black and Reformed*, 30.

55. See for example Boesak, *Tenderness of Conscience*, 156–57.

56. In a sermon on Ps. 82:3, *Opera*, 46, 406.

57. The new, multi-racial elite (20 percent of the population receives 74 percent of the GDP, while the poorest of the poor (53 percent) received 6–8 percent. Archbishop Njonkongkulu Ndugane describes poverty as a "time bomb." See *African Monitor Poverty Report* (Cape Town: African Monitor, 2010).

58. Michael O. Emerson and George Yancey, *Transcending Racial Barriers: Toward A Mutual Obligations Approach* (New York: Oxford University Press, 2011), 13.

59. As a very recent practical example of a phenomenon that repeats itself regularly, see the heated public debate on the selection for the Springbok rugby team for the 2012 Rugby world cup, *Cape Argus*, 2 June 2011. For a more systematic, theoretical argumentation see

M. Cromhout, "Die Vermyding van Etniese Spanning en Konflik in Suid Afrika: Wat kan Paulus se ervaring ons leer?" *HTS Teologiese Studies/Theological Studies* 67, No. 1 (2011) Art.#782. DOI:10.4102/hts.v67i.782. Cromhout refers to the pervasiveness of "racism" in, for example, the (Afrikaans) "language debate," the changing of street names and names of towns, and the South African government's "ideology of transformation."

60. Donald W. Sue, Christian M. Capodilupo, Gina C. Torino, Jennifer M. Bucceri, Alisha M. B. Holder, Kevin L. Nadal, and Marta Esquilin, "Racial Micro-aggressions in Everyday Life: Implications for Clinical Practice," *American Psychologist* 62, No. 4 (2007): 271–86.

61. See Wilmore, *Black Religion*, 120.

62. "Covenanting for Justice in the Economy and the Earth, Accra Confession," *Accra 2004: That All May Have Life in Fullness. World Alliance of Reformed Churches 24th General Council Proceedings* (Geneva: WARC, 2005), 153–60.

63. See David D. Daniels III, "'Doing All the Good We Can': The Political Witness of African American Holiness and Pentecostal Churches in the Post-Civil Rights Era," in R. Drew Smith, ed., *New Day Begun: African American Churches and Civic Culture in Post-Civil Rights America* (Durham, NC: Duke University Press, 2003), 178.

64. See Michael Eric Dyson, *I May Not Get There With You: The True Martin Luther King, Jr.* (New York: Simon & Schuster, 2000), 87, 88. See also Allan A. Boesak, *Coming in Out of the Wilderness: A Comparative Interpretation of the Ethics of Martin Luther King, Jr., and Malcolm X*, Kamper Cashiers No. 28 (Kampen: Kok, 1974), 38–41.

65. See Farid Esack, *Qur'an, Liberation and Pluralism: An Islamic Perspective of Interreligious Solidarity Against Oppression* (Oxford: OneWorld Publishers, 2000).

66. "A Time To Break the Silence," *A Testament of Hope*, 240.

Shape-Shifting: Cultural Hauntings, Contested Post-Racialism, and Black Theological Imagination

Walter Earl Fluker

The fact is that the comments that have been made and the issues that have surfaced over the last few weeks reflect the complexities of race in this country that we've never really worked through—a part of our union that we have yet to perfect. . . . But I have asserted a firm conviction—a conviction rooted in my faith in God and my faith in the American people—that working together we can move beyond some of our old racial wounds, and that in fact we have no choice if we are to continue on the path of a more perfect union.
—Senator Barack Obama, "A More Perfect Union," March 18, 2008

What the cynics fail to understand is that the ground has shifted beneath them, that the stale political arguments that have consumed us for so long no longer apply.
—President Barack Obama, inaugural address, January 20, 2009

Introduction: The Cultural Haunting of Barack Hussein Obama

The 2009 inauguration of our first African American president was a proud moment for the United States of America, a jubilant moment for the world, and a surreal, fantastical, disembodied experience for most of us who live and breathe, work and think about the black church. And yet, there was a troubling dimension to this incredible passage. Something said to me, maybe to all us—that *the ground had shifted*—indicated that maybe we lost something precious even as we had gained what so many fought for, prayed for, hoped for, and died for. For some of us, the moment was, and still is, strange and mixed with anxiety or angst, a distrust of feelings that were too joyful, too hopeful, and perhaps superficial. Did this moment bring with it erasure of memory—a type of anomie as in loss of world? Are we now in a post-racial America? A post-American world?

On November 5, 2008, the day after the historic election of Barack Hussein Obama as the forty-fourth president of the United States of America, I wrote an article for *U.S. News & World Report* in which I raised the issue of the cultural haunting of race in America.[1] I wrote that for many, Obama's presidency marked a new beginning, but for others it provoked suspicion, fear, and distrust because our nation is haunted by an old ghost. It is a ghost not quite like the ghosts with which we have become comfortable: Banquo visiting his cunning and power-hungry murderers; Washington Irving's headless horseman spooking the quiet village of Sleepy Hollow in Ichabod Crane's early America; Edgar Allan Poe's telltale heart pounding from beneath the floorboards; or the ghosts of the framed portrait subjects on the walls of the staircase in Hogwarts in the Harry Potter chronicles.

No, this was a different kind of eerie visitation, a twenty-first-century cultural haunting of America. This ghost is more like Toni Morrison's Beloved, who is a full-bodied, central character in the American narrative. In America, to use the language of literary scholar Kathleen Brogran, the ghost "serves to illuminate the shadowy and more repressed aspects of our national character" that played out disastrously in the campaign and election, and continues to haunt the presidency of Barack Obama. During his first presidential campaign, this old ghost showed up everywhere: in an elderly woman in Milwaukee expressing her suspicion and distrust of the "Arab"; in an old man screaming, "I am fed up and mad as hell!"; at Republican political rallies in the unidentified shouts of "Kill Obama!"; on the cover of the *New Yorker* that featured a cartoon showing Barack Obama wearing a turban and his wife Michelle toting an AK-47; and in a foiled assassination plot that was—thank God—hatched by simpletons.

Since the election, Obama has been verbally assaulted by an irate Republican congressman in the House of Representatives itself during the president's healthcare address; insulted by the Tea Party-backed demand that he submit his birth certificate to authenticate his American citizenship; and erased by thousands of backwater creeks and romanticized hegemonic imaginings of a nostalgic America that never really existed. Imagine that! A sitting American president who has to present his birth certificate as a pass card to prove his American citizenship! These were all signs of the ghost that stalks the shadows of the American collective consciousness. It is alive, well, very dangerous—and it will not go away.

The Shape-Shifting Ghost of Post-Racialism

At the heart of these cultural hauntings is a revelation of how deeply race is embedded in American culture, and of the ways in which race as a cultural and social ghost shape-shifts and re-invents itself in myriad figurations. My use of shape-shifting borrows a form of critical signification from black church traditions.[2] Historically, the black church has taken its metaphors, its parody and transformation of western stories and ideas, too literally. It has mistaken these rhetorical devices for preordained things, essences. For example, I argue that the idea of exodus is not a fixed reality, but a metaphorical device that must be revisable if the black church is to survive and fulfill its mission in this century. Along the same lines, I am arguing that the notion of God as an unchangeable reality is best understood as a relational reality that participates in human experience.

Shape-shifting, here, constitutes a form of postmodern, self-reflexive analysis of all signs claiming to be absolute, including race, blackness, and theological metaphors. In some respects, this method draws on the image of the trickster, as in Ananse, Esu, or the Signifying Monkey, as a shape-shifter in terms of the changing, indeterminate meaning of language.[3] I am suggesting, therefore, that the black church remain open to reversibility and remember its own tradition of shape-shifting, signifying, and reinterpreting in preaching, liturgy, and playing on words. In this sense, I am asking for a return to a type of process metaphysics that is already present in the traditions of the black Atlantic and in Africa.[4]

Eliminativists and Conservationists on Race as Fiction or Fact

The metaphor of race as a ghost-like social entity that shape-shifts into different guises in order to adapt to changing cultural and socio-political situations is hotly contested in contemporary academic discourse. On the one hand, eliminativist philosophers such as Kwame Anthony Appiah argue that since the concept of a race is a biological fiction, it is a meaningless term that should be discarded in academic, cultural, and socio-political life. To continue to employ the concept of race as though it were a scientific fact simply reinforces and encourages historical oppression and divisiveness on the basis of skin color. Describing the eliminativist thesis as an Enlightenment ideal, Richard Jones wrote in 2005, "[A]ccording to the eliminativists, if race is not a scientific fact, it must be a sociohistorical convention that can be eliminated by the construction of a counterconsciousness based on the delivery of the high egalitarian promises of the Enlightenment" (Jones, p. 626).

Conservationist thinkers such as Jones, Lucius Outlaw, and Charles Mills, argue that eliminating the concept of race will not lead to an egalitarian society. The opposite is actually true. If we eliminate the concept of race from our academic and socio-political discourse, we render racism and its consequences beyond rational critique (Jones, p. 621). The danger of post-racial thinking is that it easily degenerates into an outright denial of racism, a theoretically sophisticated mutated, shifting form of racism in the name of anti-racism. This perspective, reminds us of the proverbial ostrich, which hides its head in the sand in the presence of imminent danger in order not to see what is happening. The danger of this position, of course, is that when we bury our heads in the sand, more is exposed than is hidden. Those who adopt this perspective must also attend to a type of double jeopardy to non-white oppressed classes. In 2000, philosopher Naomi Zack wrote,

> It's one thing to understand within a safe forum that race is a biological fiction. [But] in American culture at large, the fiction of race continues to operate as fact, and in situations of backlash against emancipatory progress, the victims of racial oppression, non-whites, are insulted and injured further for their progress against oppression. If those who practice such second-order oppression begin to employ the truth that race is a fiction, gains already secured against first-order oppression (or in redress of it) could be jeopardized. (Zack, p. 53, brackets added)

So how do we employ the concept of race in academic and socio-political contexts without reinforcing it as biological fact or treating it is as social fiction? Here I follow Richard Jones in thinking about race as a resilient, shifting, and revisable historical reality that is constantly adapting to new social situations.

The Revisability of Race: Racing and Languaging

Drawing from American pragmatism and Du Bois, Jones redefines race as a linguistic tool, infinitely revisable, that we use in a myriad of ways to ascribe meaning to ourselves and others. As it assigns difference and value to varying configurations of class, gender, sexuality, and tribalism, race also ascribes and inscribes notions of identity and otherness, and definitions of human flourishing. In this sense, race is as a "tool in a language game, or a tool for achieving viable forms of life—that is infinitely revisable as the dynamic relationships (processes) between frameworks (or environments) and agents (or organisms) [that] evolve over time as they work out internal inconsistencies. In this instrumentalist view, race as a linguistic concept can be seen diachronically as having been a tool for domination and subordination in master/slave scripts," [and] it can be viewed "synchronically as a developing linguistic instrument for human liberation" (Jones, 627). Thus, positing race as a tool in the creation of meaning recognizes that race is not a biologically or historically fixed reality; rather, such a positing encourages us to be aware that race exists in mutable social forms that constantly adapt and blend into new socio-political situations. As a shape-shifting social phenomenon, race can be seen as something *conjured* in our lives, and as conjuring agents we have the responsibility to discern whether or not we use race effectively as an emancipatory instrument in the exorcism of social evil, or for demonic oppressive ends. Hence, the double jeopardy of racing as fact or fiction is simultaneously instrumental and revisable, and, therefore, potentially a tool of the spirit that can be used in the art of conjuring liberative practices.

Toni Morrison's work on race as metaphor also informs my thinking on shape-shifting and the revisability of race. In *Playing in the Dark: Whiteness and the Literary Imagination*, she writes,

> Race has become metaphorical—a way of referring to and disguising forces, events, classes, and expressions of social decay and economic division far more threatening to the body politic than biological "race" ever was. Expensively kept, economically unsound, a spurious and useless political asset in election campaigns, racism is as healthy today as it was during the Enlightenment. It seems that it has a utility far beyond economy, beyond the sequestering of classes from one another, and has assumed a metaphorical life so completely embedded in daily discourse that it is perhaps more necessary and more on display than ever before.

I apply this pragmatist conservationist perspective of the revisability of race (against post-racialism) to the United States black church context to consider how the major metaphors that shaped the social/political, theological/ethical, and aesthetic/existential dimensions of this phenomenon in the previous century have become inadequate guiding paradigms for this ecclesiological community in the twenty-first century. The meta-metaphor guiding this re-evaluation of the black church is, "The ground has shifted but ghosts still haunt us." "The ground has shifted but ghosts still haunt us" is a symbolic marker that pushes us to think together about ways in which African American religious scholars and church leadership must engage a new time and rhythm, a shift of lifeworlds and systems in what is being called a post-racial, post-American world.

Three Shifts in US Black Church Activism in a Contested Post-Racial World

As part of the constructive task of this presentation, I want to first analyze the guiding, diachronic, and synchronic metaphors that have shaped the black church's social/political, theological/ethical, and aesthetic/existential understanding of itself and its potential forms and functions. In particular, I would like to suggest experimentation with three dynamically and integrally related metaphors/moments that speak to the shifting markers of the American black church agenda in the twenty-first century. I structure each moment respectively as from dilemma to diaspora, from exodus *to* exile, and "from the frying pan to the fire."

1. From Dilemma to Diaspora: Social Political Contexts of Black Church Practices

Since publication of Gunnar Myrdal's classic study *An American Dilemma*,[5] the metaphor of "dilemma" has come to represent broad and conflicting ideologies in respect to African American life and culture.[6] The subtitle of Myrdal's work, however, underscores the fundamental character of the issues at stake. He characterizes the dilemma as "The Negro Problem and Democracy." The Negro problem (sometimes called the "Negro question") has been the staple ideological statement defining and representing the life and place of the African in American society since slavery. The Negro problem, formulated by all segments of the male-dominated white power elite, was, "What shall we do with the Negro?"[7]

In his meditation on doubleness, W. E. B. Du Bois posed the dilemma as a personal/existential question: "What does it *feel* like to be a problem?" More precisely, the question implies a social/political inquiry: "What does this mean for the social life and personal sanity of African American citizens?" His question, however, does not simply address a personal, sociological, or historical problem, but a religious and theological problem that demands historical, sociological, and cultural analysis. W. E. B. Du Bois's famous question is both an existential query denoting the angst inherent in the doubleness of African American life and practices, and an interrogation of the socially-constructed *habitus* that framed the practice of dilemma in social policy and the quest for citizenship at the dawn of twentieth-century America. It is also a critical signification on the bitter cry of dereliction and abandonment (remember, Du Bois also asked, "Why did God make me an outcast and a stranger in mine own house?"). The bitter cry lament is also a plea of theodicy arising from the deep processes of social alienation and estrangement in a world constructed in the image of whiteness, where black subjectivity is subjugated and incarcerated by its own agency—a consciousness that monitors and participates in its own confinement. The discursive features of the problem, of course, precede and succeed Du Bois's eloquent, poetic analytic of black agency and the concomitant structural injustices of race that have received wide scholarly attention.[8]

The dilemma is hardly resolved; it still exists at the heart of African American life and practices and has far-reaching implications for the ways African American church leaders understand and participate in civic life, and how they interrogate the ghost of post-racialism. Preoccupation with dilemma is unproductive, akin to riding two horses galloping in different directions—which is a strain on the anatomy. In recent years, a number of scholars working in critical race theory, historical, literary, cultural, multicultural, and philosophical studies have addressed the problematic in other terms.[9] More progressive critiques look at the question of dilemma with respect to macro-economic and political variables and their relationship to cultural and aesthetic meanings, and the place of the *body*.[10]

Most relevant to the purposes of our present discussion is the treatment afforded by cultural critics who ask the question of dilemma as it pertains to binary oppositions in black life that grow out of adaptation to a North Atlantic aesthetic. These studies seek to understand the ways in which attachment to the heroic ideal of the European aesthete prevents and further complicates progressive critiques and strategies for agency and peoplehood.[11] Under the title "Autonomy in Dilemma," Peter Paris discusses the long-standing struggle within African American communities between loyalty to faith and loyalty to the nation. The dilemma, Paris informs us, is how we reconcile these contending demands for loyalty: the inclusive moral demand of faith, versus the more particularized, and often self-annihilative demand of the nation. These loyalties, he suggests, "represent, respectively, theories of politics and ecclesiology that imply moral conflicts in theory and practice" (29). Historically, we have tended not to reconcile them at all, but rather to acquiesce to the demands of the nation. Our participation in the two world wars, the Korean and Vietnam wars—and now, Iraq and Afghanistan—are illustrations of this position. Such a posture has stymied not only our "power" within the political scenario of the United States, but has prevented the American black church from authentically participating in the global community.

In this sense, for the American black church, dilemma is a boundary metaphor, or what Robert Neville, in *The Truth of Broken Symbols* (1995), calls a religious symbol. According to Neville, religious symbols are complex phenomena that arise out of the imaginative engagement of persons and communities with "finite/infinite boundary conditions" in the world through the use of signs. As potential vehicles for revelations of the ultimate, these signs or symbols point beyond themselves to an infinite source, even as they remain partial, finite, and "broken" by the particular cultural, social, and political concerns of the subjects they embody (Neville, 1995). Analysis of the boundary metaphor of dilemma, I would like to suggest, is a beginning point for passage toward reconstructing a new political and ecclesiological ground for a globally conceived and engaged black church. While dilemma may have been helpful in the past, however, it cannot point us towards a global future where the American black church may fully participate in the project of human flourishing.

The second movement within the paradigm is emerging as a reconstructed metaphor of diaspora. The metaphor has always been present within African American sociopolitical and cultural discourse, for example in the illustrious examples of the call for pan-Africanism in Robert Alexander Young, David Walker, Henry Highland Garnett, Anna Julia Cooper, Ida Barnett Wells, Martin Delaney, Marcus Garvey, W. E. B. Dubois, and Malcolm X. As part of another tradition within the African American Christian community, the metaphor was ably articulated by King in his excoriation of the Vietnam War and the call for a "World House."

"Diaspora", in King's perspective of a "World House," is a shape-shifting metaphor that emerges from dilemma as a way of addressing issues of identity which are not confined to nationalistic ideologies that bind one to potentially narrow visions of peoplehood. Rather, diaspora, in this sense, places African Americans within the world context as global citizens. What diaspora ultimately does is to give the US black church a more appropriate paradigm and symbol from which to talk about ministry in global perspective. And it affords a prophetic position relative to the loyalty to nation motif that has, in many respects, prevented African Americans from more fully approximating the ideal of their faith convictions and racial/ethnic solidarity. A nagging question that accompanies this kind of thinking is, "Can a complex notion of Diaspora as we have understood it in *nation language* and in *migratory patterns* of black religious and cultural practices serve as a foundation for a more radical proposal for national and global citizenship?"[12]

In 2005, Harvard cultural anthropologist Lorand Matory began to answer this question in his work on Black Atlantic religion. Starting with the transatlantic slave trade, Matory argues that the "Black Atlantic" was the first self-conscious transnational modern community that was and is simultaneously "a geographical focus, an identity option, and a context of meaning-making, rather than a uniquely bounded, impenetrable, or overdetermining thing" (Matory, p. 274). In other words, the existence of the Black Atlantic has always represented an argument against modernity, nationalism, and master narratives about the homogeneity of human cultures—even if this fact has been ignored in the literature on modernity, postmodernity, and transnationalism (Matory, 2005).

For this reason, Matory prefers the metaphor "Black Atlantic" over "diaspora" to refer to the ways in which passing ships carried various human cargoes in multiple directions to create a multidirectional black culture. For Matory, the metaphor "African diaspora"

> shares some of the misleading implications of the *arborescent* metaphors, insofar as the diaspora concept suggests that homelands are to their diasporas as the past is to the present. Candomble and many other African-diasporic phenomena are not simply outgrowths of their homelands but also, and just as important, outcomes of an ongoing dialogue with a coeval homeland. African homelands and diasporas—much like Europe and its American, African, Middle Eastern, and Australian settler colonies—have engaged in a long and influential dialogue of mutual transformation. (Matory, pp. 280–81)

Instead Matory suggests borrowing from Deleuze and Guattari (1987) to describe black Atlantic communities as co-directional entities. Deleuze and Guattari encourage the use of "rhizome metaphors that mimic the network-like roots of grasses, which unite multiple roots with multiple shoots. Deleuze and Guattari thus reject monocausal narratives, single source constructions of group history, and inattention to the multidirectional ramifications of any genealogy of events" (Matory, p. 280). In my explication of shape-shifting diaspora, I mean something similar to the rhizome analogy, in which the US black church recognizes its multi-directional affiliations and interconnections, with several roots and shoots around the globe. This metaphor is also resonant with the black church's ultimate affiliation with the God of all creation, who has guided us beyond our exodus from enslavement into a new global exilic reality of struggle and transnational possibility.

2. From Exodus to Exile: Theological/Ethical Contexts of Black Church Practices

From our earliest beginnings, exodus has been the central paradigmatic theological and ethical statement of black church life and practices. The idea of exodus has served multiple functions in an ongoing cultural narrative "deeply anchored in themes of captivity, Exile, enslavement and deliverance." Exodus has referred to the language of nation espoused by early nineteenth- and twentieth-century church leaders and activists. It marked the transition from slavery to freedom in the historical events of Emancipation and Reconstruction. It evolved into "the second Exodus" during the Great Migration, which began around the time of the First World War, when large numbers of African Americans left the Southeast, mid-South, and Southwest for the urban Northeast, the northern Midwest, Canada, and the Southwest for "the warmth of other suns."[13] And in the modern civil rights movement, exodus language was a powerful symbol of the journey to the promised land of full citizenship and equal opportunity.[14]

However, according to theologian Sallie McFague (writing in 1974), all theological metaphors are human constructions of the divine and may never fully reveal the divine presence. McFague argues that the metaphors theologians draw upon to construct theologies should remain relevant to the current situation, rather than relying upon the authority of the past as if language about God were somehow static or fixed (Carroll, 1991). For her, theological metaphors that remain fixed upon the past led church communities to misrepresent their present condition in the world in relation to divine presence. In this sense, all guiding theological metaphors reveal and conceal aspects of the human relation to the divine. No exception, the African American attachment to the exodus motif has been helpful and hurtful in the black church's quest for evidence of activity of the divine in history. No one can read the great orations of the African American past or listen to the spirituals without knowing that the exodus has played a prominent role in our thinking about liberation, God, and history. Martin Luther King's, "The Death of Evil on the Seashore," or his last public address, "I've Been to the Mountaintop," are excellent examples of the kind sermonizing that utilizes exodus as a symbol of the historical plight of African Americans. During the rise of black power, James Cone's theology took as its point of departure the exodus of God's oppressed peoples from the bondage of Pharaoh. Womanist theologians, on the other hand, have complicated the exodus metaphor by introducing the idea of "wilderness," placing more emphasis on Hagar's triple oppression (owing to the intersectionality of gender, race, and class) than on Sara and Abraham.[15] Senator Barack Obama effectively utilized the exodus metaphor as a political rhetorical strategy early in his presidential campaign, comparing the civil rights movement to "the Moses generation" and the new post-civil rights activism to "the Joshua generation."

> I'm here because somebody marched. I'm here because you all sacrificed for me. I stand on the shoulders of giants. I thank the Moses generation; but we've got to remember, now, that Joshua still had a job to do. As great as Moses was, despite all that he did, leading a people out of bondage, he didn't cross over the river to see the Promised Land. God told him your job is done. . . . We're going to leave it to the Joshua generation to make sure it happens. There are

still battles that need to be fought; some rivers that need to be crossed. Like Moses, the task was passed on to those who might not have been as deserving, might not have been as courageous, find themselves in front of the risks that their parents and grandparents and great grandparents had taken. That doesn't mean that they don't still have a burden to shoulder, that they don't have some responsibilities. The previous generation, the Moses generation, pointed the way. They took us 90% of the way there. We still got that 10% in order to cross over to the other side.[16]

William R. Jones, in what was probably the most controversial book written during the nascent days of black theology, *Is God a White Racist?*, challenged the appropriateness of using the "Exodus metaphor" in the context of the experiences of African American people. However historically situated, Jones argued, exodus suggests that there has been or will be an actual, historically verifiable liberating act from the hand of God for black people. Jones contended that we could not point to such an act in history. I agree with Jones that the historical plight of African Americans cannot be equated with the biblical exodus of the Hebrews. Neither can we point to an eschatological event with historical certainty. The eschatological event of the future is based on the claims of a liberating exodus event from the past. Since we cannot refer to an actual historically verifiable exodus of the past, we risk serious error in anticipating an eschaton in which God will deliver the oppressed.

The exodus motif also prevents the masses of black church folk from thinking deliberatively and historically about their present political and social predicament. Theodore Walker Jr., writing in 2004, suggests this eventuality may result from modern interpretations of the exodus event, which tend to draw from antiquated metaphysical notions of God as an abstract authoritative author of history (Walker, p. 25). Drawing from the process philosophy of Alfred North Whitehead and Charles Hartshorne's neoclassical metaphysics,[17] Walker argues that an adequate postmodern black theology would entail a relational God who struggles alongside God's creatures in the quest for freedom. One only has to walk the streets of any major urban center, or to witness the proliferating phenomenon of black bodies in correctional facilities around the country and see the sheer carnage of black humanity, to know that there has not been a definitive historically verifiable exodus from Egypt or Mississippi or Chicago for African Americans. The affinity for exodus also has striking parallels for African American discourse globally. With respect to the global community, from what have we been liberated? From whom? Where? And When? In a manner reminiscent of the dilemma motif, African Americans have tended to respond out of an antiquated notion of exodus that may be, at this point in our history, more hurtful than helpful when it comes to articulating a global vision of ministry.

I would like to suggest some experimentation with the biblical and cultural notion of exile as a more appropriate mode of discourse for the present socio-political situation of African Americans. Paris makes this point in his discussion of "moral agency in conflict":

> Whenever persons are rejected by society, the result is a loss of place; the result is Exile. Whenever a pattern of oppression persists from one generation to another and is firmly rooted in an ideology, the rejected ones become destined to a veritable permanent state of Exile wherein they have no sense of belonging, neither to the community nor to the territory. Since it is necessary for persons to be nourished by a communal *eros* in order to become fully human, an imposed Exile necessitates the formation of substitute community, and ... that has been one of the major functions of the black churches. Born and reared in an alien socio-political context, blacks have had little hope for any sense of genuine national belonging. (59)

"Exile," like "diaspora," speaks to a more world-oriented, historical picture of African American oppression in a contested post-racial world, and allows black churches to take seriously their socio-historical location as agents of world history, rather than passive nation-bound spectators. Exile as a shape-shifting metaphor, likewise, is a corrective to what political scientist Frederick C. Harris refers to as "the dualistic orientation of black oppositional civic culture." Harris captures in this statement the paradoxical strivings of black leaders, which combine the quest for social dignity with political activism within a parochialized theological/ethical context that militates against a more globalized ethic of engagement. The exilic predicament of African Americans provides fertile ground for theologizing about our relationship with other brothers and sisters in diaspora; it also confronts us with the question of our existential and aesthetic estrangement; and the question of the "stranger" (maybe our other sisters and brothers from whom we have been estranged).

3. From the Frying Pan to the Fire: The Existential and Aesthetic Contexts of Black Church Activism

A number of scholars have begun to look more deeply into the existential and aesthetic contexts of black church life and activism along the lines of thinking presented here.[18] They invite us to carefully straddle the diverse worlds of religious meaning and tradition, leaving space for a sustained conversation between black church scholars and religious humanists—which, in my opinion, may be the most difficult, yet most salient public conversation in a contested post-racial and post-American world.

Anthony Pinn's new book, *Understanding and Transforming the Black Church*,[19] is a prolegomenon to a larger, more complicated set of questions that black churches will need to rethink in light of the nagging historical problems of racialized, sexualized, genderized politics in the church and the larger culture. More importantly, he challenges scholars working in these traditions to reframe these questions in reference to the shifting grounds of political and social realities that shape-shift toward complex subjectivity, diversity, openness, and inclusiveness. A critical dimension of this shape-shifting will involve a new aesthetic sensibility and appreciation of the *body*, the many colored and estranged bodies that are heirs to Somebodyness.[20] As Cornel West asserts, "[T]he notion that black people are human beings is a relatively new discovery in the modern West. The idea of black equality in beauty, culture, and intellectual capacity remains problematic."[21]

What about the body as a somaesthetic site for pondering new and fresh approaches to dilemma/diaspora and exodus/exile? I pause to reflect on a picture placed on my altar to my mother, showing her in her church usher's uniform, as a site for imaginative theological reflection on the somaesthetic. My mama took me to church two or three times a week. It was a little storefront located between a barbershop and two houses on 43rd Street in Chicago infamously known as "the Bucket of Blood." A pool hall and Princess's Restaurant were located farther down the street. Across the street were a rib joint and a tavern. The church was a sanctuary and social center that enveloped my youth like an old package used to transport fragile cargo to safe quarters. It shape-shifted over time to adapt to new urban realities. The building originally served as a church, then an animal hospital, and was later refashioned to accommodate black saints, mostly women, mostly migrants from Mississippi.[22] Mama was an usher. Every Sunday she would dress up in her white uniform with a black handkerchief delicately placed over a badge that read "Centennial M. B. Church." Mama was the proudest person alive as she greeted the congregants with an extended arm and a swift turn and escorted them to their seats. Those simple movements—the extended arm and swift turn—were what Milan Kundera calls "gestures of immortality":

> A gesture cannot be regarded as the expression of an individual, as his creation (because no individual is capable of creating a fully original gesture, belonging to nobody else), nor can it be regarded as that person's instrument; on the contrary, it is gestures that use us as instruments, as their bearers and incarnations.[23]

My mother's body—the outstretched arm, the swift turn and the ritualistic garment of the usher extending hospitality to the other—is a site for reflection on aesthetic sensibilities and an authentically human initiation of *global communitas*. They are gestures of immortality in which the intersectionality of race, politics, economic, cultural, and spiritual signs and meaning meet and transgress proscriptions on complex incarnate subjectivity bound in nation language—the language of empire that simultaneously binds the US black church to the essentialism of cultural domination residing in worn out, ineffective metaphors of the past (dilemma and exodus).

Is not my mother's outstretched arm an invitation to share in her humanity by "facing the other" in all her/his strangeness, possibility and hope?[24] My mother's ritualistic performance as an usher provides entre to a global picture of "recurring incarnations" in the swift turn and act of "gesturing" and "facing the other," greeters of disaporic bodies, lost and found in the black Atlantic middle passage. This experience of facing the other reveals the deep longing and yearning to be in unity with ourselves—our exiled and diasporic bodies—and with others from whom we are estranged.[25] In the complexity of those grand gestures, the outstretched arm and swift turn, she not only faces the other, she turns. The turn is conversion from something fixed toward something beyond, new, more, and dynamic. The act of turning towards the other is an act of shape-shifting, of leaving the old self in order to embrace a newer dynamic self that includes a "more" or an "other." The swift turn points to Martin Buber's and William James's ideas of movement from divided self to a more integral sense of self in communion with the other.[26] It is a turn from Du Bois's doubleness to a truer sense of self. Moreover, my mother's ritualistic performance is a shape-shifting, signifying movement that calls on the deity Esu, the Holy Ghost, to turn, to shift towards the other within and the other without, to signify on black figuration of language and being—or what Anthony Pinn calls a "hermeneutics of style."[27] This effect is embedded in her body language; she is the great trickster, a black interpreter god, signifying on culture and calling upon us to turn. She is a Kumina dancer, incarnating the spirit of life, filled with the Holy Ghost and a mighty burning fire!

What if we were to take this aesthetic/existential approach of shape-shifting, of turning, seriously in considering the shifting grounds of American black church tradition? What would our churches look like if we took shape-shifting metaphors of diaspora and exile seriously? What would be the content of our preaching and the form and shape of our liturgy and our "gesturing" to the stranger? I am suggesting that we would be turning, (to use an old metaphor from my mother) "jumping from the frying pan to the fire." The fire metaphor, like diaspora and Exile, takes us beyond the temptation to quietism embodied in the metaphors of dilemma (which suggests "standing still," indecisiveness, or what Robert Michael Franklin calls "the strenuous self")[28]; beyond exodus (which suggests that the liberating event has already happened and conspires with the temptation to quietism); and beyond the frying pan (a static notion in which African Americans are seen as passive objects subjected to present social/political arrangements that act as a literal hell, a "lake of Fire burning day and night, forever and ever"). The frying pan seems the appropriate context in which to talk about the historic ways in which we have wrestled ambiguously in dilemma and hoped in exodus. Turning and jumping into the fire, on the other hand, takes the black church to a deeper dimension of discourse and practice already present. Fire is far more terrifying than the frying pan, far more dangerous, far more costly—but fire is also purgative and shape-shifts toward what Howard Thurman called the search for common ground.

With respect to the shape-shifting ghost of contested post-racial discourse, let us re-imagine what it means to be bodily "baptized by Fire and the Holy Ghost." "I indeed baptize you with water unto repentance: but he that cometh after me is mightier than I, whose shoes I am not worthy to bear: he shall baptize you with the Holy Ghost, and with Fire" (Matt. 3:11). Fire, as a shape-shifting metaphor, is universal and purgative. What I have in mind here is akin to Diana L. Eck's experimentation with cross-cultural and religious themes associated with the Spirit. One of the common themes that binds traditional religious cosmologies is the element of fire as symbol for spirit (also breath, wind).[29] African American religious discourse is anchored in practices that seek the fullness of baptism in the Spirit which is "Fire shut in our bones."[30] As Allan Boesak reminds us in his excellent collection of sermons, *The Fire Within: Sermons from the Edge of Exile*, there is indeed a place for black Jeremiahs/Jeremiads, whether in South Africa or in the United States or in the United Kingdom. Preaching in exilic contexts where prophetic voices have been silenced, black church leaders must confront their own "intensely personal" narratives, "framed within the perplexity of their own voicelessness," in order to answer the question, "How can the one made voiceless be speaking the Word of God to others?"[31] The confrontation between my good friend Dr. Jeremiah Wright and then Senator Barack Obama is an example of the challenge that "Fire shut in our bones" demands of us.

Fire and Recurring Incarnation

The metaphor of fire also reminds us of the importance of the shape-shifting character of the Holy Ghost (spirit) in constructing a global theology of the

African diaspora. Womanist scholar Diane Stewart Diakete's 2004 work on the Kumina religion, a BaKongo tradition of Central Africa that became widely practiced by slaves in Jamaica and their descendants, argues that a proper understanding of spirit in the African diaspora would include the notion of "recurring incarnation" (Stewart, p. 61).[32] Rather than emphasizing men's preoccupation with death, recurring spirit possession in these women focuses on women's ability to give life. Diakete believes that Kumina women's acknowledgment of the need to be in continuous touch with the spirit of the ancestors is a much more fulfilling pragmatic approach to the everyday problems Afro-Jamaican women face, and provides an important critique of Christian doctrines of redemptive suffering. Through her womanist analysis of Kumina rituals of possession, Diakete thus critiques less helpful Christian doctrines and points toward a more inclusive global diasporic theology, one that embraces the continual renewing power of spirit within women's bodies, even those of different religions (Stewart, p. 61).

Indeed, the spirit of fire demands that our commitments to the nation and to institutionalized religion in a contested post-racial world be judged by a more inclusive and prophetic norm, not unlike the tongues of fire at Pentecost. Our commitments to the nation would be judged in the context of a greater loyalty to the world community, particularly to people of African descent and other oppressed peoples of the world. When Martin Luther King made the fateful decision to talk about a world house in which the triplets of war, poverty, and racism had to be removed, he was prophesying in tongues of fire. This courageous vision of world community cost him dearly—some of us think he paid with his life. In many respects, King's prophetic vision of the world house mirrors what we have in mind when we consider the idea of fire, or reverence that sees the interrelatedness and inherent value of all life. It was his sense of community that led him to identify the great new problem of humankind as the challenge of divided loyalties— loyalty to the particularized and local visions of race, ethnicity, and the state, versus the demand for global community:

> We have inherited a large house, a great "world house" in which we have to live together—black and white, Easterner and Westerner, Gentile and Jew, Catholic and Protestant, Moslem and Hindu—a family unduly separated in ideas, culture and interest, who, because we can never again live apart, must learn somehow to live together with each other in peace.[33]

For King, the remedy for this problem of loyalty was a "revolution of values and priorities." At the heart of such a revolution (or turning) is the question of loyalty. "A genuine revolution of values means in the final analysis that our loyalties must become ecumenical rather than sectional. Every nation must now develop an overriding loyalty to mankind as a whole in order to preserve the best in our individual societies." King suggested that this spiritual revolution would lift us beyond tribe, race, class, and nation to a worldwide fellowship of love.[34] At once, in this singular vision of reverence and possibility, King articulated the dream of the beloved community in which civility was inspired and supported within the context of global communion. Many believe he was speaking in many languages as the Spirit gave utterance—languages that speak in loving and just ways of the agonizing, yet redemptive possibilities inherent in recognition, respectability, and reverence for a beloved community more grand that even the nation and the world can ever hope for, *a new heaven and a new earth.*

Notes

1. http://www.usnews.com/opinion/articles/2008/11/05/president-elect-barack-obama
-race-has-been-haunting-this-election?PageNr=1 (accessed June 19, 2014).

2. Henry Louis Gates, *The Signifying Monkey: A Theory of African-American Literary Criticism* (New York: Oxford University Press, 1988), argues that people of African descent have always understood language as a shape-shifting, symbolic conductor of meaning that is difficult to decode because it has many forms and guises. In African American literature in particular, the themes of shape-shifting and language are often represented in the character of the "Signifying Monkey," who is an "ironic reversal of a received racist image of the black as simian like, the Signifying Monkey—he who dwells at the margins of discourse, ever punning, ever troping, ever embodying the ambiguities of language—is our trope for repetition and revision, indeed, is our trope of chiasmus itself, repeating and simultaneously reversing in one deft, discursive act" (Gates, 686).

As a metaphor of African American uses of language, the Signifying Monkey is a trickster figure, able to reverse circumstances and meanings by simply speaking and interpreting words. "The Signifying Monkey is a trickster figure, of the order of the trickster figure of Yoruba mythology, Esu-Elegbara in Nigeria, and Legba among the Fon in Dahomey, whose New World figurations . . . speak eloquently of the unbroken arc of metaphysical presuppositions and patterns of figuration shared through space and time among black cultures in West Africa, South America, the Caribbean, and the United States" (Gates, 687). This shape-shifting character, as Gates explains, is a black god of interpretation, and he tricks by using language, which apparently has one meaning, but actually signifies something else. This ability to shift the meaning of language without being detected by others often translates into undermining or reversing situations of exploitation and unjust power relations, particularly around race relations in the African American experience. An excellent example of this racial reversal, cited by Gates, is T. Thomas Fortune's rhetorical parody of Rudyard Kipling's "The White Man's Burden." In his "The Black Man's Burden," Fortune writes:

> What is the Black Man's Burden,
> Ye hypocrites and vile,
> Ye whited sepulchers
> From the Amazon to the Nile?
> What is the Black Man's Burden,
> Ye Gentile parasites,
> Who crush and rob your brother
> Of his manhood and his rights? (Gates, 693)

In this text, Fortune repeats the structure of "The White Man's Burden," but with an entirely different content, thus undermining the poem's apparent meaning. What Fortune is saying is that the apparent meaning of Kipling's poem (the presumed superiority of whiteness) can actually been seen to have a different meaning entirely (the tyranny of whiteness)—if you know how to decode it. Signification thus becomes a technique of social empowerment and personal survival in black culture. Moreover, what is critical for our purposes is the notion that as a central metaphor that organizes African American cultural uses of language, the Signifying Monkey expresses an openness to the reversibility of language and its plurality of meanings. The ability to shift the meaning of language has indeed been a central tool of physical survival and psychological resistance in African American life. In the same way, Gates goes on to show through literary criticism how black literary tradition signifies upon itself—especially when black writers mistake their own rhetorical devices and metaphors for "some preordained reality or thing. To read these figures literally, Reed tells us, is to be duped by figuration, just like the signified Lion. Reed has secured his place in the canon precisely by his critique of the received, repeated tropes peculiar to that very canon. His works are the grand works of critical signification." Henry Louis Gates Jr. "The 'Blackness of Blackness': A Critique of the Sign and the Signifying Monkey," *Critical Inquiry* 9, No. 4 (June, 1983): 723.

   3. "The Signifying Monkey is a trickster figure, of the order of the trickster figure of Yoruba mythology, Esu-Elegbara in Nigeria, and Legba among the Fon in Dahomey, whose New World figurations . . . speak eloquently of the unbroken arc of metaphysical presuppositions and patterns of figuration shared through space and time among black cultures in West Africa, South America, the Caribbean, and the United States. Thee trickster figures, aspects of Esu, are primarily *mediators*: as tricksters they are mediators and their mediations are tricks" (Gates, 687). "The versions of Esu are all messengers of the gods: he interprets the will of the gods to man; he carries the desires of man to the gods. He is known as the divine linguist, the keeper of ase ('logos') with which Olodumare created the universe. Esu is guardian of the crossroads, master of style and stylus, phallic god of generation and fecundity, master of the mystical barrier that separates the divine from the profane world. In Yoruba mythology, Esu always limps, because his legs are of different lengths: one is anchored in the realm of the gods, the other rests in the human world. The

closest Western relative of Esu is Hermes, of course; and, just as Hermes' role as interpreter lent his name readily to 'hermeneutics,' the study of the process of interpretation, so too the figure of Esu can stand, for the critic of comparative black literature, as our metaphor for the act of interpretation itself. In African and Latin American mythologies, Esu is said to have taught Ifa how to read the signs formed by the sixteen sacred palm nuts, which, when manipulated, configure into 'the signature of an Odu,' 256 of which comprise the corpus of *Ifa* divination. . . . Above all else, Esu is the Black Interpreter, the Yoruba god of indeterminacy, the sheer plurality of meaning. . . . As Hermes is to hermeneutics, Esu is the Esuotufinaalo ('bringing out the interstices of the riddle')" (Gates, 689).

"Esu's functional equivalent in Afro-American profane discourse is the Signifying Monkey, a figure who seems to be distinctly Afro-American, probably derived from Cuban mythology which generally depicts Echu-Elegua with a monkey at his side" (Gates, 688).

4. "The trickster speaks—and embodies—a vivid and subtle religious language, through which he links animality and ritual transformation, shapes culture by means of laughter, ties cosmic process to personal history, empowers divination to change boundaries into horizons, and reveals the passages to the sacred embedded in daily life." Robert Pelton, *The Trickster in West Africa: A Study of Mythic Irony and Sacred Delight* (Berkeley: University of California Press, 1989). "One of the Ashanti trickster tales strikingly illustrates the way in which Ananse, the spider-trickster, seizes the Ashanti mind by fooling with its ordinary categories. Ananse has promised to cure the mother of Nyame, the High God, and has pledged his life as a forfeit if he fails. When the old woman dies, Nyame insists that Ananse too must die. Then, as the executioners are preparing to carry out the sentence, Ananse plays his hidden trump. He has sent his son to burrow under the place of judgment, and at the last moment the son cries out as Ananse has bidden him: 'When you kill Ananse, the tribe with come to ruin! When you pardon Ananse, the tribe will shake with voices!' Nyame's chief minister turns to the High God and says, 'This people belongs to you and to Asase Yaa. Today you are about to kill Ananse, but Yaa, Old-mother-earth, says that if you let him go, it will be well.' Nyame complies, and thus it is, the Ashanti say, that the expression, 'You are as wonderful as Ananse,' has gained currency among them."

"Tricksterlike, Ananse speaks the truth by dissembling. The Ashanti cherish him for his gall and he delights them with his tricks, but the echoes of the complex relationships between Nyame and Asase Yaa, Queen Mother and King, that float through the story hint that Ananse has become synonymous with everything amazing for deeper reasons. Somehow, his slipperiness fulfills the nation's need for healthy commerce between what is above and what is below, between male and female, between apparent and hidden order. Without him the demands of the earth will be stifled, wholeness will vanish, and the people themselves will lose their coherence" (Pelton, 1989).

5. Gunnar Myrdal, *An American Dilemma: The Negro Problem and American Democracy* (New York: Harper and Brothers, 1944).

6. Harold Cruse, *The Crisis of the Negro Intellectual: The Failure of Black Leadership*; Kevin K. Gaines, *Uplifting the Race: Black Leadership, Politics and Culture in the Twentieth Century* (Chapel Hill: University of North Carolina Press, 1996), 5. Darlene Clark Hines, "Rape and the Inner Lives of Black Women in the Middle West: Preliminary Thoughts on the

Culture of Dissemblance," in *Unequal Sisters: A Multicultural Reader in U.S. Women's History*, ed. Ellen DuBois and Vicki L. Ruiz (New York: Routledge, 1990), 292–329; and Joy James, *Transcending the Talented Tenth: Black Leaders and American Intellectuals* (New York: Routledge, 1997). See Carl P. Henry, *Culture and African-American Politics* (Bloomington: Indiana University Press, 1990), 10–11. See Henry's critique of Cruse's dilemma-oriented polemic, which leaves unresolved the ideological premise that black elites must provide an adequate social theory based on living ingredients of African American history. The challenge for Cruse, as for other black elites, tends to be this unresolved problematic often couched in dilemmalistic language.

7. Ralph Luker, *The Social Gospel in Black and White* (Chapel Hill: University of North Carolina Press, 1991); Sidney M. Wilhelm, *Who Needs The Negro?* (New York: Anchor, 1971); Benjamin Quarles, *The Negro in the Making of America* (New York: Collier, 1964).

8. Since Gunnar Myrdal's classic 1944 study, *An American Dilemma*, the term "dilemma" has come to represent broad and conflicting ideologies with respect to African American life and culture. The subtitle of Myrdal's work, however, underscores the fundamental character of the issues at stake. He characterized the dilemma as *The Negro Problem and Democracy*. The "Negro problem" (sometimes called the "Negro question") has been the staple ideological statement defining and representing the life and place of the African in American society since slavery. The Negro problem/question, formulated by all sides of the male-dominated white power elite, was: "What shall we do with the Negro?" The problem, however, reached its most significant historical impasse during the last two decades of the nineteenth century and the first two decades of the twentieth. With increased African American political participation and economic development, and the large population of blacks in the South during Reconstruction, these years witnessed a rise in racially motivated violence and legislative and judicial practices aimed at stripping agency from freed men and women and returning the country to a place that was safe for "white women." At the same time former abolitionists, emigrationists—mostly Northern white religious leaders, politicians, industrialists, and philanthropists—worked diligently to solve the Negro problem through education as a means of "civilizing" the child/savage generally depicted in bestial and minstrel images. Such was the social and political context that greeted the African American entrance into the twentieth century and informed the moral and civic practices of many black intellectual elites and religious leaders, Du Bois included. Myrdal's formulation of the American Dilemma, however, betrayed a deeper and more fundamental problem seldom echoed in quiet, genteel places where the problem of whiteness was suppressed and ignored.

The "problem of whiteness," as I am using the term, refers not only to the negative pole of race as a social and structural form, but as a sacralized tool of oppression that limits, distorts, and disfigures agency. As Toni Morrison suggests in *Playing in the Dark: Whiteness and the Literary Imagination*, race is a metaphor in American culture; it exists as a surrogate and enabler of social, political, and economic forces that conspire against African presence. In its subtle, yet not-so-subtle figurations, it perpetuates itself as a sign of difference, a signal to the modernist project, as an agency that "limns out" and enforces the social construction and dreadful implications of "whiteness." In sum, race serves as a cultural means of meditation for "white humanity" (or better, "white divinity"). It functions as a normative gaze that universalizes the project of whiteness as the ultimate standard for judging truth, beauty, and goodness.

9. C. Eric Lincoln, *Race, Religion and the Continuing American Dilemma* (New York: Hill and Wang, 1984), and Victor Anderson, *Beyond Ontological Blackness: An Essay on African-American Religious and Cultural Criticism* (New York: Continuum, 1995). See Cornel West's observations on "doubleness" in *Black Strivings*—specifically, its relationship to despair, destruction, and death, using Du Bois's metaphor. Henry L. Gates and Cornel West, *The Future of the Race* (New York: Knopf, 1996). See also Robert Michael Franklin's discussion of "strenuous life" in *Liberating Voices: Human Fulfillment and Social Justice in African-American Thought* (Minneapolis: Fortress Press, 1990).

10. Anthony B. Pinn and Dwight N. Hopkins, *Loving the Body: Black Religious Studies and the Erotic* (New York: Palgrave MacMillan, 2004).

11. Victor Anderson, *Creative Exchange: A Constructive Theology of African American Religious Experience* (Minneapolis: Fortress Press, 2008), 151–57. See especially Anderson critique of "the Apollonian rhetoric of heroic genius." He writes, "That is, the black church is understood to be symbolic of the heroic, moral guiding virtues of black manhood and womanhood; strong, surviving, resistant and self-determined. Such rhetoric structures the meaning and significance of the black church within the cultural logics of masculinity, moral manliness, heroic discontent, and racial pride. The rhetoric crystallizes the black church's prophetic character, which is resistant to those elements of difference or differentiation that structure black life today. African American religious thinkers and theologians tend to rally their intellectual gifts in support of African American religious experience in the black church where the qualities of survival, resistance and the creation of a revolutionary institution are discussed in mythical proportions" (154–55). See also Victor Anderson, *Beyond Ontological Blackness* (New York: Continuum, 1995, 1998), 120–32.

12. See Walter F. Pitts, *Old Ship of Zion: The Afro-Baptist Ritual in the African Diaspora*, Religion in America (New York: Oxford University Press, 1996); Albert Raboteau, *Slave Religion: The "Invisible Institution" in the Antebellum South* (New York: Oxford University Press, 1978); Eddie S. Glaude Jr., *Exodus! Religion, Race, and Nation in Early Nineteenth-Century Black America* (Chicago: University of Chicago Press, 2000). The terminology around global citizenship is highly problematic with respect to definitions of "globalized," "globalization," "citizenship," etc. I take my cue from Jochen Fried, who suggests that we begin not with a concrete definition of the term, but with a workable conceptual framework of "world-interconnectedness" and look at ways in which this world-interconnectedness has impacted change around the globe. He writes, "By and large, these four criteria—extension, intensification, velocity and impact—are providing a workable conceptual framework for mapping the transformations that characterize the worldwide interconnectedness that we are part of—from eating MacDonald's in Cairo to SARS and the avian flu or the calling center in India to which we are connected when we have a problem with our computer." Moreover, the language of "citizenship" as a philosophical and political signifier has been around for along time, from ancient Stoic notions of being a *kosmon polites* (literally a "world citizen") to the more contemporary "solidaristic approaches" of Sen, who addresses

"our inescapably plural identities." Amartya Sen, *Identity and Violence: The Illusion of Destiny* (New York: Norton, 2006). Kwame Anthony Appiah has suggested that the future of what he calls "cosmopolitanism" hinges on how well we distinguish between thin and thick moral arguments in public debates. He identifies three kinds of disagreement about values: failing to share a vocabulary of evaluation; giving different interpretations to the same vocabulary; and giving the same values different weights. The challenge, however, is not always to come to consensus on right and wrong or good or bad, but to seek ways of understanding because the particularity, or the thickness, of some arguments do not allow for ready agreement through moral argumentation. Appiah suggests that in the final analysis, learning to live with different interpretations of values relies more on practice than on argumentation. Appiah also suggests that "a tenable global ethics has to temper a respect for difference with a respect for the freedom of actual human beings to make their own choices. That's why cosmopolitans don't insist that everyone become cosmopolitan. They know they don't have all the answers. They're humble enough to think that they might learn from strangers; not too humble to think that strangers can't learn from them. Few remember what Chremes says after his 'I am human' line, but it is equally suggestive: 'If you're right, I'll do what you do. If you're wrong, I'll set you straight.'" Kwame Anthony Appiah, *Cosmopolitanism: Ethics in a World of Strangers* (New York: Norton, 2006).

   13. Isabel Wilkerson, *The Warmth of Other Suns: The Epic Story of America's Great Migration* (New York: Random House, 2010).

   14. Eddie S. Glaude Jr. *Exodus! Religion, Race, and Nation in Early Nineteenth-Century Black America.* (University of Chicago Press, 2000); Wallace D. Best, *Passionately Human, No Less Divine: Religion and Culture in Black Chicago, 1915–1952* (Princeton University Press, 2005); Anthony B. Pinn, *Understanding and Transforming the Black Church* (Eugene, OR: Cascade Books, 2010).

   15. Delores S. Williams, *Sisters in the Wilderness: The Challenge Of Womanist God-Talk* (Maryknoll, NY: Orbis Books, 1993); Carolyn Rouse, *Engage Surrender: African-American Women and Islam* (Berkeley: University of California Press, 2004); and Diana L. Hayes, *Hagar's Daughters: Womanist Ways of Being in the World*, Madeleva Lecture in Spirituality 1995 (New York: Paulist, 1995).

   16. Senator Barack Obama made a compelling claim on the black church's theological understanding of the connection between the sacred and the political. Memorializing in March 2007 the anniversary of the March 1965 protest march in Selma, Alabama, referred to as "Bloody Sunday," Obama articulated a vision for his leadership drawn specifically from a racialized, biblical tradition. Senator Obama argued, "I'm here because somebody marched. I'm here because you all sacrificed for me. I stand on the shoulders of giants. I thank the Moses generation; but we've got to remember, now, that Joshua still had a job to do. As great as Moses was, despite all that he did, leading a people out of bondage, he didn't cross over the river to see the Promised Land. God told him your job is done. . . . We're going to leave it to the Joshua generation to make sure it happens. There are still battles that need to be fought; some rivers that need to be crossed. Like Moses, the task was passed on to those who might not have been as deserving, might not have been as courageous, find themselves in front of the risks that their parents and grandparents and great grandparents

had taken. That doesn't mean that they don't still have a burden to shoulder, that they don't have some responsibilities. The previous generation, the Moses generation, pointed the way. They took us 90% of the way there. We still got that 10% in order to cross over to the other side." The Exodus narrative, in which Moses leads the people of Israel out of bondage by the authority of God, is the single most important anchor of black religious thought. Martin Luther King Jr.'s final "sermon" drew on these same themes of leading the people to the Promised Land, but not himself entering.

17. See Alfred North Whitehead, *Process and Reality* (New York: Macmillan, 1929), and Charles Hartshorne, *The Logic of Perfection and Other Essays in Neoclassical Metaphysics* (La Salle, IL: Open Court, 1962).

18. Norm R. Allen Jr., ed., *African American Humanism: An Anthology* (Buffalo: Prometheus, 1991); Norm R. Allen, *The Black Humanist Experience: An Alternative to Religion* (Buffalo: Prometheus, 2002); Victor Anderson, *Beyond Ontological Blackness: An Essay on African American Religious and Cultural Criticism* (New York: Continuum, 1995); Victor Anderson, *Creative Exchange: A Constructive Theology of African American Religious Experience* (Minneapolis: Fortress, 2008); Dwight N. Hopkins, *Being Human: Race, Culture, and Religion* (Minneapolis: Fortress, 2005); Kelly Brown Douglas, *The Black Christ*, Bishop Henry McNeal Turner Studies in North American Black Religion 9 (Maryknoll, NY: Orbis Books, 1994); Kelly Brown Douglas, *Sexuality and the Black Church: A Womanist Perspective* (Minneapolis: Fortress, 1999); Kelly Brown Douglas, *What's Faith Got to Do With It? Black Bodies/Christian Souls* (Maryknoll, NY: Orbis Books, 2005); Mike Featherstone et al., eds., *The Body: Social Process and Cultural Theory* (London: Sage, 2001); Henry Lewis Gates Jr., "The Face and Voice of Blackness," in *Facing History: The Black Image in American Art 1710–1940*, ed. Guy C. McElroy (San Francisco: Bedford Arts, 1990), xxix–xlix.

19. Pinn, *Understanding and Transforming the Black Church*.

20. "Somebodyness" places emphasis on the body as a critical source for the somaesthetic/ethical life. One can hardly imagine living ethically or unethically without a body. Moreover, the body constitutes a critical frame of reference for the aesthetic life, apart from which ethics as a narrative quest is impossible. The concept of body as critical framework is especially important for ethical reflection in African American life and culture. Ethics, as a discipline, not only seeks answers to questions of right and wrong, but responses to beauty, balance, and symmetry, which are equally significant for the moral development and deportment of leaders, in this case black church leaders. In a discussion on what he calls "somaesthetics", Richard Shusterman makes the lively argument that the body is the occasion for ethical life and practices. He calls attention to a long tradition of philosophers who have made similar claims, among them Socrates, Zeno, Aristippus, Diogenes, and more recently, Michel Foucault, F. M. Alexander, Wilhelm Reich, and Moshe Feldenkrais. Therefore, it is incumbent upon leaders to care for and develop their sensory capacities in the pursuit of ethical living. "Every man," said Thoreau, "is the builder of a temple, called his body, to the god he worships, after a style purely his own, nor can he get off by hammering marble instead. We are all sculptors and painters, and our material is our own flesh and blood and bones. Any nobleness begins to refine a man's features, any meanness or sensuality to imbrute them." Richard Shusterman, "Somaesthetics: A Disciplinary Proposal,"

Journal of Aesthetics and Art Criticism (1999), 57. Thoreau's quote is also found in this article. Reflecting on the "New Negro" involved in the Montgomery campaign, King wrote, "Once plagued with a tragic sense of inferiority resulting from the crippling effects of slavery and segregation, the Negro has now been driven to re-evaluate himself. He has come to feel that he is somebody. His religion reveals to him that God loves all His children and that the important thing about a man is not 'his specificity but his fundamentum'—not the texture of his hair or the color of his skin but his eternal worth to God." King, *Stride*, 167.

21. West, *Prophesy Deliverance!*, 47; see also Anthony Pinn's discussion on the discipline of economy as the leverage of control over black bodies, black beauty, and hence, black freedom. Pinn writes, "The Black body had to be controlled and in this sense the manifestation of will by those with power in North America marks an economy of discipline reaching into every sphere of existence for the 'Other'—those of African descent. The taming of Black flesh through violence and intimidation in order to secure the 'consent' of the victim to his/her own victimization was the function of this economy of discipline. This economy also connotes a wider framework by which Whites sought to maintain societal order with myths of creation and meaning that made sense of the world through a mythology of Whites' aesthetic superiority. The projection of Black Americans as lacking beauty made abuse of Black bodies easier to undertake. To understand this, one need only consider the numerous stories of whippings, mutilations, and disfigurements provided by slaves and White observers alike." *Understanding and Transforming*, 69. West as quoted in Pinn.

22. See Wallace D. Best, *Passionately Human, No Less Divine: Religion and Culture in Black Chicago, 1915–1952* (Princeton University Press, 2005), 48, N40 (p. 208).

23. Milan Kundera, *Immortality* (New York: HarperCollins, 1991), 7.

24. This gesture of immortality, writes Milan, "cannot be regarded as the expression of an individual, as his creation (because no individual is capable of creating a fully original gesture, belonging to nobody else), nor can it be regarded as that person's instrument; on the contrary, it is gestures that use us as instruments, as their bearers and incarnations." Milan Kundera, *Immortality*, 7.

25. "Facing the other" in ritualistic performance is profoundly spiritual and ethical. In this sense, spirituality refers to a way or ways of seeking or being in relationship with the other who is believed to be worthy of reverence and highest devotion. The extension of the arm in recognition, respect, and reverence of the other is inclusive of both individuality and community. The other is not impersonal but intimately related to who I am and who I become. According to Emmanuel Levinas, the other has a face, and the face of the other is the foundation of ethics and the origin of civil society. "The face of man is the medium through which the invisible in him becomes visible and enters into commerce with us." Emmanuel Levinas, *Difficult Freedom*, trans. Sean Hand (Baltimore: Johns Hopkins Press, 1990), 140.

Beyond our private quests for meaning and authenticity, we are connected to others. Indeed, in order to be fully human and ethical, we must "face the other," and in facing the other we must face ourselves. How can the gods speak to us face to face till we have faces? And how shall we face ourselves until we have faced the *other*? C. S. Lewis, *Till We Have Faces: A Myth Retold* (Grand Rapids, MI: Eerdmans, 1956). Spirituality involves facing the other as we face ourselves.

26. Conversion is "based on a triadic structure of: (1) confrontation by historical identity, often presented in terms of existential pain and some type of terror; (2) wrestling with the old consciousness and the possibility of regeneration—or in William James's language, a reconstitution of the soul; and (3) embrace of new consciousness and new modes of behavior affecting relationship with the community of believers" (159–60). This is a kind of conversion of death into new life. "Religious experience hence entails a human response to a crisis of identity, and it is the crisis of identity that constitutes the Dilemma of ultimacy and meaning. In some ways, this may be described as a form of mystical experience, a type of transforming experience that speaks to a deeper reality, guided by a form of esoteric knowledge. Nonetheless, I argue that even this depiction of black religion . . . ultimately points back to this yearning for complex subjectivity. And it is conditioned by culture and thereby related to history" (173–74). According to William James, in *Varieties of Religious Experience* (New York: Modern Library, 1902), "To be converted, to be regenerated, to receive grace, to experience religion, to gain an assurance, are so many phrases which denote the process, gradual or sudden, by which a self hitherto divided, and consciously wrong inferior and unhappy, becomes unified and consciously right superior and happy, in consequence of its firmer hold upon religious realities. This at least is what conversion signifies in general terms, whether or not we believe that a direct divine operation is needed to bring such a moral change about."

27. A "hermeneutics of style" calls our attention to the ways in which the black-skinned body as a site of exploitation and creativity. Pinn argues that since there is a profound connection between the visible movement of black-skinned bodies and modes of exploitation, the "process of struggle for new ontological and existential status unfolds through black bodies" (Pinn, 2003, p. 140). And because there is almost always dissonance between the "social body" and the "physical body" in African American cultural life, we need to pay attention to style or aesthetics for the ways in which the body signifies a creative struggle for a new humanity, i.e., a new way of experiencing one's body as free and unencumbered by social regimens.

28. Examples in African American life and history abound with this problem, variously referred to as "double consciousness," "normative gaze," and the crippling labels of intellectual and social inferiority based on race, class, and gender. Du Bois's depiction of doubleness is a meditation on the psychosocial condition of the African American at the turn of the twentieth century—but it is even more. At the core of the problem is the plea for recognition. Recognition, respectability and loyalty were also cornerstones of racial uplift ideology, which dominated post-Reconstruction activities among black leadership. These civic goods were sought through education, suffrage, political leadership, and jury service, based on natural rights arguments. W. E. B. Du Bois, *The Souls of Black Folk* (New York: Bantam, 1989), 45–46, and Robert Michael Franklin's discussion of "strenuous life" in *Liberating Voices: Human Fulfillment and Social Justice in African-American Thought* (Minneapolis: Fortress Press, 1990).

29. "I indeed baptize you with water unto repentance: but he that cometh after me is mightier than I, whose shoes I am not worthy to bear: he shall baptize you with the Holy Ghost, and with Fire" (Matt. 3:11). Fire is universal and purgative. What I have in mind here is akin to Diana L. Eck's experimentation with cross-cultural and religious themes

associated with the Spirit. One of the common themes that bind traditional religious cosmologies is the element of fire denoting spirit (also breath, wind). See Diana L. Eck, "The Breath of God: The Fire and Freedom of the Spirit," in *Encountering God: A Spiritual Journey from Bozeman to Banaras* (Boston: Beacon Press, 1993), 118–43. An interesting possibility inherent in the fire metaphor as an aesthetic/existential response to the diasporic and exilic situation of African Americans is its correspondence to the global citizenship criteria (extension, intensification, velocity, and impact) outlined by Fried, above.

30. See Albert J. Raboteau, *Fire in the Bones: Reflections on African-American Religious History* (Boston: Beacon Press, 1995); Harvey Cox, *Fire from Heaven: the Rise of Pentecostal Spirituality and the Reshaping of Religion in the Twenty-First Century* (Reading, MA: Addison-Wesley, 1995).

31. Allan Boesak, *The Fire Within: Sermons from the Edge of Exile* (Cape Town: New World Foundation, 2004).

32. Mainly passed down and practiced by women, Kumina rituals emphasize the Afro-Jamaican woman's body as a site of spirit possession, healing, and continuous revelation. For Stewart, part of the reason so many Afro-Jamaicans have more faith in Kumina religion than in Christianity during times of tragedy is because problems are solved less from soteriological beliefs about Jesus' death, than by beliefs and practices of recurring incarnation in lived experience of Kumina women.

33. Martin Luther King Jr., *Where Do We Go From Here: Chaos or Community?* (Boston: Beacon Press, 1967), 167.

34. King, *Where Do We Go From Here*, 190.

II. Race, Social Divisions, and Restructured Ecclesial Spaces

High School Students, the Catholic Church, and the Struggle for Black Inclusion and Citizenship in Rock Hill, South Carolina

Luci Vaden

In 1970, the United States Fourth Circuit Court of Appeals ordered South Carolina school districts to terminate their dual public education systems. The school board in Rock Hill, South Carolina, located thirty miles south of Charlotte, North Carolina, responded by closing down the all-black schools in the district and hurriedly rezoning black and white students into previously all-white schools. But once in their new schools, black students were marginalized and mistreated. In response, more than two hundred black students at Rock Hill High School, in conjunction with the all-black St. Mary's Catholic Church and Rock Hill Oratory, a local Catholic mission, led a two-month protest that challenged the vestiges of Jim Crow in desegregated Rock Hill High.

Drawing on oral histories, Oratory records, archives at the South Carolina Department of Education, and contemporary newspaper reporting, this paper analyzes the ways in which the black Catholic community and Oratory supported student protest and became a bedrock for civil rights activism in this predominantly Protestant community. The legacy of Jim Crow in America forced black students to bear the full burden of school desegregation, but the black Catholic community ensured that students were not alone, giving them the confidence and resources to wage direct action protest in formerly all-white Rock Hill High. Their activism signaled that the civil rights movement was still evolving in communities across the American South, and through their protest, black students worked to define the very meaning of desegregated public education.

Black students at Rock Hill High School built upon a larger tradition of community and church activism. The Oratory, established in 1934, provided a forum for discussions of civil rights and helped to initiate and sustain student protest in Rock Hill for over two decades. Because the Oratory was established as a mission, and not a parish, it received no funds from the diocese and maintained its staff, facilities, and programs with private funding. Financial autonomy allowed the Oratory to pursue an independent agenda for social justice, unlike many other Southern Catholic communities.[1] Oratory members established the first desegregated school in South Carolina in 1954, supported the Friendship Nine sit-ins of 1960 and 1961, launched voter registration drives in partnership with the American Friends Service Committee in 1963, and bolstered community activism in conjunction with the Congress of Racial Equality throughout the 1960s.[2] Through continued activism, the Oratory provided the infrastructure for sustained student protest, even after the Civil Rights Act of 1964—and particularly after 1970, when Rock Hill fully desegregated its school system. While other local black student protest movements emerged, many of them lasted only a few days, with little more than a newspaper article describing their cause and actions.[3] In contrast, the Oratory provided students with a forum for their grievances, a forum that not only sustained protest, but ensured that their activism was not lost to the historical record.

On January 26, 1972, two hundred African American students walked out of Rock Hill High School. Students protested unfair discipline policies, academic tracking by race, exclusion from Rock Hill High's clubs, and the lack of black teachers and coaches in their newly integrated school. Students wanted courses in black studies and demanded that the memory of Emmett Scott High School, the former all-black school that was shut down due to desegregation, be incorporated into their new school's alma mater, colors, and mascot. As students walked out of Rock Hill High on that January morning, they marched several miles to the abandoned Emmett Scott building, but did not know where to turn or what to do when they arrived. After crowding around Emmett Scott for several minutes, the students decided to discuss their grievances with Brother David Boone, who worked at Rock Hill's all-black St. Mary's Catholic Church. When students reached the church, Boone called the superintendent of Rock Hill School District and Rock Hill High School's principal, but they refused to assist him or to talk to the students. At that point, Brother Boone instructed students to go into St. Mary's Bannon Hall to organize their grievances against the Rock Hill school board and administration.[4]

It had been more than fifteen years since the United States Supreme Court unanimously voted to overturn school segregation in the historic *Brown v. Board of Education* decision of 1954. States and local communities were urged to move towards full integration "with all deliberate speed." Instead, most

Southern communities resisted federal law, making few attempts to prepare for the challenges that desegregation would bring.[5] In 1970, when the Fourth Circuit ordered the immediate desegregation of South Carolina schools, Rock Hill School District was ill-prepared to handle the transition. School district administrators decided to shut down Emmett Scott completely, forcing all the high school students from the district, both black and white, into what became an overcrowded Rock Hill High School. A few black students had broken the color line at Rock Hill High in 1964 (with considerable difficulty) under magnet school choice policies, but only a handful of black students had ever attended.[6]

Emmett Scott Senior High, named after Emmett J. Scott, who served as Booker T. Washington's chief aide, opened in the 1920s and not only educated students, but also served as a vital center of community life.[7] Its students, teachers, parents, and administrators went to church together, participated in community events with one another, and lived in the same neighborhoods. Emmett Scott High was connected to the city's all-black recreational sports league and the young men's and women's clubs that facilitated social events, student activism, and student leadership. Recreational activities and club activities were hosted at St. Mary's Church, which the kids called "the Catholic," just a short walk from Emmett Scott Senior High. Together, Emmett Scott and the Catholic formed the center of social, academic, political, and financial activity within the community, launching voter registration drives, sit-ins, and educational programs for the black community of Rock Hill. As a result, the entire black community mourned Emmett Scott's closing in 1970.[8]

While newspapers and school boards celebrated the smooth start of the 1970–71 academic year, many unspoken problems emerged regarding discipline, classroom management, and communication, affecting students' self-awareness, personal and social identities, academic success, and perceptions about the larger society. Overcrowding exaggerated physical tensions and agitated all students as they adjusted to their new school environment. Many black students were placed in remediated academic classes, because it administrators and counselors that these students would not be able to perform on the same level as white students. Discipline issues became much more complex. Black parents were uncomfortable with white teachers disciplining their children, and white parents mistrusted the classroom management methods of black teachers. Racial discrimination persisted in some teachers' classrooms, and many teachers were unprepared to handle the cultural diversity of their students.[9]

From the fall of 1970 through the fall of 1971, black students at Rock Hill High continued to feel discounted, and tensions mounted. Administrators left school colors and mascots unchanged, reflecting only Rock Hill High's history and all-white student body. Black students were excluded from the all-white school government system and several athletic teams. Black students felt that they had no means of expressing their grievances and resented the all-white Rock Hill School Board, which was elected at large.[10]

On Friday, January 21, 1972, Rock Hill High School hosted a conference on "black personalities," which black students found offensive and protested by walking out. They were all punished for cutting class and given no chance to explain what prompted them to leave the assembly. On Tuesday, January 25, as a silent protest of their treatment at Rock Hill High, seven students at a basketball game refused to stand for the national anthem and the Rock Hill High alma mater. The black student body supported the protest, but the following day, seven of the students who refused to stand were identified and asked to leave the school premises by the school administration. All seven students were indefinitely expelled.[11]

Making matters worse, on January 26, the same day the seven protesters were expelled, band director Robert Williams made students—eight of them African American—rehearse "Dixie" in band practice. One of the black students refused to play the song and was sent to Principal Calvin Burleson's office. On her way out, five other black students joined her in protest. When other students began to follow, the band director told all band students that if they did not like playing the song, "they could get the Hell out."[12] News if the incident began to spread among black students, and their anger grew. That afternoon, over two hundred African American students walked out of Rock Hill High School, walked to their old Emmett Scott School, and later turned to Brother David Boone for help.[13]

Brother Boone began working in Rock Hill in 1951 after being recruited from his seminary in Kentucky by the Oratory, a residential community initiated in the 1930s and intended for Catholic clergyman who wanted to devote themselves to community and church service. The mission of Oratory members was to establish and entrench themselves in Rock Hill's community, where they were to advocate for the poor and unfortunate. Rock Hill's all-white Catholic parish, St. Anne's, was established in the 1920s, but members of the Oratory felt that the black community would benefit from a recreational facility and set out to build a church that could meet those needs. Oratory members led by Brother Joseph Wahl raised the necessary money and constructed St. Mary's Catholic Church, which opened its doors in 1946 just a few blocks from Emmett Scott. At the time of the opening, only a handful of black Catholics lived in Rock Hill. Equipped with sports and recreational facilities for the black youth, "the Catholic" was soon a huge social and political force in the community.[14]

The unique nature of the Catholic community in Rock Hill provided a bridge for interracial communication within the wider community. In 1949, for instance, St. Anne's and St. Mary's started the Catholic Interracial Council. Members gathered together for breakfast, discussed community matters, and got to know one another. In addition, the priests and administrators at both Catholic churches all lived together at the Oratory, an arrangement that facilitated communication between the two churches and therefore the white and black communities. After *Brown* declared segregated schools unconstitutional in 1954, members of the Oratory decided the Rock Hill Catholic parochial schools should set the example for the rest of the community and integrate, which they believed was not only legally required, but morally necessary. So in the fall of 1954, St. Anne's Catholic School integrated and remained the only desegregated school in South Carolina until 1963.[15]

By 1959, large numbers of black youths were involved in St. Anne's recreational sports programs, including basketball and softball. Through the sports leagues, "the Catholic" initiated the young men's and young women's clubs in Rock Hill. The clubs organized social events, discussed current events, and carried out community service projects. Each club was completely independent and run by students, who elected their own president, secretary, and treasurer. The purpose of the clubs was fourfold. Club members vowed to be better Christians, regardless of their church affiliations. They also vowed to be better students and better citizens, and to take part in their community. Through this forum, many young men and young women received leadership and organizational training. The adult sponsors of the clubs brought in politicians, writers, and activists to work with the students, and meetings often served as fora for discussions of black activism and civil rights. A club entry written on February 20, 1969, by the secretary of the Young Women's Club stated, "Current events [were] brought up. The topic of negroes playing 'Dixie' brought about an interesting discussion. Brother [David] mentioned the Human Relations Committee would meet here Monday and all Club members were encouraged to come. Brother would bring articles concerning Afro-styles and using 'black' instead of 'negroes' to the next meeting." Another 1969 entry by the Young Men's Club secretary stated, "An article was also read concerning the Clemson walkout. The Human Relations meeting with the black students at Rock Hill High was discussed. Discussed Vietnam, the Kenneth Minor case, L.S.D., and diet foods as a cause of cancer." Club members were able to discuss even national issues national and relate those issues to their own lives. Skills learned in the clubs provided students with leadership tools essential to the struggles they would face in the transformative years of community desegregation.[16]

Through the clubs and recreational events, the Oratory was also able to work with parents and the larger community, often in conjunction with representatives from activist groups such as the Congress of Racial Equality (CORE), the National Association for the Advancement of Colored People (NAACP), and the American Friends Service Committee (AFSC). In 1960, the Catholic worked with Guilford College and the AFSC to start the first large-scale voter registration drive in Rock Hill. Late, in 1961, Boone worked with CORE and the local NAACP to support the Friendship Nine, the eight local college students from Friendship College who, together with a CORE field representative, led the sit-in movement in Rock Hill. Coining the term "Jail No Bail," the Friendship Nine served thirty days hard labor in prison, rather than paying their bail for sitting it at an all-white lunch counter. All eight of the local Friendship Nine students had been active participants in the Young Men's Club.[17]

Since St. Mary's was essentially in the backyard of Emmett Scott School, the programs initiated by Boone and the Oratory had a particularly profound impact, and owing to his service, Boone, though white, was a respected personality in the black community. Nathaniel Barber, who served as secretary and president of the Young Men's Club remembered, "BroDavid used to do a lot of stuff. . . .The Catholic was the center of activity in the community. You had the black high school right next door. Then you had St. Mary's Catholic Church. We used to have dances there. We used to play basketball out there. He had a league put together. We played basketball out there. We had The Young Men's, The Young Women's Club. So this was a very active part of the community. Everybody knew BroDavid. Everybody. Men, women, young, old, black, white . . . everyone knew him. So when he said something, it mattered what he said." So when Rock Hill High students went to find Brother David on that January day in 1972, they were drawing on a long heritage of black Catholic activism in Rock Hill in an effort to tear down racial barriers and reshape the post-Jim Crow South.[18]

Following Rock Hill High's student walkout on January 26, Oratory members worked with students at Bannon Hall to organize their protest, inviting former members of the Young Men's and Women's Clubs to support students. For instance, Willie T. (Dub) Massey, who had been involved in the Young Men's Club, and was one of the Friendship Nine, helped students refine their list of almost one hundred grievances down to seven major complaints. Those seven objections addressed lack of leadership positions for black students, the need for black studies courses, the lack of a just system to deal with punishment for black students, the exclusion of Emmett Scott colors and mascots in Rock Hill High's displays, and the lack of black Rock Hill school board members.[19]

Students decided to return to school on January 27, and on the morning following their initial walkout, they boarded the school bus as usual. Because Rock Hill's neighborhoods were still largely segregated, most of the students rode to school on segregated buses and used their rides to and from school as an opportunity for communication. On their ride, students grew distressed as they replayed the events from the previous day, and decided to confront Burleson about the injustices they faced. Upon their arrival at school, more than two hundred angry students surrounded Principal Burleson, demanding to speak with him. Burleson, in a panic, told students to go to the auditorium so that he could work things out with them in an orderly manner. As soon as they were in the auditorium, Burleson called state and city law enforcement officers and informed them a riot was about to occur. Officers quickly arrived in full riot control gear, and state patrol cars lined the streets of Eden Terrace Road, where Rock Hill High School was located, ready to get involved if necessary. At 10:30 a.m., Burleson dismissed the entire student body and, largely due to pressure from Superintendent Jeff Savage, refused to speak with students about their concerns. In the process, Burleson slammed the door of his office in the face of several black students, was allegedly verbally abusive to some students, and refused to speak with others. The students walked out again, passing the officers in their riot control gear, and headed for Bannon Hall. In the meantime, all students involved in the walkout were suspended for three days by Superintendent Savage.[20]

That evening, 150 students gathered at Bannon Hall to discuss the events that had taken place, to clarify their list of grievances, and to elect a student advisory committee to lead the group. The students elected ten representatives: Leroy Ervin, Faye Smith, Bernard David, Nathaniel Barber, Jerome Anderson, Karen Brice, Jackie Chisolm, Ordel Griffin, Willie Hope, and Jerome Glover. Students also refined their twenty grievances into seven major complaints. Those seven addressed lack of leadership positions for black students, presented the need for courses in black studies, called for a more just system to deal with punishment of black students, demanded the inclusion of Emmett Scott colors and mascots in Rock Hill High's colors, and demanded that black members be elected to Rock Hill's school board. School board members told students that, tentatively, a special advisory committee would meet with them on Friday, January 28. Schools across the district were completely closed on that day because administrators feared violence. The district also left police on alert.[21]

On Friday, January 28, students presented their seven grievances to the advisory committee of the school board and to Wes Boone. But the following day, before the committee announced any decisions, the *Evening Herald* newspaper of Rock Hill published a press release issued by Superintendent Jeff Savage. In this release, Savage claimed that the advisory committee of the school board no longer existed, and that if students wanted to submit a list of grievances, they were to do so through the regular (all white) student body on Friday February 4. Even though Chairman of the Board Frank Kiser appointed an ad hoc committee to investigate the discord that started on January 24, Savage argued that the committee was not authorized to handle the problems. Savage declared that school would open on Monday as usual, and that students who protested would be expelled.[22]

After a meeting held between Savage and school administrators on Sunday, January 30, however, the group decided that opening school on a normal basis was too risky and could spark violence and more protest. Instead, school opened on a limited basis. Sophomores, juniors, and seniors were given separate days to attend the week. During the limited opening, black students continued to protest. They rode to school on the bus, but before entering the building, they assembled and then marched to Bannon Hall. Students reasoned that if they did not step into the school building, they could not technically be expelled. Police continued to monitor the situation at school, wearing riot control gear.[23]

On February 3, Superintendent Savage sent a memo to all teachers in the district, encouraging them to talk with parents of students who were involved in the walkouts. He also asked teachers to talk with students and tell them that "demonstrations and violence" would solve nothing. Savage instructed teachers to encourage parents to pull their students out of the walkout, telling teachers that students would only be able to speak with the board as a last resort. He encouraged teachers to handle problems with individual students at the school level. Savage also put multiple articles in the paper claiming that student walkouts were uncalled for and promising the community that he would handle the situation. But the walkouts continued. Students refused to give up until the school board heard their demands.[24]

As protest continued, community members complained about increasing chaos linked to student unrest. Merchants worried that businesses were suffering because black students were walking through town every day on their way to Bannon Hall. Parents voiced concerns about school being canceled. Jeff Savage came under increasing pressure to resolve the conflict. He finally agreed to meet with students on Friday, February 5, but afterward, he promptly dismissed their grievances and declined to overturn the expulsions of the seven students who had refused to stand during the alma mater in late January.[25]

The student advisory committee did not give up. On February 7, the students wrote a letter to Frank Kizer, chairman of the board, again insisting that they should have an opportunity to be heard. In the meantime, Leroy Ervin, president of the committee, also wrote a letter to the United States Department of Health, Education, and Welfare (HEW) in Atlanta about events in Rock Hill and continually tried to build support for the student movement growing in Rock Hill. On February 10, Jeff Savage responded to the committee's letter to Frank Kizer, once again agreeing to meet with students on February 12. Savage requested that only two student leaders be present, each in the company of an adult. In addition, students were asked to keep their presentation under thirty minutes. The student advisory committee wrote back insisting that it was important for all members to attend and insisted they attend without parental accompaniment.[26]

On the morning of Friday, February 12, the members of the committee readied themselves to present their grievances to the school board. As they began, they reminded board members that they were there to tear down the racial barriers that prevented Rock Hill High from becoming truly integrated. Jackie Chisolm was the first student to speak. She declared, "Our procedure will be a simple one. We shall state each grievance. We shall give each an explanation. Whatever time remains we would be pleased to spend in discussion or in answering your questions." Next, Karen Brice approached the podium and described the first grievance, saying that "a school committee with student representation is needed to deal with school problems." She explained, "The student Council has not, in our opinion, been truly representative of all students nor has it been functional." When she was done, Bernard Davis spoke up. "Black students should be amply represented on such a committee because black students represent an ample percentage of the student enrollment." Next up was Willie Hope, who insisted that "blacks are not given proper recognition for their achievement." He went on to declare, "Recognition is a very human need. Black people have had to struggle for their rights and acceptance. We feel blacks are generally not recognized for their achievements. There seems to be a lack of sensitivity to their human needs which we share as brothers and sisters."[27]

The board continued to listen as the fourth student, Thomas Gilmore, declared, "There is need for reform of school identity, symbols, school mascots, etc. We desire to be proud of our identity. The identity of Emmett Scott High School is gone and along with it our black community's identification with past achievements. Could not, for example, Scott's colors be added to

Rock Hill High's as a gracious sign of acceptance of former Scott students?"
Eddie Caldwell then proclaimed, "There is need for a Black Studies program. Blacks have made many contributions. These should be recognized to
complete the education of students." Jerome Glover insisted, "There is need
for black representation on the Rock Hill School Board. We recognize election is the way to gain seats. However, lacking the ward system or any other
system which would make the election of black people possible, we have
lacked the voice of anyone who lives as a black person lives." Lastly, Jerome
Anderson insisted

> that no disciplinary action be taken against those students who in conscience
> do not feel compelled to stand during the playing of the national anthem or the
> alma mater. We do not wish to be unpatriotic. We do not wish to offend our fel-
> low Americans. While each person must speak for himself, the grievance here
> is directed at the alma mater song, for it too falls into the same category as our
> grievances over the school colors and mascot. We ask only that some of our past
> loyalties are permitted to be carried over to our new integrated situation. Garnet
> and black need not be changed, but could not blue and gold be added?

Leroy Ervin closed the session with a reminder that the goal was to create
a learning environment that insured the inclusion of black students in the
classrooms, athletic departments, student councils, and community of Rock
Hill High. He then opened up the floor for questions.[28]

Over the next few weeks, board members deliberated. Students returned
to school on a normal basis and anxiously awaited the decision of the board.
In the last days of February, the board announced their decision. They over-
turned the expulsions given to the seven students on January 27. The Board
decided not to include Emmett Scott's colors officially in Rock Hill High's
school colors, but to add "some gold" over the next two years to represent
Emmett Scott. They did so by putting a gold stripe down the side of the
sleeves of the school's uniforms. The bulk of the students requests were
ignored.[29]

Insulted by the board's decision, black students once again decided to
speak out. On Friday, March 2, when the homeroom bell rang, 180 students
walked out of Rock Hill High. This time they went directly to Superintendent Jeff Savage's office. Lacking the restraint exhibited during the previous walkout, many students broke windows and streetlights. They demanded
that Rock Hill High's school colors be officially changed, along with the
alma mater. Despite their march, the school board refused to meet any of
the students' demands. After an hour and a half, administrators convinced

the students to leave the superintendent's office in school buses provided by the district. When asked about the walkout by a reporter, Brother Boone responded, "The board members missed the point of the issue." He went on to say that the students marched down to the office "to explain how deep the feeling is about Emmett Scott by those in all the black community."[30]

As a result of the protest, all schools in the district closed early that day, and over the weekend, the superintendent declared that all 180 students who protested in his office would be suspended for three days. In anticipation of the black students' reaction to this move, schools opened the following Monday only for the tenth grade; eleventh and twelfth grade students were scheduled to attend separately on each of the following two days. The following day, twenty black female students rode the bus to Rock Hill High, led a protest in the hallway, and then left for home. Savage requested that Rock Hill principal Cal Burleson identify as many of the student participants as possible. Savage then suspended them indefinitely, and later recommended they be expelled.[31]

On March 14, concerned parents and community members carried their children's fight forward. Parents took their grievances to the York County legislative delegation. They declared:

> As we are all aware, recent events in our school district have brought our community to the brink of open confrontation. As individuals we may or may not agree with the arguments expressed or the actions taken in recent weeks. But as responsible community members, the worst thing we could do is pass off these events as unimportant or unworthy of our attention.
>
> We have come here today as representatives of the black community to seek the ways to avoid imminent, or future confrontations, and to express some of the underlying problems in our schools. However, the problems do not affect the black community alone, they affect the entire city of Rock Hill and all of School District Three. The request to meet with the County Delegation has come after attempts to solve the problem through other channels have failed.

After speaking out about what they considered "surface issues" such as school colors and mascots, parents complained that larger issues were involved. They stated:

> The surface issues about school colors, administrative rules, and representation are not new. The kids have been talking about it for two years. The black community has watched white children bussed pass Fairfax and Hillcrest Schools (both of which were black schools) and into white schools. We have subsequently seen

Fairfax closed to avoid sending a white child into a school that was previously all black. And Hillcrest closed, then one year later it opened as Leslie School Two, why? West End Elementary School was closed rather than integrated, and finally closure was invoked on an educational landmark, in, and for, the black community, Emmet Scott Senior High. No thought was, or has been given the colors, mascot, or any other symbols to which the black community has identified with for over fifty years. You can give all the arguments about Federal Laws and Court Decisions as justification for the form that changes took, but when it comes down to local decisions not prescribed by the federal law, the black community always loses.

Black community leaders went on to request that the school board be expanded to nine members from seven so that two African American members could be added. They also wanted to create an expulsion review committee so students could no longer be expelled so easily. The York County delegation refused to meet any of their demands. With no black voice on the school board or delegation, and little voting power to ensure their voices would be heard on the school board, the burden to fight the inequities inherent in desegregated Southern schools was carried on the backs and in the hearts and souls of Rock Hill's children—and children across the country—on the daily basis.[32]

From early in the twentieth century, the legal campaign for desegregated education was at the core of the African American struggle for quality education and civil rights. Civil rights organizations and black communities fought for equitable public education because many saw the denial of equal educational opportunity as fundamental to the inequalities black citizens endured. But when desegregation became a reality, black students were left to find their way in hostile environments that offered little guarantee of academic, physical, or emotional protection. As a result, many students became casualties of the very system that was supposed to offer them a promise of something better. School expulsions, disillusionment, and physical intimidation denied many black students their right to a quality education. Almost forty years earlier, W. E. B. Du Bois foresaw the problems faced by black students during the desegregation era. He declared, "[A] black man . . . has a right to protest any separation of schools by color, but what, then, of his helpless child, sent into a mixed school, where white children kick, cuff, or abuse him, or where teachers openly and persistently neglect or hurt or dwarf his soul? The dilemma is complete and there is no escape."[33]

Yet the struggles of students and their communities during the arduous first years of desegregation, and their endeavors to contest the day-to-day insults that persisted in desegregated public schools were a spirited part of the longer struggle for civil rights and an integral step towards the realization of black citizenship in American society. Through their attempts to reform Rock Hill School District, students in the black community collectively exercised their right to protest. For the first time in this historically white school, black students shifted the struggle to secure equality and freedom to one that incorporated civil rights organizing, direct action protest, and a celebration of black power and black pride in the desegregated system.

In Studs Terkel's 1961 interview of James Baldwin, Baldwin discussed the bravery and strength of Elizabeth Eckford, one of the Little Rock Nine, who was spit on by an old woman as Eckford entered Little Rock High School in 1957. Baldwin argued that Eckford was able to endure because "[s]he knew who she was. She *knew* who she was. After all, that child has been coming for a very long time. She didn't come out of nothing."[34] Like Elizabeth Eckford, Rock Hill High students *knew* who they were. The Oratory built an infrastructure of support for student activism in Rock Hill, and rooted black students in a community that bolstered their identity and citizenship within the desegregated system. In a system that marginalized black students, the Oratory and the black Catholic community reinforced the principle that black students mattered, and students asserted their voices in a system dominated by white administrators, school board members, and educators. While the outcome of the protest failed in many respects, the process of the movement laid the groundwork for continued community protest in the post-Jim Crow South, giving students the courage to carry on.

Notes

1. See Bently Anderson, *Black, White, and Catholic: New Orleans Interracialism, 1947–1956* (Nashville: Vanderbilt University Press, 2008).

2. On May 4, 1961, the Congress of Racial Equality, under the direction of James Farmer, initiated freedom rides through Southern communities. Thirteen freedom riders, seven black and six white, left Washington, DC, on Greyhound and Trailways buses. They planned to ride through Virginia, the Carolinas, Georgia, Alabama, and Mississippi, ending their ride in New Orleans. When they entered Rock Hill, John Lewis, Al Bigelow, and Genevieve Hughes were beaten. The Friendship Nine was a group of African American men who went to jail after staging a sit-in at a segregated McCrory's lunch counter in Rock Hill in 1961. The group gained nationwide attention because they followed an untried strategy called "Jail, No Bail," which lessened the huge financial burden civil rights groups were facing as the sit-in movement spread across the South. The men became known as the Friendship Nine because eight of the nine were students at Rock Hill's Friendship Junior College. They are sometimes referred to as the Rock Hill Nine.

3. For instance, in neighboring Fort Mill, South Carolina, just a few miles from Rock Hill, black student unrest led to a black student walkout at Fort Mill High School just a few weeks prior to the one in Rock Hill. In Fort Mill, police attacked protesting black students with tear gas and arrested all participants. Administrators suspended most involved, and with little organized support from the community, the walkout ended in just a few days.

4. Student advisory committee list of grievances, 1972. Other information compiled from multiple oral history interviews: David Boone, interviewed by author, Rock Hill, South Carolina, September 9, 2010; Abby Caveny, interviewed by author, Rock Hill, South Carolina, November 19, 2008; Sam Foster, interviewed by author, Rock Hill, South Carolina, October 30, 2008; Deborah Harris, interviewed by author, Rock Hill, South Carolina, November 25, 2008; Bob Jenkins, interviewed by author, Rock Hill, South Carolina, November 3, 2008; Dub Massey, interviewed by author, Rock Hill, South Carolina, September 16, 2010; Robert Parker, interviewed by author, Rock Hill, South Carolina, September 13, 2010; Bobby Plair, interviewed by author, Rock Hill, South Carolina, September 7, 2010; Elizabeth Ann Reid, interviewed by author, Rock Hill, South Carolina, September 11, 2010; Wade Witherspoon, interviewed by author, Rock Hill, South Carolina, September 9, 2010; Nathaniel Barber, interviewed by author, Columbia, South Carolina, September 30, 2010.

5. Vernon Burton and Lewie Reece, "The Palmetto Revolution: School Desegregation in South Carolina," in *With All Deliberate Speed*, ed. Brian Daugherity and Charles C. Bolton (Fayetteville: University of Arkansas Press, 2008), 87.

6. Freedom of choice plans allowed children in a school district to attend the school of their choice. These plans were widely used as a system to maintain segregation under the guise of desegregation in order to retain federal aid. Most black students who applied to attend white schools under freedom of choice rules were routinely denied and even when accepted had to provide their own transportation, a requirement which was often impossible to meet.

7. Terrance Allridge, "A Case Study of Emmett Scott High 1965–1970" (thesis, University of South Carolina, 2009).

8. Interviews: Boone, Plair, Witherspoon, Reid, Harris, Massey, Parker, Barber.

9. Ibid.

10. Stephen Smith, Karen Kedrowski, and Joseph Ellis, "Electoral Structures, Venue Selection, and the (New?) Politics of School Desegregation," *Perspectives* 2, No. 4 (December 2004): 794–97.

11. While it is not clear exactly what was said that upset students, some tension arose from the administration's insistence that black students attend separate assemblies from white students. Information based on an interview done with Leroy Ervin, October 29, 2010; Jim Clark, "Minor Disturbance Mars School Opening," *Evening Herald*, March 6, 1972; Lynn Willoughby, *The "Good Town" Does Well: Rock Hill, S.C., 1852–2002* (Orangeburg, SC: Written in Stone, 2002), 213; Jim Clark, "Board Members Briefed on School Problems," *Evening Herald*, January 30, 1972, 1.

12. Clark, "Board Members Briefed on School Problems."

13. Bob Miller, "Rock Hill High Dismissed Early After Protest," *Evening Herald*, January, 29, 1972; oral interviews with Boone, Barber, Witherspoon, Plair, Smith.

14. History newsletter published by St. Anne's Catholic Church, 2004; interview, Boone.

15. Ibid.

16. Young Men's Club Journal, 1969; interview, Barber.

17. Interview, Boone.

18. Interview, Barber.

19. Records kept by student advisory committee; Betsy Perone, "Black Students Present Grievances," *Evening Herald*, January 28, 1972; Betsy Perone, "Burleson Tells Faculty He 'Made a Mistake,'" *Evening Herald*, January 28, 1972.

20. Bob Miller, "Rock Hill High Dismissed Early After Protest"; interview Boone, Barber, Witherspoon, Plair, Smith.

21. Miller, "Rock Hill High Dismissed Early After Protest."

22. "Savage Says Protest Misdirected," *Evening Herald*, January 29, 1972, 1.

23. Interview, Boone.

24. Jim Clark, "Board Members Briefed on School Problems," *Evening Herald*, January 31,1972; Betsy Perone, "Savage Sees 'Progress' with Black Students," *Evening Herald*, February 2, 1972, 1.

25. Record of letter sent to Department of Health, Education, and Welfare, 1972.

26. Letter of correspondence between Jeff Savage and student advisory committee, February 1972.

27. Notes from student advisory committee, February 1972.

28. Ibid.

29. Compiled from interviews with Caveny, McCleave, Jenkins, Foster, Barber, and Boone.

30. Perone, Betsy, "Schools Dismiss Early After Student Walkout," *Evening Herald*, March 3, 1972.

31. Ibid.

32. Parents draft of grievances to York County Delegation, 1973.

33. Du Bois, "A Free Forum," *Crisis*, February 1934, 52.

34. "An Interview with James Baldwin," by Studs Terkel (1961), in *Conversations with James Baldwin*, Fred R. Standley and Louis H. Pratt, eds. (Jackson: University Press of Mississippi, 1989).

Christian Youth Activism and South African Black Ecclesiology

Reggie Nel

Introduction

The world stood in awe recently at the power of younger generations in challenging oppressive governments in North Africa, thus demonstrating that youth and student movements remain a critical force in transforming societies and faith communities. What occurred in North Africa was not a new phenomenon. The question is whether church communities and theology are willing to be challenged again.

Steve Bantu Biko is perhaps the most well-known, inspirational figure in what became popularly known as the Soweto[1] youth riots against racism in South Africa that took place in June 1976. Barney Pityana says of Biko, "He became a figurehead of the new generation of political activists and would-be revolutionaries that we fancied ourselves to be."[2] Yet Biko died violently at the hands of the South African police force on 12 September 1977. He was twenty-nine years young, he was black, and he was a Christian activist. Biko saw his role in the struggle to overcome racism in apartheid South Africa as a struggle against theological justification, a struggle against what he called "the colonial-tainted version of Christianity."[3]

In this contribution, I analyze a particular trajectory of Christian youth activism, or what I have called elsewhere "youth in the mission to overcome racism,"[4] by revisiting Biko's challenge to the black church in the 1970s. I then present an analysis of a few responses—in particular from proponents of South African black theology of liberation—in relation to Christian youth activism, after which I conclude with a narrative on the current challenges and questions raised by post-apartheid Christian youth and student ministries in South Africa. Behind this approach is an understanding that the church's prophetic witness and mission to overcome racism are at heart an ecclesiological struggle. A prophetic witness is not merely about the conversion of individuals, or mere political activism, it is also about the conversion of the church.[5] Black theological thought has been engaged in a struggle against a colonial conception of church and mission, where non-theological factors, rooted in racism, shaped the reading of the gospel, which in turn led to a particular structuring of church and society. It was understood in this struggle that the formation of community, which transcends the boundaries of language, ethnicity, and racial identities, would induce social as well as personal healing and transformation. It is from this community that witness/activism would emerge, in what Russell Botman calls "world transformative discipleship."[6]

I utilize a South African remixed, praxis cycle,[7] appropriated as a missiological hermeneutical tool,[8] in analyzing the interplay between social struggle/activism and the faith community, where the angles of insertion or agency, contextual and ecclesial analysis, inform the reading of the tradition, with the view of creating an appropriate witnessing response. These angles are different facets of an integrated struggle, which are often not distinguished as such, yet remain critical for our analysis of this praxis of youth activism. In my remixed version, I play with the spirituality at the center of all these angles.

The Church as Seen by a Young Black Layman

In 1972, Biko addressed a conference of black ministers of religion, organized by the Black Community Program,[9] under the theme, "The Church as Seen by a Young Layman."[10] He started his address by stating the two ways in which he personally differs from his audience. First, he is a "layman" speaking to religious professionals, and second, he is a "young man talking to fairly elderly people."[11] He, however, sees this self-conscious attempt to close the generation gap as fundamental to "the re-examination of any hitherto orthodox" situation. Moreover, he sees this situation as "fast becoming obsolete in the minds of young people."[12]

In trying to understand the context, Biko first presented his view of religion in general, and then the particular introduction of Christianity to South Africa, after which he moves to analysis of the "Church and its operation in modern-day South Africa."[13] He refers to the "appalling irrelevance of the interpretation of Scripture,"[14] the preaching of "stern-faced ministers who stand on pulpits every Sunday to heap loads of blame on black people in townships for their thieving, house-breaking, stabbing, murdering, adultery, etc." whilst "no-one ever attempts to relate all these vices to poverty, unemployment, overcrowding, lack of schooling and migratory labour."[15] He also refers to the "bureaucracy" of the church and its control by white people, and laments, "This bureaucracy and institutionalisation tends to make the Church removed from important priorities to concentrate on secondary and tertiary functions like structures and finances, etc. And because of this, the church has become very irrelevant and in fact an 'ivory tower' as some people refer to it."[16]

Biko concluded this analysis with an important challenge, not only for the church leaders present, but also for us today: overcoming the tendency to make the interpretation of religion a "specialist job." This is the hermeneutical challenge, and he suggested as an alternative a reading strategy that is communal. He said, "Young people nowadays would like to feel that they can interpret Christianity and extract from it messages relevant to them and their situation without being stopped by orthodox limitations. This is why the Catholic Church with its dozens of dogmas either has to adjust fast to a changing world or risk the chance of losing the young constituency. In various aspects, this applies to all Churches in the Christian world."[17] His answer to this church's witness response or action, which for him is modeled along Western lines, is to work for fundamental change. Fundamental change means that blacks are to "first [to] gain ascendancy over them (whites) in that white model, then thereafter turn that model into one we cherish, we love, we understand, and one that is relevant to us."[18] He referred to the concrete strategies of caucusing and building a thorough understanding of black theology in order to "save Christianity from falling foul with black people particularly young black people."[19] In summing up this challenge, he reminded his audience, "God is not in the habit of coming down from heaven to solve people's problems on earth."[20]

Biko had a clear activist understanding of the role and calling of Christians. He also worked with an implicit praxis method, which would serve the struggle for liberation and provide an appropriate theological perspective on the sources of the Christian tradition. Tinyiko Maluleke sees the significance of Biko as far greater. He states, "As an activist social theorist, Biko stands proudly and firmly in the tradition of Frantz Fanon, Martin Luther King, Jr. and Malcolm X."[21] He marvels at the youth of Biko and his contemporaries, as they led the intellectual charge to overcome racism. He does on to say, "Indeed, the revolution Biko led was a revolution led by people in their early twenties, most of whom were banned and restricted by the time they were twenty-six."[22] In his view, "Black Theology (BT) was born, not through the pen or mind of a solitary academic, but by a product of the self-same college student politics; inspired by SASO and born within the University Christian Movement."[23] I would, however, surmise that Biko's method—perhaps underdeveloped at this stage—was critical in this instance. The question now is how this challenge, as it erupted a few years later with respect to the role of younger people in the Soweto riots, was answered by the church—in particular, the black church.

Black Ecclesiology, in Struggle

Allan Boesak

While it is generally accepted that the advent of a more articulate and scholarly expression of black theology can be traced back to the late 1960s and early '70s, most key proponents[24] argue that the roots of this post-colonial theology are much deeper and can be found in the earliest forms of black religious resistance against slavery and colonialism.[25] Allan Boesak links this history of struggle to the actions of what became later known as the African independent churches, those who "walked out of the established, white-controlled churches to form their own churches."[26]

The question is how the thinking of the youth and student activists impacted on this formal articulation of black theology, in particular its ecclesiology. As a leading voice within what became known as the first pioneering phase of South African black theology, Boesak delivered a classic speech[27] at the annual general meeting of the South African Council of Churches in July 1979 in which the challenge of Biko's thought clearly surfaces. This speech, given in the aftermath of the 1976 riots and the violent death of Biko, reflects on and also responds to the challenges posed by actions and activism of the youth. Boesak states, "We had all heard Biko, and we all knew we had to respond. We were facing a new generation of young black Christians: politically astute, sensitive to what they were being told, knowing the dilemmas of the black church, and articulate in their anger, critique and aspirations."[28]

The speech, titled "The Black Church and the Future," starts with a reflection on the relevance of its theme, making it clear that it is out of the legacy of struggle that the reconceptualization of the black church emerged as

a broad movement of black Christians, joined in the black solidarity that transcends all barriers of denomination and ethnicity. It shares the same black experience, the same understanding of suffering and oppression, and the same common goal of liberation from all forms of oppression. It is a movement deeply imbued with the belief that the gospel of Jesus Christ proclaims the total liberation of all peoples, and the God and Father of Jesus Christ is the God of the oppressed.[29]

In attempting to understand the context, Boesak continues to assert that the black church faces various challenges. One critical challenge concerned changes in political consciousness since 1976. Some young people indeed left the church (as Biko predicted) in disappointment and disgust, whilst others stayed. Those younger generations who stayed, emerged with a highly sensitized political consciousness, with probing, critical questions about the nature and witness of the church. Boesak surmises, "It is my contention that the black church does not yet know how to deal with this new generation."[30]

In his analysis of the church, he refers to the crisis of authentic identity. This crisis relates to what he calls "white control." This is not simply administrative control; for him it is "the predominantly white image of the black church: in style, in witness, in commitment."[31] The authentic black church must therefore identify with the community it serves, so that it can understand the joys, sorrows, and aspirations of the people. For him it was, however, a community in a struggle, "not merely against an oppressive political and exploitative system; it was also a struggle for the authenticity of the gospel of Jesus Christ."[32] For Boesak, political authenticity does not mean that the Christian has to condone and justify everything done in the course of the struggle. It does mean that the Christian has the duty to make a difference and not be absorbed or dictated to by the world. By adhering to the criteria of the gospel, the church can make a meaningful contribution to the struggle of the people. For future church action he suggests two alternatives: first, adopting a policy of accommodation urging people to accept concessions; and second, standing firm and actively challenging the status quo.

In strategizing for the black community, he sets the agenda for Christian youth activism. Boesak's thought inspired many of the strategies for nonviolent protest actions by resistance movements within communities, which followed in the 1980s under the banner of the United Democratic Front (UDF) and also from the black church. While the focus of youth ministries was traditionally only on spiritual development, now under the influence of some student chaplains and youth leaders from the University of the Western Cape and the various teacher training colleges, it also started to play a key formative role in the social and political consciousness of church youth. Under the raised clenched fists[33] and the "black power" slogan, various freedom song chants, as well as struggle art—articulated in posters, banners and clothing—were developed in the 1970s and then in the middle 1980s, raging against and subverting the hegemonic power of what became known as "the system." In the 1980s, various local movements, organized under the banner of the South African Youth Congress (SAYCO), student representative councils (SRC) of various high schools organized student action through school and consumer boycotts. There were also sports boycotts associated with the South African Council of Sport (SACOS). These became known as "non-racial sport," which turned the traditional playgrounds of young people into sites of struggle. Most of these movements were affiliated with the then non-racial UDF, and in the late 1980s and at turn of the decade with the Mass Democratic Movement (MDM).

Within the Dutch Reformed Mission church, the growing tension,[34] between a colonial mission theology and the black theology of liberation that inspired many of the younger ministers and challenged and shaped engagement in vigorous debates, political stances, and protests through the ecclesial youth congress movement, as well as the student movements. The Christian youth associations[35] within these churches remained in dialogue with the resistance movements, and so the various church youth camps, conferences, and worship services became the space for "critical" and "relevant" Bible studies by leaders who led the struggle—and because they did, were often jailed. The Dutch Reformed Mission Church, to which I also belonged, was forced to wrestled with these issues theologically, and consequently a unique witnessing self-identity[36] emerged, which gained a strong reformed emphasis and articulation with the adoption of the Belhar Confession between 1982 and 1986. The eventual adoption of the Belhar Confession needs to be seen as a key moment in responding to these contestations.

Takatso Mofokeng

In his book *The Crucified amongst Cross-bearers: Towards a Black Christology*, Takatso Mofokeng, a representative of the second generation within South African black theology, the meaning of a new missionary ecclesiology also emerges in an oppressive situation on the one hand, and in the struggle for liberation on the other. Mofokeng situates his insertion and reflection in the context of his struggles as a pastor with the reality of younger generations, who have left the church and joined the various liberation movements in exile. He struggles with the question of decolonization and whether it promotes dechristianization. For him, to be a blessing in the world, a sacrament, the church needs a new self-understanding (identity) that sheds the ecclesiocentric perspective. Mofokeng states, "The church exists in a horizon of salvific work instead of itself being the sole custodian and centre of salvation. It has its centre outside itself."[37] Therefore, Mofokeng's ecclesiology is defined in terms of service to all humanity. The church is a subject as well as an object of evangelization with the world as subject. By implication, the church is placed in a dialectical relationship with the poor, a reconversion to the Third

World in order to become a church of the poor and also to find its place "on the outside, like the poor it has to serve."[38] This church cannot be neutral in situations of oppression, and the Christological dialectic of death and resurrection becomes the structure of the transformation of the church that is so critical for its new mission.

The implicit result of this understanding is a new partnership between the church and the working-class poor in communities and movements and therefore the transformation of the church. In the context of the time, it meant the deconstruction of the racially based, colonial churches, and the struggle towards a new church dealing with the poor and landless black communities. These ideas translated into the emergence of the uniting church. Mofokeng was himself part of this new struggle for a post-racial church, but also the various efforts for the transformation of public institutions—in particular tertiary institutions.

The question is whether this impetus lasted into the democratic turn in South Africa. It seems as if the "miracle" of the 1994 democratic transformation also called for a new ecclesiology, which impacted on the prophetic witness of the church.

Black Ecclesiology, Struggling in the New South Africa

In an article, "Culture and the Church: the Quest for a New Ecclesiology" (1995), Barney Pityana says of the 1990s, "Successive annual conferences of the South African Council of Churches (SACC) since the Rustenburg Conference in 1990, have added their voice to the South African search for a *new* ecclesiology."[39] His article aims to trace what he calls the "emerging trends towards a relevant ecclesiology for South Africa." In his analysis of the new South African context, he states, "[T]he transformation of South Africa has been described variously as breath taking, miraculous and even as a godsend." The flagship of the new government's policy addressing the legacy of colonialism was the Reconstruction and Development Programme, popularly known as the RDP. Pityana declares, "We have begun to see a government with a human face," and "the development of a culture of human rights has been going apace." His analysis for the "new South Africa" continues, describing the progress taking place in South Africa as nothing short of a major transition of the moral character of this nation. But he also notes, "[T]he truth though, is that while this effort is underway, crime is escalating. . . . more frighteningly, there are concerns about a deteriorating public morality—even amongst those who have responsibilities in national life." He laments what he calls a "culture of entitlement," a "culture of waiting," and states, "A culture of demand has set in and in pursuit of our narrow interests we see no need to consider wider issues, such as the need of the most needy. Those who have the muscle apply the most pressure to get their way and the weak fall by the wayside."[40]

Pityana then asks, where is the church? For him, the new South African churches regularly gather in large numbers for worship, yet it would appear that Christian teaching has only a marginal influence on "personal life." He reminisces about how prophetic witness was once testimony to a vibrant and integrated Christian life and had a great social influence. Now, in the new South Africa, however, Christians learned only too well the strategies and tactics of struggle, and inevitably these were applied in the life of the church. This means that Christians were cultured in the art of struggle, which influenced behavior and practice within the church. Accordingly, there were constant conflicts with youth, with activists, with women. Whilst everything else was changing and dynamic, the church remained conservative and unchanging).[41]

In working out his plan of action, Pityana deals with the question "Whereto for the church and what were the lessons learnt?" For Pityana, the struggle against a common enemy forged a common spirituality and devotion detected in songs, dances, style of prayer, and preaching, activities that continue to sustain many communities even in changed circumstances. He calls theirs an "ecumenical spirituality," which is spontaneous and which is not the property of any one denomination. Further, there are lay people who have learnt leadership in the streets. They are assertive, articulate, and industrious. The language of the political struggle, he argues, has become the language of theology, concepts like workshops, networking, accountability, transparency, and so on. The church now has had to cope with a more assertive cultural expression, especially in African congregational life. Indeed, popular culture has found expression in church life—even if this development has received insufficient recognition. As a result, the livelier worship—songs sung spontaneously, with dancing and extempore prayer—have been added to the very formal and stuffy European worship of our traditions. More and more African Christians have become both African and Christian without shame, and without a feeling of being torn apart. The church, however, has taken no account of this transformation, and the "new South Africa" theology, for Pityana, has not begun to deal the change. Pityana argues that one can say that the church during transition shows no readiness to change. Instead, many churches have withdrawn back into cozy denominationalism and pietism. What seems to be happening is that engagement with the changing political reality is often uninformed and somewhat hostile. The church has to learn the rudiments of democracy fast. The church is being challenged, often painfully, to embrace the culture of democratic transformation.

These awkward issues seem to have seeped into youth activism as well. There would currently seem to be a lack of youth activism, which has characterized the youth ministry of black South African churches and student movements since the late 1960s. Initially, the popular explanation in the South Africa of the 1990s was in line with Pityana's analysis. The church seemed to believe "the struggle is over," and that it should return to its "normal spiritual business" and celebrate the "new" South Africa. The fundamental question is, however, whether the participation of Christian youth in popular struggles against "the system" departed from a more "biblical" expression of youth in mission, or whether it was an authentic expression of contextual mission praxis, as indicated in the analysis of the challenges in the earlier part of this paper. If the latter is the case—and I argue that it is—then it follows that the particular theological method that guided and sustained this mission praxis, or social activism of Christian youth, is still relevant for purposes of unearthing the authentic expression of a youthful, but also ecclesial praxis today. I therefore argue that today the assessment of this new, united South Africa—with the formation of new uniting churches, and the ongoing struggles of uniting faith-based youth movements, what I would term post-racial youth ministry—is critical, as it will shed light on emerging conceptualizations of church as the critical basis for dealing with the new, post-colonial context.

Christian Youth Activism Today

We've seen that Christian activism was a struggle against a tainted colonial version of Christianity. It was a struggle against a conception of church and mission where non-theological factors, rooted in racism, shaped the reading of the gospel, which in turn led to a particular structuring of the church and society. It was understood in this struggle that the formation of a faith community that transcends the boundaries of language, ethnicity, and racial identities, would induce social as well as personal healing and transformation. This new understanding of the church as a witnessing community is stated in the Belhar Confession:

> [W]e believe that God has entrusted the church with the message of reconciliation in and through Jesus Christ; that the church is called to be the salt of the earth and the light of the world, that the church is called blessed because it is

a peacemaker, that the church is witness both by word and by deed to the new heaven and the new earth in which righteousness dwells.

This confession presented an ecclesiology to transcend, but also subvert the colonial ecclesiologies forged in a particular context, and thereby the dismantling of a regime. [42] The way churches, in their reading of the gospel, structured the church became a life-threatening statement of political intent and action. The embrace of church unity and of non-racial youth movements[43] was understood to be God's mission for the church, a mission where unity, reconciliation, and social justice were indeed critical interweaving linkages intended to transform both church and society. Ecclesiology and ethics could not be separated. In the "new" South African context, various churches, such as the Apostolic Faith Mission, one of the biggest Pentecostal churches in South Africa, the Presbyterian church in Southern Africa, the Congregational Church in Southern Africa, and student and youth movements such as the Christian Youth Movement (CYM), the Uniting Christian Students Association(UCSA), and the Students' Christian Organization, amongst others, united to form non-racial, post-apartheid faith communities. Aiming to understand their calling as Christians, both CYM and UCSA made explicit reference to their social vocation as they listened to the word of God.

The CYM came about in 1995, the result of a merger between youth ministries of the black Dutch Reformed Church in Africa (DRCA), such as the Mokgatlo wa Bodumedi ba Bokreste (MBB),[44] the coloured Dutch Reformed Mission Church (DRMC), and the Christelike Jeugvereniging (CJV). [45] The UCSA came into existence in 1997 as a result of the merger between the predominantly coloured Vereniging vir Christen Studente (VCS) [46] and the all-white Afrikaanse Christen Studente Vereniging (ACSV).[47] The structure and practice of these ministries were steeped in imagery of the white Dutch Reformed Church's official collusion with apartheid, and formed during the apartheid period as racially defined colonial structures.

As indicated earlier, decisions recorded by the youth congresses, particularly the former CJV and ACS (1985–93), indicate that serious attempts were made to understand and contextualize the gospel (à la Boesak's ecclesiology) in terms of black youth resistance, and later (à la Mofokeng's ecclesiology) in terms of working-class cultures and struggles of the day, that is, the struggle against colonialism and colonial-tainted versions of Christianity (as Biko challenged). The emphasis was indeed on forging a missionary self-understanding, where the pursuit of unity, reconciliation, and justice, and a focus on the black poor, the oppressed, and the needy was central. It was also understood that black liberation was key to unlocking all humanity. Indeed,

here we find the articulation of post-colonial thinking, which has relevance
for oppression in the rest of Africa and other former colonies, the mission to
overcome racism. Not merely aimed at unity or reconciliation, it was about
establishing justice. In this vein, Nico Koopman, then student chaplain of
University of the Western Cape, reflects in the official newspaper of the then
DRMC, *Die Ligstraal/Ligdraer*, on the historical significance of the scope of
activism by South African Christian students:

> Our youth is blessed with wonderful skills which are demonstrated in their abil-
> ity to arrange a national event of this magnitude so effectively. Their discipline,
> loyalty to the church and love for Jesus Christ, struck me. The theme and con-
> tents of the conference reflects the spiritual growth of our youth, but it also indi-
> cates that our youth is grappling with the most important issues of the day. And
> very important, they are not discouraged, they are hopeful about the dawning of
> a new unifying church and a unified South Africa. May the young members of
> the church encourage all of us.[48]

The process of merger between VCS and ACSV to form UCSA (VCSV)
started with a historic meeting January 24–25, 1992, in Stellenbosch, of the
various student bodies, including the Students' Union for Christian Action
(SUCA), Scripture Union (SU), Students' Christian Movement (SCM), and
the Students' Christian Association (SCA). At this meeting the principle of
merger was agreed, and the various stages were set out. It was affirmed. We
repent of the unbiblical division that occurred in 1965. We commit ourselves
to the vision of united ministry/movements in schools and tertiary institutions *for the sake of our Christian witness in the world*[49] (italics RWN).

The first phase of the unification was forming UCSA and SCO (as a
result of a merger between SCM and SCA), whilst a second stage of unification involved UCSA and SCO. Questions were asked as to whether the
church could still become a place where race is transcended, and whether
black and white Christian youths could come together and make a difference
in transforming unjust realities? I will explore how the search for answers
to these questions manifested in the current journey of CYM and UCSA
after more then fifteen years of being structurally united. Although CYM
and UCSA have formed new organizations, the on-going journey of unification, reconciliation, and justice has been central to its recent reflections and
ministry focus. These remain guiding principles, but also challenges, in how
the leadership develops policy and aims at transforming their practice at a
deeper level.

"Internal Unity" within a Black Christian Youth Movement

Within the CYM, the question of internal unity is often debated, as illustrated by events at the general congress in 2007. The then chairperson, Molefe Morake, noted in his address that the challenge of racism and dealing with diversity still haunts the ministry. In the aftermath of the congress, vigorous and often bitter debate raged via email, and later Facebook, among young people, ministers, youth leaders, and former youth leaders. This was mainly a debate amongst coloured members of CYM, and was sparked by an incident at the general congress, where a prominent black minister and member of the church's executive called the meeting null and void because of administrative and constitutional errors. This action was about the perceived incompetence of the leaders, but behind it were layers of unresolved matters.

In the debate that stretched from July to October 2007, often referred to as the "e-congress," various alignments and loyalties pertaining to the CYM emerged. From some, there was a lament that CYM was loosing its footing administratively, but also in terms of its mission with young people. Some participants, steeped in the history of struggle, remained loyal to and invoked an older CJV culture and identity, whilst others in various senior management positions, held strong views on the corporate governance of the organization and called for a sort of corporatist management paradigm shift in the youth ministry and in the church. These managerial leaders felt that the church was not doing enough to ensure efficiency and effectiveness. Yet a growing number of younger voices expressed their alienation from the corporatist, old school language and style of the "comrades." They hoped for an affirmation of their own unique needs and articulations of transformation and community. Indeed, they gave voice to a new sound, born or schooled in the new South Africa, where the older "struggle" language and working class cultures were unknown. They were born into a new struggle against exclusion in the church, and in educational and economic prospects linked to economic globalization.

The irony was, however, that this conversation excluded the black young people who, in terms of the official documentation and reports, were beginning to protest the absence of the coloured members and branches at official gatherings and that they were being dominated in certain regions where they were numerically stronger. The central executive committee wrestled with a spate of resignations, especially from coloured members, yet tried to maintain the vision of a unity through close ties with the formal structures of the church. Indeed, it seemed that the challenge of unification, reconciliation,

and justice remained high. While unification took place structurally, the need
for reconciliation and justice in new contexts remained. This had become,
seemingly, a long journey.

What is "Transformation" within UCSA?

Within UCSA, in-depth conversation on the future of the organization was
sparked by a discussion document, submitted at the national executive meeting in November 2007 by senior staff members in response to the challenge
of bringing about transformation. The document was an honest assessment
of their varied experiences. It came in the year UCSA should have celebrated
a decade years of being reunited, but it became a critical assessment of the
post-unification process.

The document states that transformation, as it was being implemented,
was one of the major stumbling blocks for spiritual and professional growth
for individual staff members and for the organization. There was a dearth of
people still seeking the will of God and praying for the future of the UCSA.
The national executive committee read this document and wanted to engage
in a dialogue with senior staff in order to discern a way forward.

In these dialogue sessions, which took place the weekend of March 1–2,
2008,[50] UCSA was said to stand at "a critical cross-roads." UCSA had to
search harder for the will of God through prayer and Bible study, and in the
voices of sisters and brothers in the organization. The process of listening to
one another using a methodology called "outsider witness" helped clarify the
issues. In the process, it became clear that certain coloured members within
the national executive and staff of the organization felt that some white members viewed the challenge of transformation and the needs of young coloured
students as a lower priority. White members within the national executive,
along with certain staff members in the organization, however, maintained
that one of the major challenges within the UCSA concerned obsession of
coloured members with race and with social transformation, or "koppetel."[51]
These coloured members, it was believed, were still bitter over the past and
had yet to deal with their own pain and resentment over apartheid. It was
time to forgive and forget and move on.

There seemed to be a tension between the policy of transformation (on a
personal and spiritual level) and transformation as a policy for employment
equity. It emerged that economic considerations were critical. Ironically, more
young people from the white community are growing poorer, even as younger
people from black communities gained access to wealth and opportunity. The

co-chairperson, who came from the former coloured VCS, responded in this debate: "We will have to make a shift to a more inclusive accent . . . . I hear . . . speaking too exclusive about the brown[52] child. We cannot continue to think like this . . . we need an inclusive approach." But I hear him; the brown life experience is not always taken up in the new UCSA program planning. But we are making progress. I was at a recent national camp, where I took part in some very fruitful programs.

The Landscape Is Risky

Out of these difficult but honest processes, the landscape of student and youth ministry is shifting. Attention is shifting toward the dire socio-economic and educational needs of the poor students, but also toward tensions derived from older notions of race and antagonism between economic classes. Often in these conversations, clashes occur between poorer, working-class young students (whose circumstances are linked both to the colonial legacy and to current policy, including an inability to pay for services rendered), and affluent, young learners (whose historical privilege transfers in the current context in multiple ways, including access to all the latest gadgets and technology to enhance their lives). Therefore, while unity has been achieved in a structural sense, interrelatedness between unity, reconciliation, and justice remains incomplete. Achieving these more comprehensive and interrelated goals will require further critical dialogue with emerging voices, so that current challenges rather than outdated concerns become the focus.

Notes

1. In *Running with Horses: Reflections of an Accidental Politician* (Cape Town: Joho Publishers, 2008), Dr. Allan Boesak opens his reflections on his years of activism with a telling anecdote. He was requested by students at the University of the Western Cape to speak on "the meaning of Soweto for us." He surmises that Soweto, in the minds of these young people, meant more than a township in Johannesburg. Already, "Soweto was a condition, a symbol, a compelling call upon the suppressed anger" (22).

2. B. Pityana, "Reflections on 30 Years Since the Death of Steve Biko: A Legacy Revisited," in C. W. du Toit, ed., *The Legacy of Stephen Bantu Biko: Theological Challenges* (Pretoria: Unisa Press, 2008), 3.

3. Stephen Biko, *I Write What I Like: A Selection of His Writings*, Aelred Stubbs, ed. (Johannesburg: Picador Africa, 2004), 60.

4. Reggie Nel, "Youth in the Mission to Overcome Racism: The Formation and Development of the Christian Youth Movement in Southern Africa (1995–2005)," *Studia Historiae Ecclesiasticae* 36, No. 2 (October 2010): 178–205.

5. Ibid., 201.

6. Russell Botman, "Towards a World-Transformative Christianity," in *An African Challenge to the Church in the 21st Century*, M. Guma and L. Milton eds. (Cape Town: Salty Print, 1997), 72–80.

7. Cochrane, de Gruchy, and Petersen, *In Word and Deed: Towards a Practical Theology of Social Transformation* (Pietermaritzburg: Cluster Publications, 1990), 13.

8. M. Karecki, ed., *The Making of an African Person* (Pretoria: Daan Roux Printers, 2002), 138–41.

9. This program, along with the black theology project, were the key ventures supported by the Christian Institute, begun in 1968. See also Pityana (2008), 9.

10. Biko (2006), 58–65.

11. Ibid., 58.

12. Ibid.

13. Biko, 60.

14. Ibid.

15. Biko, 61.

16. Ibid., 62.

17. Biko, 62–63.

18. Ibid., 63

19. Biko, 64.

20. Ibid., 65.

21. T. S. Maluleke, "May the Black God Stand Please!" in A. Mngxitama et al., eds., *Biko Lives!* (New York: Palgrave Macmillan,2008), 116.

22. Ibid., 117.

23. Ibid.

24. Cf. S. Maimela and A. Konig, eds., *Initiation into Theology* (Pretoria: J. L. van Schaik, 1998), 112–13, and M. Motlhabi, *African Theology/Black Theology in South Africa* (Pretoria: UNISA Press, 2008), 1–3.

25. Cf. Allan Boesak, *Black and Reformed: Apartheid, Liberation and the Calvinist Tradition* (Johannesburg: Skotaville Publishers, 1984), 23; Boesak, *Running with Horses*, 50; Maimela, 112; M. Motlhabi, *African Theology/Black Theology in South Africa* (Pretoria: Unisa Press, 2008), 18; D. J. Bosch, *Het Evangelie in Afrikaanse gewaad* (Kampen: Kok, 1974), 92–93.

26. Boesak, *Running with Horses*, 50.

27. This speech was also published in Dr. Allan Boesak's most recent book reflecting on his years of activism, *Running with Horses*. Here it appears under the title "The Black Church, Politics, and the Future: Responding to Biko and the Children".

28. Boesak (1984), 22–35, and (2008), 84.

29. Boesak, (1984), 23–24; see also B. Goba, "Towards a 'Black' Ecclesiology," *Missionalia* 9/2 (1981), 53.

30. Boesak, (1984), 22.

31. Ibid., 25.

32. Ibid.

33. J. N. J. Kritzinger, "Black Theology: Challenge to Mission" (DTh dissertation, University of South Africa, 1988), 43–44, refers to the "clenched black fist," as the "most visible symbol" and "trade mark" of black consciousness, expressing the determination of black people to affirm their dignity and humanity in the context of white racism.

34. Cf. Adonis, *Die afgebreekte skeidsmuur weer opgebou* (Amsterdam: Rodopi, 1982); P. J. Robinson, "Die Belhar-belydenis van 1982 in sendingperspektief," in G. D. Cloete and D. J. Smit, eds., *'n Oomblik van Waarheid* (Kaapstad: Tafelberg, 1984), 49–59; and E. D. C. Jacobs, "Swart teologie: missionêre implikasies," in J. Du Preez, C. M. Pauw, and P. J. Robinson, eds., *Sendinggenade: Feesbundel vir W. J. van der Merwe* (Bloemfontein: NG Sending, 1986), 164–80, for critical analysis on Dutch Reformed Mission policies and, later, the challenge from within the ranks of the Dutch Reformed Mission Church.

35. The relevant youth associations, for me in this context, were the CJV-*Christelike Jeugvereniging*, meaning Christian Youth Association, and the VCS-*Vereniging vir Christen Studente*, which translates as Association for Christian Students, affiliated with the World Students' Christian Federation.

36. Cf. P. Robinson, "Die Belhar-belydenis van 1982 insendingperspektief," in Cloete and Smit (1984), 49–59.

37. T. A. Mofokeng, *The Crucified Amongst Crossbearers* (Kampen: J. H. Kok, 1983), 58.

38. Ibid., 59.

39. Pityana, (1995), 87.

40. Pityana, (1995), 89.

41. Ibid., 90.

42. D. J. Smit, "Reformed Faith, Justice and the Struggle Against Apartheid," *Reformed World* 55, No. 4 (December 2005), 355–67.

43. Apart from the more formal church and para-church youth ministries, we also found non-formal activist student formations in this theological climate, such as the Koinonia, initiated by missiologist and pastor Nico Smith, the Student's Union for Christian Action (SUCA), Youth Alive, and others led by evangelical activists like Moss Nthla and Caesar Molebatse.

44. Association for Christ's (or Christian) Youth.

45. Christian Youth Association.

46. Association for Christian Students (ACS).

47. Afrikaans Christian Students Association.

48. H. Hendriks, "Missional Theology," *Die Ligdraer/Ligstaal* (Aug 1993), 10.

49. G. van der Merwe, *Jesus is Koning: Die verhaal van die Christen-Studentevereniging van Suid-Afrika, 1896–1996* (Stellenbosch: CSV van Suid-Afrika, 1996).

50. Just after the revelations of four young university students who made a video showing some female black workers being fed a concoction, seemingly mixed with urine.

51. Counting heads.

52. Within the Southern African context, "coloured" and "brown" (bruin) are used interchangeably, although some now prefer to speak of "people of mixed descent."

White Theology amidst White Rhetoric on Violence

Cobus van Wyngaard

Introduction

Public shame associated with the explicit religious rationale for legalized racism in South Africa, and the racialized formation of institutionalized religion—particularly as found in the reformed churches—perhaps predictably led to a situation where any blatant racism is actively rejected by the white church. However, it would be naïve to assume that race has been ousted from religion and theology, and as reflection on post-apartheid whiteness continues, we would be wise to also consider how theology and religion continue to manifest as markedly white, even while (and at times exactly by) actively joining in the post-apartheid non-racial chorus.

This essay explores Afrikaner[1] whiteness[2] as inherently theological, and interprets important elements of post-apartheid whiteness as a continuation of an underlying theology running throughout the construction of Afrikaner nationalism and apartheid. It will seek to describe what parades as objective social analysis as a continuation of key religious and mythological elements from the perspective of white Afrikaners. To be specific, the essay will seek to show how contemporary white rhetoric on violent crime is connected to the Day of the Vow and the Anglo-Boer War of 1899–1902, and to a quasi-soteriology that calls for white withdrawal into a *laager*. The essay is an attempt to unravel further one thread from the theological core of whiteness, and to present a theological alternative that actively dismantles the continued racialization of society.

One of the most important threads of white discourse in post-apartheid South Africa concerns the public reaction to violent crime.[3] Working from a critical insider's position, this essay will explore the way in which white (particularly Afrikaner) discourse on violence remains theological in a post-apartheid South Africa. This discussion will be related in particular to traditional Afrikaner quasi-soteriology underlying apartheid, pointing out how elements of contemporary white discourse on violence and crime manifest as a continuation of a similar quasi-soteriology. In dialogue with black soteriology, a theological challenge to white responses to violence and crime is then articulated.

Whiteness as Salvation: A Soteriology of the *Laager*⁴

While the importance of explicit theological reflection in the formation of apartheid—such as through the influence of Dutch Reformed Church mission policies—has been widely noted, this section starts by taking a step back in order to recognize the entire construction of race as inherently theological. I will first point to interpretations of whiteness as a soteriological marker, before discussing the particular mythological and theological construction of a white soteriology in the formation of Afrikaners and the development of apartheid. This strategy will provide an interpretive lens to assist in describing post-apartheid white responses to violence as inherently theological, continuing a particular soteriological vision.

While the construction of race is often seen as a development of the Enlightenment, with voices such as that of Immanuel Kant considered the first to develop proper theories of race,⁵ race has been shown to function soteriologically much earlier. In describing the work of the sixteenth-century Jesuit Alessando Valignano, William Jennings illustrates how early notions of race, drawing on aesthetics and culture, provide a rationale for a theological interpretation of people discovered during early phases of colonialism. Working from the assumption that white Europeans are the elected people of God, the Christian social space was reinterpreted around black and white bodies. Whiteness became the marker of salvation, with blackness the reminder that salvation was unlikely or impossible.⁶

Such a racialized soteriology organized social life in the real. This for Valignano is connected to the capacity for self-governance, the designation of the kind of labor an individual can be involved with, and a marker of intelligence. Such categorizations became more elaborate over time, and as racism take on its later pseudo-scientific character, became seen as ever more fixed. Whiteness is the position considered elected by God, deserving of privilege, and, as a soteriological construct, a mythic presumption of wholeness.⁷

Somewhat disconnected from the European discourse, the construction of whiteness in South Africa took on a life of its own, while maintaining the broad interpretive gaze of the white European. Scientific racism, important in nineteenth- and twentieth-century Europe, played a lesser role in South

Africa during this time, and was even actively rejected when the scientific consensus on race shifted after the Second World War.[8] Rather than scientific racism, a *realpolitik* seeking to defend white privilege and justified through theology and mythology formed the whiteness of Afrikaners in the twentieth century.

Afrikaners can be described as a deeply mythologized people,[9] and the mythological construction of Afrikaners is connected to a self-understanding of being a threatened group. Two key elements of this mythological construction of Afrikaners need to be discussed in brief: the Day of the Vow and the Anglo-Boer War of 1899–1902.

On December 16, 1838, a military encounter between the Voortrekker expedition under the leadership of Andries Pretorius and the Zulu army took place at Ncome/Blood River. In the days preceding the clash, a covenant had been made by Pretorius and other leaders of the expedition in the form of a prayer, in which a promise was made that a church would be built and the day celebrated with thanksgiving if God provided them with a victory. The Voortrekkers gathered into a strategically well-placed *laager* and defeated the Zulu army.[10] However, in the ensuing years little was made of the celebration of the covenant by those who were present at the encounter. In 1880, the covenant was renewed by burgers of the Transvaal Republic as they prepared for a revolt against Britain, and after the successful military campaign the Transvaal government organized a state festival on December 16, 1881, that was to be repeated every fifth year thereafter to celebrate both the victory over Britain and the victory at Blood River.[11] Over the course of the twentieth century, December 16 would be continuously reinterpreted in relation to the struggles of the day—as a celebration of Nationalist victory after the 1948 elections, or as a metaphor for the battle against decolonization in the 1960s and 1970s, when the *laager* at Blood River became the image for the small group of white people positioned against the threat of Black Africa.[12]

If the *laager* at Blood River runs as a continuing thread throughout the development of Afrikaner nationalism in the nineteenth and twentieth centuries, the war of 1899 to 1902 is the defining moment in the formation of Afrikaner identity. This event is generally regarded as having provided the vital stimulus for the development of Afrikaner nationalism as a mass movement.[13] Bosch writes, "For Britain, the war was no more than a passing episode; for Afrikaners, who lost eight times as many women and children in the concentration camps as soldiers on the battlefield, this was the most crucial event in their history, the matrix out of which a new people was born."[14] This event reinforced an already existing *laager* mentality among the Afrikaners, who found security by a turning within and fortifying against the externalized, experienced threat.[15] One of the most distinct features to emerge in Afrikaner self-understanding in relation to the war was that they could triumph through suffering.[16] This internalization of Afrikaner identity was to have dangerous consequences for the nation as a whole during the apartheid era.

Using biblical passages, such as the narrative of Nehemiah, and applying it to the Afrikaners, salvation for the Afrikaner was found in racial purity and racial separation as instituted by God.[17] Just as God was on the side of Israel, God was seen to be on the side of the Afrikaner, the chosen people of the Lord.[18] Differences according to race were considered to be so fundamental that it became impossible to imagine a racially integrated future to be good in any way, to lead to any form of salvation whatsoever.[19]

There are various ways in which separation and withdrawal into the *laager* is considered a precondition for salvation can be identified. Politically, self-determination was considered essential to safeguard the social and economic interests of Afrikaners. Socially, integration was assumed to lead to a loss of Afrikaner identity, and strength and salvation was therefore found in isolation. For Afrikaners this relates to a deep sense of cultural superiority and a way of finding protection against the "sea of barbarism," and underlies the importance of uplifting "poor whites," lest they should move closer to black groups (considered a threat by the white elite in a context where a class overlap between black and poor white exists). On a military level (important for the topic under discussion), the threat of the "total onslaught" and the "swart gevaar"[20] to the well-being of white existence was ever-present as a reminder that salvation cannot be found outside the *laager*.[21]

Salvation was found through racial separation, and God was seen as the protector against the threat of both black and British. The continuation of these theological notions into a post-apartheid South Africa begs further discussion.

White Soteriology and the Racialization of Violent Crime

A key aspect underlying this essay is the importance of violence—specifically violent crime—in white rhetoric in post-apartheid South Africa. Violence and crime are used in defining white people as a threatened group, the victims of society, although research indicates that poor black and coloured people continue to be disproportionately affected by violent crime.

In white discourse, crime, rather than poverty or economic inequality, is considered to be the biggest problem of the post-apartheid South Africa.[22]

White people tend to blame violent crime on the inability of the ANC-led government to govern.[23] Black people are portrayed as criminogenic and violent,[24] and as hating white people.[25] White people—specifically Afrikaners—are described as the primary targets of violent crime,[26] while black people are stigmatized as perpetrators.[27] On occasions, some white exponents even state that the apparent inability of the government to end violent crime is actually a hidden agenda of the ANC government to get rid of Afrikaners.[28]

Research on violent crime reveals a picture that contrasts with popular white discourse. Although South Africa is not entirely unique with reference to its levels of violent crime, it is indeed part of a relatively small group of countries in the world with exceptionally high rates of violent crime.[29] Murder rates peaked in the 90s, at approximately sixty murders per hundred thousand per year, and current figures in the high 30s per hundred thousand per year continue to be exceptionally high.

But South Africa has been an exceptionally violent country throughout its history of colonialism and apartheid. Extensive (often foreign) military power was used to control indigenous groups,[30] and police use of excessive violence during apartheid is well documented. Urban violence connected to gang culture can be seen developing in the late nineteenth century around mining cities (particularly Johannesburg), with pass laws, migrant labor and the criminalization of black laborers creating a constant flow of inmates through prisons, often the place where the violent culture was strengthened rather than defused, contributing to a culture of urban violence.[31]

There is evidence to support the fact that significant differences in the prevalence of violent crime exist between different racial groups, and is also tied to class locations. Although violent crime affects all racial groups in South Africa, African and coloured South Africans experience a higher incidence of murder than Indian and—especially—white people.[32] No evidence can be found to support any systemic victimization of white people.[33] Violence affects people of all economic groups, although poorer areas experience higher levels.[34] Financial resources for responding to crime, particularly private spending, are primarily focused on affluent areas,[35] and white people in South Africa can generally spend more providing security for themselves. The tension between white rhetoric and the above picture of violent crime in South Africa provides at least a partial background for Melissa Steyn's observation, which key to this topic: "While crime in South Africa is real enough, the choice to cast this as targeting primarily whites, and as if Afrikaners are being singled out for persecution is a deliberate rhetorical option."[36] It is this deliberate, rhetorical option, seen as a theological problem, which concerns us in this essay.

It is important to take note of a certain continuity in Afrikaner discourse. The idea of being under constant threat, of salvation being found when all stick together and fortify themselves against the outside world reminds us of the initial elements that gave rise to Afrikaner nationalism. At times this is even explicitly stated. Let us examine an explicit example from popular culture: the controversial song "Ons sal dit oorleef,"[37] written by the highly popular Afrikaans singer, songwriter, and self-identified activist against violent crime Steve Hofmeyr.[38] Hofmeyr's song take the form of a prayer for the present, reminding the Afrikaner "volk"[39] about their history of being under threat, and of the fact that they will survive as they have done in the past. Hofmeyr explicitly connects this song to the experience of violent crime at concerts.[40] "Die kakie kanon of die kaffer se dolk,"[41] is used as an example of the threats against which the Afrikaner has survived in the past, and also a reminder of the black and British threat important in the formation of Afrikaner nationalism and the *laager* mentality. Hofmeyr serves as a reminder that the formative moment in the making of the Afrikaner not only survives on a subconscious level, but is consciously remembered and used in the process of identity formation and sense-making in the post-apartheid South Africa, where talk about violence plays an important role in the formation of the post-apartheid Afrikaner. In Hofmeyr's description of the modern Afrikaner as oppressed group, religious language is explicitly employed, prayer is mentioned alongside blood and gunpowder as the means through which Afrikaners bought their freedom, and God is called in to protect the group. But what, exactly, is the function of this talk about the threatened Afrikaner today?

When reflecting on memory and violence, Miroslav Volf argues that "the memory of wrongs suffered is from a moral standpoint dangerously undetermined."[42] Among other reasons he states, this is because remembering wrongs suffered can easily led to legitimizing further injustice. How we remember the experienced injustice is of the utmost importance. How we talk about violent crime in the post-apartheid South Africa, how we are actively creating memories of injustice suffered, is of the utmost importance, since doing so carries the potential of creating further injustice justified by the experience of being a victim.

In reflecting on letters in Afrikaans newspapers using strategies to Hofmeyr's, Steyn writes:

> The victim appropriates innocence, averts the gaze of accusers, allows blame
> to be shifted, generates guilt, smudges lines of accountability, and, especially,
> transfers responsibility for the emotions generated within this resistant section
> of the community onto the broader society. The victim stance both justifies,

and stokes, feelings of outrage, indignation, and self-pity, allowing disclaimed violent impulses to be projected onto the perceived victimizers. And the more disgraceful the victimization can be shown to be, the more justified the powerfully antagonistic sentiments expressed are rendered, and the more the backlash mentality is vindicated.[43]

Centre for Violence and Reconciliation reports ended with a postscript document summarizing possible reasons for the unique situation of South Africa. To a large extent, the conclusion is that the high incidence of violence in South Africa is a continued effect of apartheid, and of the inability to correct the injustice and inequalities created by the apartheid government.[44] Could it be that recasting the Afrikaner as the victim par excellence of post-apartheid violence provides grounds for stating that no responsibility for the ongoing injustice created by apartheid should be expected from white South Africans? To take Volf's logic further, "Why expect those who are nursing their own wounds and mending their own shattered lives to minister to the needs of others?"[45] Such a strategy is indeed noted in research on white discourse on violence:

[B]y exaggerating white victimhood and stoking, even reactivating, constructions of the inimical nature of Africa and Africans to whiteness, resistant elements in white South Africa are able to underplay the dominance of their whiteness in the larger scheme of past and present global arrangements.[46]

{W}hites are not the primary victims of South Africa's social ills, and propagating the view that they are encourages ungenerous politics that refuses to acknowledge the responsibility whites have to address past wrongs.[47]

White victimhood is not a strange theme within international white rhetoric—witness affirmative action. Violent crime is one factor that is used to keep alive the idea of white victimhood, which is in turn used as motivation for diverting attention from the past role of white South Africans, as well as their continued concomitant privilege. Theologically it provides motivation for continuing to affirm that salvation is to be found by withdrawing into a *laager* and a position in opposition to a perceived threat.

Black Soteriology and White Rhetoric on Violence

In direct contrast to the soteriology of the *laager* described above, where the salvation for white South Africans was inherently tied to the racialization of society, positioning one group in opposition to another, the central symbol of salvation in black theology is liberation,[48] often understood as liberation from the very quasi-soteriological engineering of society that promised salvation to whites. That is to say, what functioned as a form of salvation in white South Africa became the oppression that provoked calls for liberation from black theologians. This argument is relevant to the above discussion about white rhetoric on violent crime in two ways: the continuation of a soteriology of the *laager* perpetuates perception of black life as of lesser importance, presenting salvation in a way which is inherently unattainable. The notion of quasi-soteriology should therefore be explicitly connected to a false soteriology, keeping its believers focused on a means to salvation that will never succeed. We focus our attention on these two aspects in this final section.

In stark contrast to the classic soteriology of the Afrikaner community described above, Isabel Phiri writes of black theology, "'Salvation' in Black Theology is the end of racism and the establishment of a new social order that affirms black humanity."[49] The challenge of black theology becomes tangible in the face of white talk about violence. The sense of being black and poor as somehow less human is most conspicuous when the death of the nameless is as of little concern. Concerning the public conversation on violent crime, David Bruce states, "[C]onsistently, it is when middle-class and, particularly, white South Africans are victimised, that violent crime is seen as a matter of concern, while the impact of violence on poorer people is disregarded."[50] Our rhetoric on violence then becomes a litmus test of a lived theology. Reactions to the death of a nameless poor black person testify of our belief in God as the creator of all people as equal—or as testimony against this belief. If violence against black people is of less concern, this feeling reinforces a disregard for the value of black humanity.

As part of a broader project of critically engaging whiteness and white theology in dialogue with North American black theology, Jim Perkinson writes,

> [W]hat if salvation actually is all about salvation, that is to say, that there indeed is no wholeness at any level without wholeness at every level? What if, in fact, we are interlinked in such a way that the first world cannot become healthy without the two-thirds world also becoming healthy? Not as a matter of prescription, but as simple description? What if the suburb cannot quiet its angst without the city finding answer to its anger?[51]

We can translate his questions in the South African context, first by expanding on the metaphor of the *laager* used above, and then by making it more concrete. What if there can be no salvation within the *laager* if health and wholeness does not come to the entire society? What if the town cannot quiet its angst without the township finding answer to its anger? What if the only way for white people to rid themselves not only of violence in the post-apartheid South Africa, but also of the constant fear that characterizes the white experience today, is to reconcile with black neighbors, to face the injustice of the past, and to recognize no salvation can be found in holding onto supposed privilege or entitlement connected with being white?

What if we were to bring such a comprehensive belief in salvation into dialogue with the reality facing South Africa? Although the continuing violence in post-apartheid South Africa cannot be reduced to a single cause, a key contributing aspect lies in the culture of violence that cannot be disconnected from the apartheid and colonialist past, as well as ongoing economic inequality (rather than merely poverty), which has often been associated with higher levels of violent crime.[52] Seen in this context, violent crime, the racialization of society and the extreme class inequalities of society become inseparable, and the liberation of those oppressed becomes a prerequisite for wholeness at any level of society.

One of the challenges of black theology to the white church in South Africa is finding an alternative to a culture that disregards the violence against the poor. The question is whether the church will be a voice challenging the discourse that disregards the effect of violence on the most marginalized in society—especially since the church at times actively participates in a discourse which considers the death of white and middle-class people to be of more concern. The question is, furthermore, whether the white church will reject the lure of a quasi-soteriology that finds salvation in withdrawal—this time probably withdrawal into gated communities.[53]

Conclusion

Our rhetoric on violent crime can be seen as a barometer of racialization in South Africa, and it reflects a particular lived theology among white people. While Bruce's reflection that violent crime is only seen as a concern when it affects the white middle-class remains true, it is a reminder that the racial hierarchies established by colonialism and apartheid continue into the present. When a *laager* mentality is supported by the constructed idea that white people are exceptional victims of violent crime in post-apartheid South Africa, the danger of perpetuating a soteriology that considers salvation something to be found in withdrawal from society, granted only to the privileged, should be noted.

At least two theological challenges are now presented to the white church by the South African context of violence. First, the church must remember the black experience of violence truthfully, taking a conscious concern with the death of the black and poor person in South Africa as an act of affirming humanity. Second, the church must take the soteriological challenge of black theology seriously, calling for the end of racist structures and actively distancing itself from any lingering belief that salvation might be achieved by separating into a *laager*. Salvation concerns wholeness on every level of society.

Notes

1. Afrikaners are white Afrikaans-speaking South Africans. Their ancestors were largely Dutch Calvinists. Afrikaners arrived in Southern Africa from the mid-seventeenth century onwards and were the dominant ethnic group prior to the institution of universal suffrage in 1994.

2. Afrikaner mythology, theology, and contemporary rhetoric is the explicit focus of this essay, and references to "white" and "whiteness," even when not qualified as Afrikaner, refer first and foremost to Afrikaners. However, the discussion is not unique to Afrikaner whiteness. English white rhetoric in post-apartheid South African speaks similarly about violent crime (although without the mythological undertones), and readers from other contexts might notice familiar patterns in discussions of violent crime and race, and the withdrawal of white people from spaces such as inner cities.

3. Melissa Steyn and Don Foster, "Repertoires for Talking White: Resistant Whiteness in Post-Apartheid South Africa," *Ethnic and Racial Studies*, 31, No. 1 (2008): 34, 36–38.

4. A *laager* was originally a group of ox-wagons gathered in a circle to form an enclosed area that could be easily defended. The *laager* was a key image in the Blood River narrative, the place from which the Voortrekkers defended themselves and gained victory over the Zulu armies. The image of the *laager* can be seen surrounding the Voortrekker monument in the city of Tshwane. This image became a metaphor for Afrikaner withdrawal from others into and seeing themselves as continuously under threat.

5. Ali Rattansi, *Racism: A Very Short Introduction* (New York: Oxford University Press, 2007), 27.

6. William James Jennings, *The Christian Imagination: Theology and the Origins of Race* (Kindle, available from www.amazon.com, 2007), chapter 1.

7. James W. Perkinson, *White Theology: Outing Supremacy in Modernity* (New York: Palgrave Macmillan, 2004), 3.

8. Saul Dubow, *Illicit Union: Scientific Racism in Modern South Africa* (Cambridge: Cambridge University Press, 1995), 2, 275–81.

9. Ibid., 246.

10. Anton Ehlers, *Desegregating History in South Africa: The Case of the Covenant and the Battle of Blood/Ncome River*, http://sun025.sun.ac.za/portal/page/portal/Arts/Departementei/geskiedenis/docs/desegregating_history.pdf (accessed November 3, 2011).

11. Ibid., 5–6.

12. Ibid., 6–11.

13. Dubow, *Illicit Union*, 248.

14. David J. Bosch, "The Afrikaner and South Africa," *Theology Today* (1986), 207.

15. Ibid.

16. David J. Bosch, "The Roots and Fruits of Afrikaner Civil Religion," in *New Faces of Africa*, J. W. Homeyr and W. S. Vorster, eds., (Pretoria: University of Pretoria, 1984), 23.

17. Ibid., 28.

18. Ibid.

19. Murray Hermanus Coetzee, *Die "kritiese stem" teen Apartheidsteologie in die Ned Geref kerk (1905–1974). 'n Analise van die bydraes van Ben Marais en Beyers Naudé* (Wellington: Bybel-Media, 2010), 37.

20. Translated as black threat, this expression referred to the security threat inferred from the existence of the majority black population.

21. Murray Coetzee and Ernst Conradie, "Apartheid as Quasi-Soteriology: The Remaining Lure and Threat," *Journal of Theology for Southern Africa* 138 (2010): 117–22.

22. Steyn and Foster, "Repertoires for Talking White", 34.

23. Charlotte Lemanski, "A New Apartheid? The Spatial Implications of Fear of Crime in Cape Town, South Africa," http://www2.lse.ac.uk/internationalDevelopment/pdf/WP20.pdf (accessed July 2010).

24. Steyn and Foster, "Repertoires for Talking White," 38.

25. Wiida Fourie, "Afrikaner Identity in Post-Apartheid South Africa: The Self in Terms of the Other," in *Power, Politics and Identity in South African Media*, A. Hadland, E. Louw, and H. Wasserman, eds. (Cape Town: HSRC Press, 2008), 267.

26. Melissa Steyn, "Rehabilitating a Whiteness Disgraced: Afrikaner White Talk in Post-Apartheid South Africa," *Communication Quarterly* 52, No. 2 (2004): 156.

27. Gavin Silber and Nathan Geffen, "Race, Class and Violent Crime in South Africa: Dispelling the 'Huntley thesis,'" *SA Crime Quarterly* 30 (2009): 36.

28. Fourie, "Afrikaner Identity," 264–65. For a more thorough overview of white discourse on violent crime, see Cobus van Wyngaard, "Race-Cognisant Whiteness and Responsible Public Theology in Response to Violence and Crime in South Africa" (master's thesis, University of Pretoria, 2012), 65–72.

29. Centre for the Study of Violence and Reconciliation, *Why Does South Africa Have Such High Rates of Violent Crime?* (Centre for the Study of Violence and Reconciliation, 2009), 4.

30. Sampie Terreblanche, *A History of Inequality in South Africa, 1652-2002* (Pietermaritzburg: University of Natal Press, 2002), 400–1.

31. Gary Kynoch, "Urban Violence in Colonial Africa: A Case for South African Exceptionalism," *Journal of Southern African Studies*, 34, No. 3 (2008), 629–45.

32. Centre for the Study of Violence and Reconciliation, *The Violent Nature of Crime in South Africa* (Centre for the Study of Violence and Reconciliation, 2007), 131–33.

33. David Bruce, *No Answers to Violent Crime*, http://www.mg.co.za/article/2011-01-14-no-answers-to-violent-crime (accessed June 23, 2011).

34. Centre for the Study of Violence and Reconciliation, *The Violent Nature of Crime in South Africa*, 114.

35. Silber and Geffen, "Race, Class and Violent Crime in South Africa," 36.

36. Steyn, "Rehabilitating a Whiteness Disgraced," 156.

37. The title translates as "We will survive this." Hofmeyr stated that the song was a response to the controversy surrounding the struggle song *Dubula ibhunu* ("Kill the Boer"). Hofmeyr threatened that if then ANCYL president Julius Malema was not barred from singing *Dubula ibhunu*, he will include the word "kaffir" in the *Ons sal dit oorleef* (http://www.sowetanlive.co.za/news/2011/05/13/steve-hofmeyr-spits-venom). Although Hofmeyr was widely condemned for the song, popular criticism focused primarily on the use of the word "kaffir," and rarely reflected on Hofmeyr's reinterpretation of Afrikaner myths amidst the context of violence.

38. Hofmeyr's language might be rejected by many white South Africans, as such rhetoric is not acceptable in a "civilized" world that prides itself on its democratic tolerance and inclusiveness (Shannon Sullivan, *Revealing Whiteness: The Unconscious Habits of Racial Privilege* [Bloomington: Indiana University Press, 2006], 187), however the singer and songwriter remains important and vocal and popular within the Afrikaner community—and as such a window into the continuing construction of Afrikaner mythology.

39. Translated as either "people" or "tribe," when used in Afrikaner nationalist rhetoric the word also has a quasi-religious undertone, a reminder that both the Afrikaner and the Israelite is God's "volk."

40. Steve Hofmeyr, *Daai toesprakie voor ONS SAL DIT OORLEEF*, http://steve-hofmeyr.co.za/website/steve-se/259-daai-toesprakie-voor-ons-sal-dit-oorleef (accessed November 12, 2012).

41. Translated as "the canon of the British or the spear of the kaffir."

42. Miroslav Volf, *The End of Memory: Remembering Rightly in a Violent World* (Grand Rapids, MI: Eerdmans, 2006), 34.

43. Steyn, "Rehabilitating a Whiteness Disgraced," 156–57.

44. Centre for the Study of Violence and Reconciliation, *Why Does South Africa Have Such High Rates of Violent Crime?*

45. Volf, *The End of Memory*, 31.

46. Steyn and Foster, "Repertoires for Talking White," 46.

47. Silber and Geffen, "Race, Class and Violent Crime in South Africa," 36.

48. Vuyani Vellem, "The Symbol of Liberation in South African Public Life: A Black Theological Perspective" (PhD dissertation, University of Pretoria, 2007), 1.

49. Isabel Apawo Phiri, "Southern Africa," in J. Parratt, ed., *An introduction to Third World Theologies* (Cambridge: Cambridge University Press, 2004), 147.

50. Bruce.

51. James W. Perkinson, "Like a Thief in the Night: Black Theology and White Church in the Third Millennium," *Theology Today* (2004): 508–24.

52. Centre for the Study of Violence and Reconciliation, *Adding Injury to Insult: How Exclusion and Inequality Drive South Africa's Problem of Violence*, http://www.csvr.org.za/docs/study/4.Book_SocioEconomic_20_03_2009.pdf (accessed May 15, 2010).

53. Van Wyngaard, "Race-Cognisant Whiteness," 110, footnote 29; Coetzee and Conradie, "Apartheid as Quasi-Soteriology," 119.

III. Religious Cultural Impairments in Assessing Racism's Social Costs

"They Must Have a Different God Than Our God": Towards a Lived Theology of Black Churchwomen during the United States Civil Rights Movement

AnneMarie Mingo

Introduction

While there were many reasons—including exploitative economic gain and political power through occupation—that Europeans and others began to make their trans-Atlantic journey to the Americas in the seventeenth century, one of the most consistent justifiers for the actions that Europeans took in the coerced captivity and enslavement of Africans and the destruction of both African and Native American cultures and lives through colonization was God, or more specifically Christianity. Despite relatively minimal evangelistic efforts in the first century of African enslavement in the Americas, Christianity and God's providence were used to support Europeans' primarily economically driven actions. The Americas became a place that was simultaneously a God-ordained promised land for Europeans and a land reminiscent of Egyptian-style bondage for Africans who were forced to labor in the heat of the day to build a new nation. Yet Africans who were being victimized, oppressed, violated, and murdered also worshiped God, and many embraced Christianity as a religion, so it must have been difficult for them to accept the notion that the same God would permit such atrocities as chattel slavery instituted in God's name.

During the enslavement of Africans in the Americas, Europeans used God and religion as a method of control, while enslaved Africans used God as a source for spiritual and physical liberation. After becoming a unified racial group that provided power and control, despite their different ethnicities, whites used God and religion in the United States as a justification for the legal segregation of blacks.[1] Blacks used God and religion to profess the equality of their creation and existence as children of God created in God's image. Today, God and religion continue to be used in American political rhetoric, predominantly around immigration and marriage equality, as a way of dividing those who seek to maintain power from those who simply seek to live out their full humanity. Yet today, those who are being marginalized and oppressed do not seem to be as engaged with liberation-centered religious activism as they once were .

For blacks in America, reliance on God has consistently been a component of large and small black freedom struggles from the early seventeenth century through today. In this chapter, in order to briefly explore a lived theology of justice and freedom constructed in contestation, I focus primarily on portions of the narratives of activists associated with traditional black churches who spent time living in and fighting for freedom throughout the Southern United States during the civil rights era.[2] The American South during the civil rights era of the mid- 1940s through the early 1970s was fraught with dualisms reflecting the *de facto* and *de jure* segregation that created two very separate and unequal worlds. "Whites Only" and "Colored" signs marked visible boundaries and created social barriers, while invisible limitations created socio-political inequities such that blacks, particularly in the South, were treated like second-class citizens.

Optimistic figures report that 43 percent of all black churches participated in the civil rights movement in some way. Most of these being were rural churches where the inequalities blacks faced were more pronounced than in some urban environments.[3] Civil rights veteran Wyatt T. Walker observed that even at the height of the movement, only about 10 percent of the ministers in Birmingham actively supported the efforts of the Southern Christian Leadership Conference (SCLC).[4] Even though the popular lore exaggerates the level of black church participation in the civil rights movement, it is clear that such involvement represents one of the most significant socio-religious mobilizations of the modern era.

Theologies were being constructed on the edges of the movement as blacks sought to make sense out of what they were experiencing and what role God was playing in their actions and the actions of others. The movement was a period of religious reassessment and identification. How could whites, who also professed to be followers of God, understand the God of those who were being oppressed socially, politically, and economically by them? As children of God, blacks fought for freedom and justice in part to have their humanity recognized by others. As the civil rights movement began to decline and the black power movement began to build, a black theological development began to grow, led by James Cone, J. Deotis Roberts, Albert Cleage, and others in the mid-1960s.

Black theology, a theology whose emphasis on black liberation posed a direct challenge to Eurocentric theologies, did not come into being solely in academic institutions. In many ways it was initiated through black radical struggles within the black church, enabling black theology therefore to come into being in the context of black striving for racial justice through such civil rights organizations as the SCLC, the National Conference of Black Churchmen (NCBC), the Interreligious Foundation for Community Organization (IFCO), and others[5] Of the forty-eight persons who signed the Black Power Statement, composed and publicized by the National Committee of Negro Churchmen in 1966, Dr. Anna Arnold Hedgeman, a leader with the National Council of Churches' Commission on Religion and Race, was the only woman and the only layperson.[6] It is therefore important to remember that black theology's fathers were a collection of pastors, preachers, seminary professors, and religious activists whose understanding of blackness and the necessity for liberation was filtered through their privileged experience as male clergy.

Both before and after the emergence of black liberation-oriented theological constructions in the mid-1960s, few black women were given access to the hallowed halls of academia or to prominent pulpits, yet many women worked out a lived theology of justice and freedom based on their experience of injustice in their encounters with white Christians. I define a lived theology as an understanding of God obtained through everyday experiences with God. As a result of personal revelations of God, which are disclosed in the mundane, a lived theology addresses concrete and practical aspects rather than distant theories, shaping ethical ways of engaging the world. This lived theology is also a liberating theology like black theology, in that its method examines lived experience first, and then reflects theologically on it—particularly in the areas of justice and freedom. In this essay, as one component of the construction of a lived theology of justice and freedom, the experiences of both individuals and communities will be examined in the context of transformative, on-the-ground encounters that occurred during the civil rights era.

Transformative Encounters

On March 31, 1968, four days before his murder, Martin Luther King Jr. preached at the National Cathedral in Washington, D.C. In his sermon, titled "Remaining Awake Through a Great Revolution," he revisited a social reality that he had mentioned on many previous occasions, declaring, "We must face the sad fact that at eleven o'clock on Sunday morning when we stand to sing 'In Christ There is No East or West,' we stand in the most segregated hour of America."[7] The Christian Church, especially in the American South, was a place where belief in the inferiority of blacks was reinforced through the actions of white Christians.

As a ten-year-old girl growing up in an all-black area of Birmingham in 1955, Marjorie (as she will be referred to here) had experiences that shaped her spiritual and theological inquiry at an early age.[8] In her own community she encountered one loving and supportive reality, but she faced a counter-reality in many white areas of her hometown. Birmingham was founded after the Civil War and therefore had no history of slavery, but segregation was nonetheless actively maintained there during the mid-twentieth century, when black and white residents were separated by both law and practice. Whites who did not see blacks as worthy of respect or acceptance often violently opposed cross-racial encounters.

The sting of segregation was even more jarring when faced in a location where seemingly there should have been the least amount of separation: on the grounds of a Christian church. Marjorie describes one such encounter. One day as she and her siblings and friends were walking to church school, they passed a white church where children near her age were playing in the yard. Upon seeing Marjorie and the other young people, the white children began to taunt and torment them, calling them derogatory names, such as "Niggers and Sambos." One white child even spat at Marjorie and her. Marjorie recalls that even at the young age of ten, she understood there was something amiss if young people capable of calling her such names worshiped the same God that she learned about in church school.

Marjorie described her experiences to her father and asked, "[H]ow could they pray to the same God?" When asked whether or not she was able to reconcile her God with the God that she thought must be the cause of such hatred towards blacks, she replied that the situation did not make sense to her because her father, her church school teachers, and her pastor all taught her that there was only one God. There could not be a separate black God and white God.

The type of experience that Marjorie had with young white church school goers on a Sunday morning in Birmingham was certainly not an isolated experience. In 1960, a Spelman College student in Atlanta, Georgia, who helped coordinate regular visits to churches for purposes of studying religious practices, had an encounter one Sunday morning at a white church in the West End section of Atlanta near her historically black college.[9] As this student (who I will refer to as Lenora) and other students walked up to the church, a white man met them and said they could not go in. As a native of New York City, Lenora was not immediately aware of the lengths to which Southern white segregationists would go to maintain racial separation. She explained to the man at the door that she and the others had come to the church to worship, and he responded that they could not come into *that* church. Stunned, Lenora then asked him, "[W]hat are you going to do when you get to heaven . . . will you segregate people up there?" To which the man replied, "[I]f I'm there and I can, I will."[10]

Lenora and the other college students who were with her had gone to the white church to worship God, but she encountered a man at the entrance who believed not only that he should prevent them from coming into the worship service, but also into heaven. He apparently thought he was not only a doorkeeper at the church, but also a gatekeeper for heaven. Unlike the white man at the church, Lenora believed that any place where God was worshiped should be open to all of God's children. In her previous church experiences, she worshipped a God who was welcoming to all, yet at this white church she encountered a man whose worship of God sanctioned segregation in both earthly and heavenly places.

Then, on the morning of September 15, 1963, tremors reaching beyond the American South announced to the world the deadly encounter that impacted worshippers at an all-black church where four young women were murdered and over twenty others were injured by a bomb placed at the church by four men who were a members of white hate groups.[11] The well-known bombing of the Sixteenth Street Baptist Church in Birmingham was yet another encounter that highlighted different understandings of God. As black persons worshiped God on a Sunday morning, white men whose Klan organization professed a love of God and a commitment to the unwavering authority of the Bible made a conscious decision to use a weapon of mass destruction on a black house of worship during Sunday morning services. Birmingham was locally known as "Bombingham," owing to the fifty or more bombs that had been detonated in the city during the twenty years leading up to the Sixteenth Street Baptist Church bombing. This act of domestic terrorism resulted in the murder of Denise McNair, Carole Robertson, Cynthia Wesley, and Addie Mae Collins, the blinding of Collins's sister Sarah, significant injuries requiring hospitalization of many others at the church, and the killing of two teenage boys in the aftermath of the bombing. Not only was the eleven o'clock hour the most segregated hour in America, as King asserted, but in many ways, as whites and blacks encountered each other on the hallowed ground of the church, it became one of the most spiritually and at times physically destructive hours as well.

The question remains, how could God lead black and white Christians toward such different theological and ethical understandings? Marjorie's inquiry rings true for each of these encounters: "How could they pray to the same God?"

Reflection on these transformative encounters raises theological issues of identity, authority, and possession. For Marjorie and Lenora, self-identification as a child of an all-loving God shaped a particular understanding of human sameness in the eyes of God, despite disparate treatment by white Christians. Marjorie remarked, "I thought about it, I said, you know, this is a shame how we cannot [come together] just because of the color of our skin, and my thing was that if you would prick my finger, I would bleed. If you did it to the white person, the same thing would happen to them."[12] As she wrestled with the differences between the black church community and the white church community, Marjorie's God was one who identified her as a child of God and did not see her as any less or any more than any other person who expressed a belief in God. Since all persons were created in the image of God, the rejection and hatred expressed towards blacks by whites reflected a rejection and hatred of God and therefore could not be of God.

The authority associated with one's understanding of God as revealed through the Bible and through lived experiences is of critical importance. Activists in the civil rights movement believed they were on the God's side, and that their theological understanding of a God of justice derived from the authority they gained by walking with God. A few years after her experience with the white children in the churchyard, Marjorie encountered another white person who seemed to worship a different God. Birmingham's segregationist commissioner of public safety, Eugene "Bull" Connor, was a Sunday school teacher who could teach Bible lessons at his white church on Sunday, and then turn dogs and water hoses on innocent black children on a Thursday.[13] One day after participating in a mass meeting at a Baptist church in downtown Birmingham, Marjorie walked out of the church with others to begin a non-violent direct action demonstration. Across the street they saw Connor directing firemen to turn fire hoses on them, but as Marjorie recalled, when the firemen attempted to turn on the hoses, no water came out. Marjorie was certain that because they were leaving church where they had been praying, Connor's attempts were thwarted on that day.[14] She and her fellows walked in the authority of God, and even when other professed Christians sought to do them harm, their God heard their prayers and protected them. Conversely, Lenora earlier encountered a white man so secure in his own sense of authority that he believed God would allow him to maintain segregation and division not only in the church he attended, but also in heaven where he sought to go.

As indicated in some of the encounters cited above, the extent to which God can become a cultural possession is a matter of contestation by both black and white Christians. The conclusion that "they must have a different God than our God" was articulated by a young girl, but it also seems to have been understood by older men who blocked the entrance to a white church, and who perpetrated mass murder in a black church. This idea of "their God" and "our God" contains echoes of the Hebrew text, with "our" God being on the side of what was deemed acceptable by the possessor of that God. In this troubling competition over possession, God takes sides, and those laying claim to God profess victory.

Lived Theological Constructions

In the sixth chapter and eighth verse of the Book of Micah, the prophet Micah states, "He has told you, O mortal, what is good; and what does the Lord require of you but to do justice, and to love kindness, and to walk humbly with your God?"[15] These words provide a model and framework for the lived theology of justice and freedom that black churchwomen engaged in, and for the ethical acts that followed from their theological beliefs. This requirement of God as outlined by Micah does not pertain only to one group of people, but is a requirement for all who follow God and seek one day to come before the Lord.[16] Black churchwomen who became active in the civil rights movement felt they had to do so. Therefore they marched, sat-in, organized, went to jail, pushed limits to showcase injustice, and did anything else they could do to participate in pursuit of justice. The requirement to love kindness motivated black churchwomen to endure white hatred and to return it with kindness that sometimes unsettled those whose actions and beliefs were steeped in hatred. Finally, black churchwomen knew that they were not carrying out justice and loving kindness on their own. The God they served was not a distant otherworldly God, but one who would walk with them through shadows of death so that they would not fear the evil that surrounded them as they took stands for justice and freedom. God was actively involved with their struggles. The understanding of God as a God of justice, kindness, love, and unity caused the women to choose actions that reflected the influence of that God.

The recognition of theological differences did not take place because Marjorie and Lenora attended all-black churches, while their tormenters attended all-white churches. Various understandings of God became evident because of the vitriolic rhetoric spewed from the steps of white congregations, and the destruction visited upon a black church in Birmingham. What should have been considered holy ground became contested theological space that gave rise to completely different understandings of the desires and revelations of God.

After these encounters in contested holy spaces a renewed desire to seek justice and freedom for all persons was born. Marjorie's theological inquiry as a young girl influenced her civil rights activism as a teen, and strengthened her resolve while a student at Tuskegee Institute to live a life focused on helping the oppressed. In college, Marjorie continued to push for the equal rights of all persons by teaching men and women in rural Alabama to write so they could register to vote. Lenora committed to a life of activism after her encounter at the white church. Her activism led to numerous arrests for participation in marches, sit-ins, and other protests after experiencing segregation firsthand while a student at Spelman College. She worked for a number of years as a field worker with the Student Nonviolent Coordinating Committee (SNCC) and other activist groups to change *de jure* and *de facto* segregation in the South.

Four months before the bombing that took the lives of the four girls in Birmingham, Martin Luther King Jr. wrote a letter from the jail of that city, questioning the white religious leaders who criticized his and others' efforts to right the wrongs of injustice. He explained:

> When I was suddenly catapulted into the leadership of the bus protest in Montgomery, Alabama, a few years ago, I felt we would be supported by the white church. I felt that the white ministers, priests and rabbis of the South would be among our strongest allies. Instead, some have been outright opponents, refusing to understand the freedom movement and misrepresenting its leaders; all too many others have been more cautious than courageous and have remained silent behind the anesthetizing security of stained-glass windows.
>
> In spite of my shattered dreams, I came to Birmingham with the hope that the white religious leadership of this community would see the justice of our cause and, with deep moral concern, would serve as the channel through which our just grievances could reach the power structure. I had hoped that each of you would understand. But again I have been disappointed.[17]

Like the questions raised by Marjorie and Lenora, King's letter challenged the white religious leaders of Birmingham whose actions did not reflect an understanding of God rooted in love and justice. Through on-the-ground encounters within contested social relationships, individuals and communities developed a lived theological understanding of God as one actively challenging and correcting American society and moving it towards justice and freedom.

For these black activists and others, one's belief in God should be consistent with one's actions on behalf of God. Their questions and assessments of the nature of God were strengthened through bad experiences, often in contested holy spaces. Profession of belief and practice of belief must be unified. Therefore the theo-ethical mandate found in Micah became a clear model to do justice, to love kindness, and to walk humbly with God. For many black churchwomen in the civil rights movement, theology was not simply a theoretical exercise to be debated, but a practical guide to be lived out in ways that created a more just society.

Conclusion

The lived theologies of the black churchwomen developed from reflections on encounters at churches in the 1950s and early 1960s, predating the formulation of black liberation theology by black churchmen responding to the radical black Christianity that grew out of the black power and black nationalism movements in the late 1960s and early 1970s. Many of these women were young when they constructed a justice-seeking understanding of God. While the encounters focused on in this essay have been at churches in the American South, practices of monolithic worship took place throughout the United States, with many black denominations forming as a result of segregationist practices within white churches that relegated black worshipers to positions of inferiority. Today less than 8 percent of churches in the United States have memberships that include at least 20 percent who are not a part of the predominant racial group of the church.[18] Almost fifty years after King's sermon, the eleven o'clock hour on Sunday morning still remains the most segregated hour in the United States. The messages that are being taught in those segregated spaces often do not lead followers to commit to the theo-ethical mandate at the core of a lived theology of justice and freedom: to do justice, love kindness, and walk humbly with God. The current social evils of economic injustice, health care disparities, mass incarceration, and educational underachievement—all with clear racial and economic lines of demarcation—indicate that the actions of individuals in this so-called

Christian nation continue to reflect different understandings of God. These actions lead one to wonder, as blacks and whites gather in their segregated churches in the twenty-first century, whether or not we are all praying to and worshiping the same God.

Notes

1. I will often refer to the civil rights movement as simply "the movement."

2. While the traditional civil rights period of 1954–68 forms the general boundary of this era, a longer period consisting of the mid-1940s through the early 1970s creates a more realistic span for the civil rights centered activism that took place throughout the United States.

3. C. Eric Lincoln and Lawrence H. Mamiya, *The Black Church in the African American Experience* (Durham, NC: Duke University Press, 1990), 189. Civil rights veteran Wyatt T. Walker pointed to an extreme example of the often limited involvement of black churches and pastors when he observed that up to 90 per cent of the ministers in Birmingham did not support the efforts of the SCLC, even during the height of the movement. Adam Fairclough, "The Southern Christian Leadership Conference and the Second Reconstruction, 1957–1973," *South Atlantic Quarterly* 80 (1981): 183.

4. Adam Fairclough, "The Southern Christian Leadership Conference and the Second Reconstruction," 183.

5. James Cone, *For My People: Black Theology and the Black Church* (Maryknoll, NY: Orbis Books, 1984), 6–7.

6. National Council of Negro Churchmen, "Black Power," in *Black Theology: A Documentary History, 1966–1979*, Gayraud S. Wilmore and James H. Cone, eds., (Maryknoll, NY: Orbis Books, 1979), 23. The black power statement was first published in the *New York Times* on July 31, 1966.

7. Martin Luther King Jr., http://mlk-kpp01.stanford.edu/index.php/encyclopedia/docu mentsentry/doc_remaining_awake_through_a_great_revolution (accessed May 24, 2012).

8. Full names of persons interviewed are not being used in this essay.

9. Located in the West End, the Atlanta University Center is the largest contiguous consortium of historically black colleges and universities in the United States. During Lenora's time as a student it comprised Morehouse College, Spelman College, Clark College, Atlanta University, Morris Brown College, and the Interdenominational Theological Center.

10. Transcript of interview by author with Lenora, 3.

11. The Federal Bureau of Investigation found evidence that four men (Robert Chambliss, Herman Cash, Thomas Blanton, and Bobby Cherry) associated with the bombing had connections to the Ku Klux Klan. http://learning.blogs.nytimes.com/2011/09/15/sept -15-1963-birmingham-church-is-bombed-by-klansmen/ (accessed May 26, 2012).

12. Marjorie, 6–7, parentheses mine.

13. The well-known children's crusade in Birmingham gained national prominence on Thursday, May 2, 1963, when Bull Connor ordered dogs and water hoses turned on children as they peacefully protested in downtown Birmingham.

14. Marjorie Wallace Smyth interview by author, August 2009.

15. Micah 6:8 (NRSV).

16. Micah 6:6a, "With what shall I come before the Lord, and bow myself before God on high?" (NRSV).

17. Martin Luther King Jr., "Letter from a Birmingham Jail," April 16, 1963, http://mlk-kppo1.stanford.edu/index.php/resources/article/annotated_letter_from_birmingham/ (accessed May 26, 2012).

18. Curtiss Paul DeYoung, Michael O. Emerson, George Yancy, and Karen Chai Kim, *United by Faith: The Multiracial Congregation as an Answer to the Race Problem* (New York: Oxford University Press, 2004), 2.

Church Youth Activism and Political and Economic Constraints within "Post-Racial" South Africa

Chabo Freddy Pilusa

I present thoughts here on the racial and ideological positioning of youth activism in "post-racial" South Africa. This is a daunting exercise, because my thoughts may be out of tune with present day perceptions of a so-called "rainbow" nation—although I am also sure that my thoughts resonate with the feelings of the majority of black people in our country.

From time to time, we do experience inklings of the kind of nation we can be, for instance in the manner with which we approached the 2010 hosting of the Fédération Internationale de Football Association (FIFA) World Cup and the celebrations of some of our sports achievements. This promise was also eloquently expressed through an episode that occurred during my activist years as a youth in Cape Town at the height of the defiance campaign in 1989 (the massive uprisings across South Africa that helped usher in the political transformations of the early-1990s). A few days before the racially segregated South African parliament held its elections, the United Democratic Front (UDF) organized a march to Parliament, which I opted to join. The marchers were confronted by a large contingent of police with armored vehicles, one of which was equipped with a water cannon laced with purple dye. When the marchers refused to disperse, the police fired tear gas at us, attacked us with batons and "sjamboks," and turned the water canon on us. Comrades who attempted to flee had their feet knocked from under them by the force of the water. In what can only be described as a strange irony, one of the comrades managed to climb onto the armored vehicle with the water cannon, where he turned the purple jet on the police. As the police regained control and led us to their vehicles, we laughed at each other because all of the protest marchers—whether black or white (and even some of the police)—were purple from the dye on that day. The following day, newspapers and graffiti all over the city proclaimed "The Purple Shall

Govern," a phrase that was a spin on the first phrase of the Freedom Charter, "The People Shall Govern." With this transformation of protest marchers from African, white, colored, and Indian to purple, there was a moment in our racialized South African history where we were all of one color and of one purpose.

With the release of Nelson Mandela and other struggle heroes from prison in the early 1990s, followed by democratic elections in 1994, hopes about prospects for moving beyond the racial injustices and hostilities of the past rose. Unfortunately, almost twenty years later, South Africa still remains, in most respects, a racially polarized nation, a nation lacking in social cohesion, demarcated into two segments: one white and rich, and the other black and poor. I will be reflecting here on the activism of young people within this new South African context, with reference to the role of the church, and against the backdrop of South Africa's post-apartheid constitution.

Enduring Constrictions on South African Progress

Black theology guided our approach to the struggle for liberation. We analyzed the context of our time and fought apartheid as a crime against humanity and a sin in the eyes of God. Our struggle, though inspired by the gospels, was nevertheless guided by the programs of action adopted by organizations like the United Democratic Front and the African National Congress. We marched in the streets in protest, we took arms by joining the military wing of the ANC, we pledged to make apartheid ungovernable, and we rejected all structures built by the regime that harbored collaborators, such as the homeland system. Though the system looked powerful and unshakeable, the messages from the gospels propelled us forward and gave us hope that any system can be defeated. Apartheid became the equivalent of the mighty Roman Empire, which also collapsed. We believed, and therefore we fought and we prevailed.

Prevailing was just the first step of our liberation. The next challenge was reversing more than four hundred years of occupation and the legacy of apartheid. The National Planning Commission instituted in May 2010 by President Zuma presented its diagnostic report in 2011. The report celebrated the few achievements made over sixteen years of South African democracy. Our economy turned around, employment has grown, the health of public finances was stabilized, and we achieved both unity on the sports field and success in the international arena. Today we are a non-permanent member of the United Nations Security Council, in part because we have taken our place

in the family of nations, striving for peace and security on our continent and
in our world.

The report, however, bemoans the level of inequality in our country, which
is amongst the highest in the world. By most measures this elevated level of
inequality, inherited in 1994, has not decreased sufficiently. In 1995, the richest 20 percent of the population earned 72 percent of national income, while
the poorest 40 percent received about 6 percent. Today the picture is almost
identical, with the richest 20 percent receiving 70 percent of income and
the poorest 40 percent about 6 percent. The pattern of poverty within South
Africa is such that the poorest South Africans are still black, mostly female,
and living in the former homelands. What is deeply concerning is that the
income received by the poorest 40 percent has shifted from wage income and
remittances to social grants. Social grants are a positive development, but
they mask deep marginalization and exclusion from the labor market.

The diagnosis identifies nine key challenges facing our country:

1. Too few South Africans work.
2. The quality of school education for most black people is sub-standard.
3. Poorly located and inadequate infrastructure limits social inclusion and
   faster economic growth.
4. Spatial challenges continue to marginalize the poor.
5. South Africa's growth path is highly resource-intensive and hence
   unsustainable.
6. The ailing public health system confronts a massive disease burden.
7. The performance of the public service is uneven.
8. Corruption undermines state legitimacy and service delivery.
9. South Africa remains a divided society.

The diagnosis is extensive, but it articulates what is common knowledge for
the majority of South Africans. How we as a nation will deal with the challenges outlined by the commission's report is the key question. The white
establishment that owns the means of production and the means of communication has foisted upon us a "kindergarten" worldview. In this worldview,
the attainment of political freedom was the purpose of our entire struggle.
In this worldview, the concerns of black people must be focused on how the
black government administers taxes, which the white establishment insists,
with efficient administration, will make the problems associated with four
hundred years of subjugation disappear. We are told to watch out for corrupt
leaders and managers, and we are told that if not for such leaders, most of our
legacy problems would be long gone.

This is the simplistic analytical framework in which most of our people are forced to operate. These issues constituted the entire focus of our 2011 national and local government elections. I personally believe that one of the largest constraining factors for us is our current constitution, in which key tenets do not reflect the core values and cultural priorities of the majority of our population. Until such a time that the presumed beneficiaries of our historical struggle can write their own script, based on their values, we can never fully realize the benefits of our freedom.

We need only examine the progress—or lack thereof—of black business in this country to fully appreciate the challenges we are facing. Black people's attempts at playing a meaningful role in our economy continue to be frustrated by an environment that is not conducive to their success. Many small and medium sized black-owned companies have collapsed due to lack of funding, political interference, suffocation by white owned businesses, or sadly, due to non-payment by some government departments and institutions. Some of the deals operating within the framework of South Africa's black economic empowerment initiative hardly qualify as economic empowerment. A common example is where a black person uses a bank loan to buy equity in a white-owned business and immediately thereafter gets projected by the media as a millionaire—before he can even service the interest of such a loan. Even here, within our kindergarten worldview, there is a perception that black businesspersons do not succeed because they have worked hard, but rather because they are lucky or criminal.

Unfortunately, most sectors of our society, including the church, have no vision for our country. Our lifestyles revolve around pursuits of upward mobility, allowing us little time to breathe or think, and, in the absence of deep reflection, we have been swayed by simplistic narratives that rarely point us in directions that will bring about long-term benefits for our people. It is not too late for us to unapologetically go back to the drawing board.

The Struggle Continues

During the early 1990s, I served as president of the Anglican Student Federation (ASF). Members of ASF felt at the time that our organization needed to move beyond its historical role as simply a pressure group within the Anglican Church, and evolve to exert ever-greater political pressure within society at large. We lobbied church leadership throughout the country, enabling young people to transform churches into centers of the struggle against apartheid, while promoting a belief in the God who sides with the oppressed and marginalized. The ASF presidency also gave me the opportunity work closely with Archbishop Desmond Tutu and other activist leaders within the Anglican Church. Archbishop Tutu was always patient with us, providing us with ample space to articulate our issues. He listened carefully and guided us when he thought our approaches were not good. We developed a strategy whereby we lobbied him privately on our issues before the issues were taken up in decision-making fora of the Anglican Church. Instead of us arguing our issues ourselves there, he would argue for us, with the result that church leaders were more readily convinced. Unfortunately, this mutuality of purpose and spirit of cooperation between activist youth and empowered elders shows signs of weakening within the contemporary South African context.

Let's evaluate what the politically aware youth of this country are discussing. The biggest political youth wing in the country, the African National Congress Youth League (ANCYL), has been making waves and creating discomfort. The centerpiece of the issues they are putting forward is demand for reassessment of aspects of our constitution that have become a yoke on our neck. ANCYL members are unhappy that the majority of South Africa's land is still in the hands of white people. They argue that the willing seller-willing buyer policy implemented by government over the past seventeen years has failed genuinely to assist black people who lost their land during the oppressive apartheid regime. Only 4 percent of agricultural land has been redistributed since 1994, with more than 80 percent of agricultural land remaining in the hands of fewer than fifty thousand white farmers and agribusinesses.

The constitutional provision addressing the willing seller-willing buyer approach to land acquisition has constrained the pace and efficacy of land reform. This clause, together with the clauses governing private property, has made it almost impossible to redress past wrongs. The ANCYL has also raised the pertinent issue of nationalization of the mines. The organization argues that wealth must be transferred to all people through this mechanism. The issues being raised by youth are gaining momentum with the Northwest ANC, as well as the Gauteng ANC, which share the same sentiments.

The subject of changing our constitution to better reflect our needs and values makes the white establishment nervous. We hear complaints about our country being at risk of becoming another Zimbabwe (by which is meant a country whose aggressive approach to economic redistribution has resulted in significant economic and political dysfunction). We are told by those who want us to view our context through their kindergarten worldview that the constitution is sacrosanct and any thought of changing it sinful. We are told by the same white establishment to block all unconstitutional attempts at transformation introduced by our leaders, no matter how badly needed those

transformations may be. This constitution is used to arbitrate what is culturally legitimate, whether or not the issue at hand is culturally beneficial, much
in the same way missionaries used their Christianity to declare certain of our
cultural traditions and pursuits heathenish and evil. Through such formulations—whether theological or constitutional—black poverty maintains an
aura of legitimacy and acceptability, while pursuit of any black goal that falls
outside such frameworks is rendered illegitimate and unacceptable.

This simplistic (and, frankly, pernicious) approach to our challenges is
unsustainable and shortsighted. If we are going to redress the past four hundred years of oppression and subjugation, we need brave solutions that will
bring us results. Equating racial harmony in South Africa with a few sports
achievements is little more than window dressing. We remain a country of
two nations: one black and poor, the other white and rich. Race is still a major
dividing line. We face as a major challenge a white establishment whose attitude continues to be that they own this country, and that black people are
mere consumers of what they produce. With the support of our constitution,
an environment has been created which fosters notions of white accommodation of an array of black social impositions. Seen in thus light, blacks are
being accommodated in white residential areas; blacks are being accommodated in white schools; blacks are being accommodated in white businesses.
A condition of this accommodation, however, is that blacks must not try to
change anything. Blacks must not introduce their way of thinking or their
values and cultures. Particularly galling is the growing belief among the white
establishment that black people must not speak of the past, but should, rather,
stay focused on the future. With increasing boldness, the white establishment
is even proclaiming that "apartheid was not that bad." Inconceivably, black
kids can be found repeating this message when efforts are made by their
elders to teach them our history.

The racial harmony that we fought for is not going to be realized through
sentimental statements. Measures of redress will have to be fully implemented
for all races to live in harmony in South Africa. Our battle for non-racialism
will not be realized by coddling the feelings of the white establishment at the
expense or disregard of the majority black population. It is in the nature of
any struggle that those holding the power will be made to feel uncomfortable,
and in the continuing struggle within South Africa, the white (and black)
establishment must be made uncomfortable.

Militancy and youth are often synonymous. The youth of the 1940s and
'50s (led by the likes of Nelson Mandela, Oliver Tambo, and Walter Sisulu)
was frustrated with the liberal tactics of the ANC leadership of the time and
introduced a militancy that became a norm in the struggle against apartheid.

They not only mobilized people against the regime, but also campaigned within the ANC itself for a change of leadership and policy in line with the thinking of young people. It is this militant approach that saw the launch of the defiance campaign and, later, a decision to take up arms against the apartheid regime.

It was young people like Steve Biko who in the 1970s introduced black consciousness philosophy and organizations to keep the momentum of the struggle against apartheid going. It was young students who defied the might of the apartheid apparatus by taking to the streets to protest against the imposition of Afrikaans as a medium of instruction in all schools. This protest led to the infamous 1976 Soweto massacre of school children by the apartheid regime. It was young people of the 1980s under the leadership of leaders such as Peter Mokaba who responded to the call of the ANC to render the apartheid system ungovernable. This militancy led to the torture and killings of many young people by the regime, but despite the risks, young people continued to join the struggle in large numbers.

South African youth policy defines "youth" as anyone between the ages of fourteen and thirty-five. I suppose that the most quoted person on earth, Jesus Christ, would be regarded as a young person when he was at the height of his ministry. Jesus Christ's ministry is a representation of youth militancy at its best. Following in his footsteps, the youth from various South African church denominations and organizations undertook militant action, turning their churches into centers of struggle. It is the young people within the churches who convinced their reluctant leaders to join them in the streets to protest against the apartheid system, a system that would eventually be condemned by various church communions, including the World Alliance of Reformed Churches, as a heresy and a sin against humanity.

The militancy of young people throughout history has made adults uncomfortable. With time, however, many wise adults joined them and played a pivotal role in guiding their militant approach to struggle. In the 1980s, the militancy of South African youth was encouraged by the leadership of the ANC and the UDF, despite the mistakes that were made. In the church, we young people introduced radical positions that made our bishops and other church leaders uncomfortable, but leaders such as Archbishop Tutu and others helped to channel our militancy.

Youth militancy is a prerequisite of change in any society. It is therefore important that as adults we give young people the space to be militant. Our role is to channel their energy and guide them. Our challenge is to engage with issues raised by young people within the church and broader society, however radical these issues may sound.

The church must remain "prophetic," meaning that it should be willing to say uncomfortable things to those in power and to advocate on behalf of policies and structures that serve the interests of the poor and the downtrodden of society. Churches must actively pursue justice and redress, and oppose corruption and abuse of power. Each of these objectives must be embraced to move beyond superficial solutions to South Africa's racial issues and achieve substantive, sustainable non-racialist solutions. Heeding the voices of South Africa's activist youth is essential to the future that well-intentioned South Africans desire and that post-apartheid, post-racial youth represent.

Black South African Christian Response to Afrophobia in Contemporary South Africa

Rothney S. Tshaka

Introduction

On the 12th of May, 2008, a chain of insurgences erupted in the townships of Alexandra in Johannesburg. At least twenty-five people were killed, and many were injured as African immigrants were targeted by the local black South Africans. Most of these immigrants were from Mozambique, Malawi, Zambia, and Zimbabwe. After the riots, these foreign nationals were displaced and in the process lost most of their scarce possessions. Soon the violence spread to other parts of South Africa, especially the coastal cities of Cape Town, George, and Durban.[1] This time immigrants from Somalia, who mostly own small convenient stores in the black townships across South Africa, were included in the violence. The degree of violence perpetrated against these fellow Africans stunned many, including South Africans themselves.[2]

When our study team visited the Central Methodist Church in downtown Johannesburg, it was sheltering African immigrants, mostly Zimbabweans, every night. We were able to see first-hand some of the struggles that our African brothers and sisters had to endure in a neighboring African country. By the time of our visit, the number of African immigrants at this center was estimated to be about three thousand men, women, and children. In the church, we listened to the stories of women and children who feared for their safety, even there. Paul Verryn, who was then bishop of the Methodist Church in the Johannesburg region, spoke to us about the struggles he encountered with the police, city government officials, and local merchants, none of whom relished having a concentration of African immigrants in the city. The xenophobia of the riots the year before was more shocking, but a very similar sentiment simmered here.[3]

The xenophobic riots shoved South African inter-group relations once again onto the international stage, and they raised a number of questions that many thought had long been resolved. South Africa, once hailed as the racist capital of the world, had stunned the nations when for the first time it conducted racially inclusive, democratic elections in 1994. Because it had avoided the expected retaliation against those who had benefited from apartheid, South Africa thereafter became the miracle child of the world. But evidently, the spirit of apartheid, with its deep fragmentation of this beautiful and beloved country, was still affecting intergroup relations.

Indeed, one cannot fully comprehend the events of May 2008 without seriously attempting to understand the situation in which many black South Africans then found—and still find—themselves. Many black South Africans, even those who have escaped poverty, remain divided on the question of how to deal with our black brothers and sisters from other parts of Africa. The apartheid legacy plays a powerful role in shaping and driving the xenophobia, and indeed "Afrophobia," that still simmers and sometimes erupts in South Africa. Only by unpacking this legacy, and understanding its enduring effects on the black South African psyche, can we make sense of the attacks by some black South Africans on their black African neighbors from north of the Limpopo River.

These attacks were characterized as "the Perfect Storm" by the South African Migrants Project (SAMP), a committee formed to investigate the riots.[4] It is indeed an explosive situation, a racial powder keg, which is compounded by the lack of basic services among the most vulnerable, the black masses. Unless something is done soon to address the living conditions of the majority of black people in this country, the perfect storm of which SAMP spoke of so passionately will prove to be nothing in comparison with what is to come. There are numerous elements, of roughly equal importance, attached to the issue of Xenophobia. SAMP rightly concedes that the fundamental, interlinked elements are historical, material, political, and managerial.[5] But here we will add historical, material, and political elements. Once all the elements outlined above receive the necessary attention, managing the situation will prove to be more efficient.

Without negating the realities of xenophobia, we need to put a finer point on it and call it Afrophobia. In order for us to understand the current problem, we must consider the impact that colonialism and apartheid had on black people. And the best way to consider these issues more deeply, I think, is to identify the dynamic components of race and racism—notably white privilege, internalized oppression by black people, and the nervous anxieties that many ordinary black people feel in present day South Africa.

This chapter has two parts. It first endeavors to understand the workings of racism, leaning heavily on the research of North American scholars. This is important work, which can dispel some common misconceptions. Secondly, this chapter will consider the condition of many black South Africans, affording insight as to why such conditions are dangerous and problematic, as well as why they pose significant challenges for the stability of this country and the larger region.

This is a study by a Christian ethicist with a confessional background. As such, I remain encouraged by the theological resources that we have at our disposal to deal with these problems. One such resource is the Belhar Confession of the Uniting Reformed Church in Southern Africa (URCSA). This confession contains clear guidelines for how Christians are to identify with those who are on the margins of society. The Belhar Confession is clear testimony to the truth that what affects the civil community affects the Christian community.

While the Belhar Confession is becoming well known and is being accepted as a gift by Christians in other parts of the world, it sadly remains a relatively unknown and sometimes controversial document for many black South Africans.[6] Even so, it has great potential, as we will see, to become an instrument to help Christians identify with the most vulnerable members of society. Clearly understanding and embracing the Belhar Confession can help black Christians see foreign blacks in our communities in a different light and relate to them with a transformed spirit.

Afrophobia in the Light of Racism's Dynamics

The Nigerian poet, pan-Africanist, and philosopher, Chinweizu, refers to Negrophobia in general, as "the fear and dislike of blacks as a great disease." This malady, he continues, "has killed more blacks in the last five hundred years than all other diseases combined; more than malaria, more than epidemics and plagues of all sorts, [and] in the coming years, it could kill more than AIDS. It is a psychological disease, a disease of the mind which harvests dead black bodies every day."[7] With regard to the name, it must be remembered that the concept "negro" has had its own evolution. In more contemporary terms, we speak of Afrophobia instead of Negrophobia.[8]

In probing the ills of Afrophobia, it is important that we realize it is fuelled by racism. At the heart of racism and the treatment meted out against the black other is the question of power. To be sure, power is more than simply having control over economic or political matters. It includes the power of ideas and perspectives, and attitudes as well. Assumptions of cultural superiority, as we shall see, are not always arbitrary, but are insinuated as assumptions, as matters of fact. But first, let us understand what racism is.

For many in South Africa, any talk about racism is considered irrelevant and backward. Some consider it passé because they want to wish the past away on account of its ugliness. Many white people, especially, claim that they were not aware of the devastation for which apartheid alone is responsible, and their relative ignorance is plausible, given the separation between black and white in this country. But others give racism a premature burial because racism has not been defined adequately, at least in the South African context. For many, the most convenient definition of racism is racial prejudice. With a simplistic division of human beings into those who are bad and those who are good, racial prejudice is a convenient yardstick to determine into which category one falls. As long as one does not verbalize his or her racial prejudices, one is considered a good person. This approach assumes that there are in fact people who do not have racial prejudices, even though they live in a world in which they are bombarded with stereotypes of the other. South Africa since 1994 has become a rather polite society in which true feelings about the other are not verbalized for fear of being politically incorrect. There is both good and bad in such an approach. The good is that we have been forced to be sensitive of the other, and the bad is that because of this political correctness, we are increasingly becoming a dishonest society, disguising how we really feel about the other.

Any attempt to speak sincerely about racism requires that we move beyond this shallow definition if we seriously want to combat prejudice based on race. There is popular talk in South Africa that we are striving toward a non-racial society. Embedded in this talk is the idea that racial prejudice must be arrested in order for us to realize this ideal. We soon realize, however, that the reason there is much talk about reverse racism in South Africa is simply because we have confined talk about racism to personal racial prejudice and have not extended it to systems and structures with power to discriminate against blacks. It is therefore imperative that in our definition of racism we include the privileges and powers that are given to whites because of their whiteness. These privileges exist whether whites ask for them or not. Popular talk about racism as personal prejudice does not seem to reckon with the fact that we are all—affected by this systemic racism.

My review of the North American literature on racism has led me to conclude that there are dimensions to systemic racial segregation with which South Africans have yet to engage. The African American psychologist Beverly Tatum points out,

[T]here is always someone who hasn't noticed the stereotypical images of people of colour in the media, who hasn't observed the housing discrimination in their community, who hasn't read the newspaper articles about documented racial bias in lending practices among well-known banks, who isn't aware of the racial tracking pattern at the local school, who hasn't seen the reports of rising incidents of racially motivated hate crimes in America. In short, someone who hasn't been paying attention to the existence of racism.[9]

In most cases those who are blind to such incidents are whites. But for blacks, too, there is no way to escape the reality of racism.[10] The impact of racism, argues Tatum, begins very early, even in the pre-school years. Even at that age, children are exposed to misinformation about people different from them. Thanks to apartheid, many South Africans grew up in neighborhoods where they had limited chances of interacting with people from different races. And because of the social segregation still omnipresent in South Africa, they continue to collect second-hand and therefore distorted information about the other. Suffice it to say that assumptions about the other occur because of what we say about the other. However, assumptions about the other also occur because of what is not said or experienced about the other. Tatum argues, for instance, that "the distortion of historical information about people of colour leads young people (and older people too) to make assumptions that may go unchallenged for a long time." She tells the story a young white male student who got angry with her thesis and responded by saying "it was not his fault that blacks did not write books." Tatum goes on to explain that although this student might not have been taught adequately at school, the fact that he was not exposed to black writers led him to that conclusion.[11] So Tatum shows that stereotypes acquired via omissions and distortions contribute to prejudice. She defines prejudice as "a preconceived judgment or opinion, usually based on limited information."[12] Human beings are prejudiced by socialization simply because we are continually exposed to misinformation about others. We are essentially, therefore, all prejudiced against those who are different from us.

Another concept, one that is critical to understanding the depth of racism, is the notion of cultural, or internalized racism. We mentioned earlier that the notion of power manifests itself in numerous ways, not necessarily just economically. Tatum defines cultural racism as "the cultural images and messages that affirm the assumed superiority of whites and the assumed inferiority of blacks."[13] We shall see that cultural racism is not confined necessarily to white vs. black, but is evident among blacks and perhaps among whites. Tatum uses smog as an analogy. Racism, she argues, is sometimes so thick and therefore visible and other times it is less apparent, yet it is always there each day and we are breathing it. The knowledge that smog is out there whether we see it or not, does not lead us to label ourselves "smog-breathers" (and so most of us do not describe ourselves as prejudiced), but if we live in a smoggy place, we cannot avoid breathing the air. By the same token, because we live in an environment in which we are bombarded with stereotypical images in the media, or are frequently exposed to the ethnic jokes of friends and families members, we will certainly develop negative categories of the other.[14]

So black and white people are affected whether they know they are or choose to ignore their own prejudices. Members of the stereotypical groups adopt categories in a process called internalized oppression. This syndrome has been described by many black leaders. Carter G. Woodson describes it as the black person knowing his or her place in society.[15] Malcolm X was thinking of it when he said, "[T]he black person was taught to use only the back door of the house his white master, to such an extent that he would cut out a back door even when there is no back door to his master's house."[16] Harold Cruse speaks of the African as being a perpetual child.[17]

Black internalized oppression essentially encourages a flight from the black self. Frantz Fanon argues that Africa is a creation of the West. Thus the better the African is able to imitate the westerner, the closer he or she is to being human.[18] Because blackness is characterized negatively, many blacks flee from such badness. This flight from the self not only happens among the blacks who become assimilated into the established order, but it is something that happens even among the masses. There is always an intense need to be a little better than the other. Woodson makes this point succinctly when he argues,

[T]his refusal of Negroes to take orders from one another is due largely to the fact that slaveholders taught their bondmen that they were as good or better as or better than any others and therefore, should not be subjected to any member of their race. If they were to be subordinated to someone it should be to the white man of superior culture and social position. This keeps the whole race on a lower level, restricted to the atmosphere of trifles which do not concern their traducers.[19]

It is this condition that causes many Africans to look at other blacks with disdain. To illustrate this point in the South African context, one often hears, as a justification for why black foreigners are not welcome in South Africa, that "they come and steal our jobs and women." Yet this is not said of white foreigners. So it is best to characterize the May 2008 attacks by South

Africans on Africans north of the Limpopo River not as xenophobia, but rather as Afrophobia.

An important but often overlooked feature of internalized racism is "colorism." Cedric Herring defines colorism as "the discriminatory treatment of individuals falling within the same 'racial' group on the basis of skin color." He maintains that it "operates both intra-racially and interracially. Intra-racially, colorism occurs when members of a racial group make distinctions based upon skin color between members of their own race. Interracially it occurs when distinctions are made upon skin colour between members of another race."[20] Herring argues that colorism, much like the notion of race, is based on longstanding supremacist assumptions. Thus in the West, race and color preferences are typically measured against putative European (white) standards. These preferences have involved physical features including skin color, hair texture, thickness of lips, eye color, nose shape, and other phenotypical features.[21]

Looking at the race problem and how it is related to colorism in Latin America, Eduardo Bonilla-Silva sees a "Pigmentocracy" at work. This hierarchy maintains white power because it fosters: divisions among all those in secondary racial strata; divisions within racial strata limiting the likelihood of within-stratum unity; mobility viewed as individual and conditional upon whitening; and regard for white elites as legitimate representatives of the "nation" even though they do not look like the average member of the nation.[22]

With these insights in hand, we need to return briefly to the events of May 2008. At the heart of the attacks is the question of power. Thus many recall that South Africans were not treated differently when they fled South Africa and sought refuge in other parts of Africa. While the top leaders of banned South African political organizations were treated kindly, ordinary South Africans had to contend with being foreigners. It is therefore not by chance that the South Africa government is dragging its feet in granting refugee status to immigrants it labels economic migrants. By giving refugee status to economic migrants, the country is bound to allow them the privileges that come with such status. Any plan instituted by government to address the problems faced by African foreigners has to contend with the conditions in which the majority of black South Africans are still trapped.

The Nervous Condition of Blacks in Democratic South Africa

The perfect storm of 2008 was caused by Afrophobia, a complex dimension of racism, rather than xenophobia, simply a fear of the stranger. In South

Africa, the events of 2008 point to fear of a stranger who is clearly African, and often darker-skinned. Township activist Andile Mngxitama is correct when he characterizes the events of 2008 as Afrophobia instead of xenophobia. While acknowledging that the definition of xenophobia refers to, as he puts it "the hatred of foreigners," he poignantly reminds us that in the case of South Africa, there are no white foreigners. Rather, he continues, "we think of these [white foreigners] as benefactors, as tourists, investors and business people who must be protected."[23]

It is, however, not enough to draw attention to the current frame of mind of the ordinary black South African; we must ask what feeds such conduct. What is happening in South Africa that makes its black citizens behave in a barbaric manner toward their fellow Africans? The present situation forces us to deal with the tension that has been prevalent in South Africa since the dawn of democracy in 1994. This tension has increased dramatically in recent years, with the upsurge of public demonstrations for the lack of service delivery. Under the new political regime, there are high expectations concerning improvement for the masses that have been marginalized for ages, and fretful apprehensions of decline on the part of those who were privileged by the apartheid regime. These expectations and apprehensions quickly turn into frustration and anxiety when the former realizes that his or her full citizenship remains an illusion. At the same time, anxiety intensifies for those who saw the depreciation of what used to be exclusively white rights and privileges.[24] Frustration and anxiety can be seen on two levels in present-day South Africa. Firstly among all South Africans, both black and white, and secondly among black South Africans alone. When venting this frustration, the African other is always a convenient scapegoat .

Let us start with the anxiety felt by whites, who have always been on the receiving end of privileges because of the color of their skin. Their anxiety forces them to find justification for why things must continue as they are. While some know not to use overtly racist language to justify the current economic system, which continues to privilege few, many engage in a different form of justifying talk. With their whiteness remaining the unexamined norm, many continue to deny that they are privileged. Tim Wise argues that white denial manifests itself in four primary ways: minimization, rationalization, deflection, and claims of competing victimization.[25]

Minimization refers to the tendency for whites to make molehills out of what may indeed be mountains when it comes to racism and discrimination. Minimizers commonly claim that black people "play the race card," or that individual success stories (à la Oprah Winfrey or Barack Obama) signify the demise of racism as a persistent social problem. These whites will also claim that attempts at racially-tinged humor are taken too seriously, and use this ploy to minimize the damage that racial subordination can wreak. It is not just overt racists who are guilty of minimization, as minimization is found amongst the best white liberals as well.

While minimization seeks to downplay the struggles of black people due to racism and discrimination, rationalizers often acknowledge racial bias, even within themselves, but then seek to justify its existence by claiming that their prejudice flows from logical and understandable thought processes informed by personal experiences. These whites will claim that their experiences with certain racial groups justify the biases that they have towards these other groups.

Whites will often seek to change the subject when racism is brought up. They will insist that the focus should be on cultural defects within the black community, and the need for black people to "take personal responsibility" for their lives instead of worrying about discrimination.

And while black people are often accused of playing the race card, many white people act as if they are victims of racism. In the case of South Africa, the phrase "reverse racism" is becoming increasingly popular.

At the heart of these defenses are systems and institutions that privilege some and discriminate against others—albeit in very subtle ways, so these matters devolve to the question of power. Steve Biko noted that behind white defensiveness was a fundamental reality. The South African white community, he said, "is a homogenous community. It is a community of people who sit to enjoy a privileged position that they do not deserve, are aware of this, and therefore spend their time trying to justify why they are doing so."[26]

South African blacks, who thought the new dispensation would give validity to their citizenry, need to understand why the black other is a convenient scapegoat. It is not unusual for South African blacks of various social levels speculate about why blacks from other African counties are not welcome in this land. Basing their research partially on an SAMP report of 1997–98, Danso and McDonald illustrated how South African media has helped to perpetuate the belief of many black South Africans that black foreigners are responsible for the upsurge of crime in South Africa.[27] Black frustration and the scapegoating of foreign blacks give new meaning to Steve Biko's condemning words of long ago, that "the black man has become a shell, a shadow of a man, completely defeated, drowning in his own misery, a slave, an ox bearing the yoke of oppression with sheepish timidity."[28] It is this frustration that renders the black person a perpetual child in his own country.[29]

Africa, it is agreed, is a fragmented world. It is fragmented not by the choice of the black majority, but rather for the benefit of the so-called "mother countries." This fragmentation goes back to the late nineteenth century, when

German Chancellor Otto von Bismarck invited the major European powers to Berlin to "carve up" Africa in the "scramble" for colonial territory.[30] Nyam-njoh reminds us that "combing the world for opportunities has historically been the privilege of whites, who have been encouraged by their imperial governments to settle foreign territories, and who have always benefited from fellow whites on the ground, from colonial officers to missionaries through business, journalists and scholars."[31] Even though white internationals have not been homogeneous, he continues, they "have always managed to tame their differences in the interest of the economic, cultural and political hege-monies of the West vis-à-vis the rest."[32]

The African, it seems, has yet to learn that his or her struggle is the same as that of brothers or sisters whose origin is elsewhere in Africa. As a result, this fragmentation has raised brother against brother and sister against sister. In response to the question, "What is wrong with the African?" Jessie Kab-wila Kapasula argued "there is nothing wrong with the African; he is simply a good student. He does what he or she was taught to do."[33]

This is the "racial smog" phenomenon of which Tatum spoke. It affects us all, whether we are able to see it or not. Seen in this way, we are all rac-ist insofar as racism is racial prejudice. If we live in a world where we are inundated with misinformation about the other, then we are bound to inter-nalize such views. Some internalize white privilege, while others internalize oppression. Since blackness, insofar as it is associated with the bad and the ugly, is a product of whiteness, associated with goodness and purity, there has always been an intense need for blacks to flee from themselves. Such blacks have often sought ways of distinguishing themselves from other blacks, so that they appear to be a least better than the rest. It is this fragmentation, which essentially encourages the flight from the black self that is responsible for the sectarian politics among blacks, across Africa and in South Africa in particular.

Biko spoke to this flight from the black self and suggested black con-sciousness as a means of interrupting such flight. In this way he wanted to engage the fragmentation or the compartmentalization of Africa and of the African.[34] To substantiate the claim that Africa is fragmented, Fanon reminds us of the division of the continent into white and black Africa, that is, Africa south of the Sahara and Africa north of the Sahara.[35] Inherent in this division, says Fanon, is the belief that white North Africa is better off than the black remainder of Africa because of the way that North Africa is able to imitate the West.

The SAMP study and a number of other studies before and since indi-cate that most South Africans, black and white, negatively perceive black

African foreigners, with whom most locals have little contact. This outlook is of course based on black frustration and white anxiety. It also has to do with a common post-colonial experience, which Frantz Fanon calls the luck of where some Africans are located. "Immediately after independence," Fanon writes, "the nationals who live in the more prosperous regions realise their good luck, and show a primary and profound reaction in refusing to feed the other nationals."[36]

The "racial smog" is once again illustrated by Antoine Bouillon, the immigration scholar who compared the ill treatment meted out against black foreigners by black South Africans:

> [T]o demonstrate that these "illegals" clearly have little to offer, South African blacks, perhaps reminiscent of the Boers who named the local black communities "hottentots" to denote "stutterers," deny black African migrants an intelligible language. All they claim to hear is "gibberish"—a "barbaric" form of "stuttering"—hence the tendency to classify them as *Makwerekwere*, among other onomatopoeic references to the strange ways they speak.[37]

The problem is compounded by the media, which portrays "illegals" as criminals. Mngxitama maintains that there is everyday public harassment of these immigrants by the police and the Homeland Affairs department as part of the undeclared war against black Africans. Yet there are no white *Makwerekwere* in our country.[38]

The concept *Makwerekwere*, when used to refer to black foreigners, means different things in different situations. When used by a black South African, it refers to a black person who cannot demonstrate mastery of local South African languages. More importantly, it refers to someone who originates from a country assumed to be economically and culturally backward when compared to South Africa.[39] This is an aspect that is always ignored by those who insist that the May 2008 events be as xenophobia instead of Afrophobia.[40] Nyamnjoh reports that colorism is always applied to foreign blacks in South Africa: "In terms of skin pigmentation, the racial hierarchy of humanity under apartheid comes into play, since the *Makwerekwere* are usually believed to be the darkest of the dark-skinned, and to be less educated even when more educated than the light-skinned South African blacks."[41] These factors are all used in determining the other and in justifying why others are to be treated with less respect. Sometimes the mere perception of economical and cultural backwardness is used to justify abuse, as is the case with the violence directed against Somalians and other groups—a phenomenon that does not meet the criteria of colorism.

One reason for South Africa's economic development has been its long dependence upon cheap black labor. One source of cheap black labor was the foreigner who had no right to claim citizenship while in this country. Nyamnjoh argues that "citizenship has been defined narrowly around the rights, entitlements and interests of nationals." So it is deeply disillusioning "to most *Makwerekwere* from beyond the borders whose labour reserves were exploited with impunity and ingratitude by the architects of apartheid," that they have no such rights in the new South Africa.[42]

South Africa is one of the leading economies on the continent. It is also far and away one of the most industrialized countries in Africa, yet it, wealth distribution is skewed distribution. It is ranked as one of the countries with the most liberal constitutions in the world, having opted for a liberal economic and political model. This liberal constitution guarantees individuals the right of private ownership and control, even of what was acquired illegally under the apartheid rule. Nyamnjoh has argued that this option of rights without justice has made the post-apartheid context very tense, as ordinary underprivileged South Africans realize that their constitutional rights are slow to deliver the material benefits of citizenship.[43]

Skewed distribution of wealth remains conspicuous in present-day South Africa, and Andile Mngxitama reminds us that it drives much of the contemporary social tensions and violence. It is "convenient for some," he says,

> to see the outbreak of black violence as some atavistic unexplained black lashing out at black. . . . To think of this violence as a consequence of the relatively comfortable lives we lead would be too much, but if we look at the wealth enjoyed by our white counterparts, if you follow the money trail, historically you will see that the creation of Sandton (that super rich suburb) was made possible by the creation of the sprawling Alexandra. Alexandra is the direct product of Sandton.[44]

When comparing these two worlds of the settler and the native, post-colonial theorist Frantz Fanon noted. "[T]he zone where the natives live is not complementary to the zone inhabited by the settlers." "The settlers' town," he continues, "is a strong-built town, all made of stone and steel. It is a brightly lit town; the streets are covered with asphalt and the garbage cans swallow all the leavings, unseen, unknown, and hardly thought about. The settler's feet are never visible, except perhaps in the sea; but there you are never close enough to see them."[45] On the other hand, argues Fanon,

> [T]he town belonging to the colonized people, the Negro village . . . the reservation, is a place of ill fame, peopled by men of evil repute. They are born there, it

matters little where or how; they die there it matters not where nor how. It is a
world without spaciousness; men live there on top of each other, and their huts
are built one on top of the other. The native town is a hungry town, starved of
bread, of meat, of shoes, of coal, of light.[46]

This description closely resembles the description of South African townships offered by the eminent South African writer Ezekiel Mphahlele. He
describes them as

an organized rubble of tin cans. The streets were straight; but the houses stood
cheek by jowl, rusty as ever on the outside, as if they thought they might as
well crumble in straight rows if that was to be their fate. Each house, as far as I
remember had a fence of sorts. The wire always hung limp, the standards were
always swaying in a drunken fashion. A few somewhat pretentious houses could
be found here and there.[47]

While a few black elites have graduated from the slums created by the
apartheid regime, the townships are still home to the majority of South Africans. To anyone who lived in that black world, Steve Biko wrote, "the hidden
anger and turmoil could always be seen shining through the faces and actions
of these voiceless masses but it was never verbalised. Even the active phase,
thuggery and vandalism, was directed to one's kind—a clear manifestation of
frustration."[48] That was the case during apartheid; it remains the case even
today in democratic South Africa.

Frantz Fanon reminds us of a fundamental aspect often ignored when
the political situation has undergone some change. He argues that while
"colonial domination has marked certain regions out for privilege," it soon
becomes clear that "the colony's economy is not integrated into that of the
nation as a whole. It is still organized in order to complete the economy of
the different mother countries."[49] All the while, a "second economy" struggles
on, an economy of informal businesses and unskilled workers, most unemployed and unable to benefit from the formal economy's growth.

Former president Thabo Mbeki rightly asserted that this second economy
is rooted in

the long period of colonialism and apartheid . . . ensuring that the white economy had access to unlimited supplies of cheap unskilled black labour, and that
this economy did not waste any money on the development of the localities
in which the black workers lived. This did not even allow for the possibility of
improving the lives of the oppressed majority through the "trickle-down effect."

Mbeki points out that "the Second Economy is caught in a poverty trap," and adds, "[i]t is therefore unable to generate the internal savings that would enable it to achieve the high rates of investment it needs. Accordingly, on its own, it is unable to attain rates of growth that would ultimately end its condition of underdevelopment."[50]

While it is fundamental that we move towards accepting the black foreigner as one of our own in South Africa, it is equally important that we realize how volatile the condition of the black South African is. For this reason Biko argued that "to look for instances of cruelty at those who fall into disfavour with the security police is perhaps to look too far. One need not try to establish the truth of the claim that black people in South Africa have to struggle for survival. It presents itself in ever so many facets of our lives." Echoing Fanon and Mphahlele, Biko notes that "township life alone makes it a miracle for anyone to live up to adulthood. There we see a situation of absolute want in which black will kill black to be able to survive."[51]

Because of such conditions, the South African black sees the black immigrant as an easy target. While it is imperative that the leadership of this country takes the nervous condition of black South Africans seriously, it is nonetheless essential that black people in this country begin to see their inter-connectedness with blacks across the Limpopo River. And it is even more important for us to begin to understand how dangerous such nervous conditions are, not only for the stability of the country and therefore of the region, but for the world at large. Economics and foreign affairs journalist Sebastian Mallaby noted that "once a nation descends into violence, its people focus on immediate survival rather than on the long term. Savings, investment and wealth creation taper off; government officials seek spoils for their cronies rather than design policies that might build long term prosperity. A cycle of poverty, instability and violence emerges."[52] It remains absolutely clear to Mallaby that this cycle is deadly dangerous and must be arrested by all means.

Christian communities are not immune to these tense conditions in civil communities. It is sad, however, to note that Christian communities, especially within the townships, have neglected the foul treatment of the black other simply because of the state in which such communities find themselves. As daunting as the task may be, Christian communities have a special responsibility to identify themselves with the stranger and with the marginalized in society. However, in meeting this responsibility Christian communities must not stop before seriously challenging the forces and conditions that have brought on the condition of the majority of blacks in South Africa. They must speak truth to power, especially in difficult times. Christian leaders will have to analyze and expose these situations, instead of being content with the kind of ambulance service that the powers that be provide to the victims. This is a rather difficult task, given the resources at these communities' disposal. Christian communities are generally still very dependent on settler communities, and as such have developed what Steve Biko called an ambivalent personality.

The Belhar Confession in the Struggle Against Afrophobia: Conclusion

If black Christian communities are going to deal with the question of the black other, they need a strong and determined black church leadership. One significant question is whether there really is a black church in the mainline church tradition from which to gain such leadership, given the dependence of the so-called daughter churches on the mother churches.[53] The answer to this question must be answered in the negative. The concepts of "mother" and "daughter" churches have their origin in the establishment of separate churches for blacks, colored, and Indian Christian communities in South Africa. The prime example of this apartheid-shaped arrangement is the Dutch Reformed Church. Its daughter churches have been very much dependent, economically, politically, and ecclesiastically, on the mother church. The levels of dependence vary, but the most dependent of them all still is the black church.

To be sure, black liberation theology in South Africa was a project undertaken by black Christians within the confessional church traditions á la Manas Buthelezi, Simon Maimela, Takatso Mofokeng, Itumeleng Mosala, Bonganjalo Goba, Buti Tlhagale, Allan Boesak, Mokgethi Motlhabi, and others. While it was successful in mobilizing black Christians to adopt a black hermeneutical approach towards the apartheid ideology, black theology of liberation failed nonetheless to integrate African cultures with the Christian faith. This failure has abetted the pseudo belief held by many that South Africa is better off thinking of itself as South African instead of African.

This failure was also brought about by the fact that these black theologians could not overcome the confessional hurdles in their way. It was important for them to wrestle with their blackness in relation to their confessional traditions and talk, for example, about being black and reformed.[54] And yet that blackness did not take seriously the question of Africanness, as suggested by the black consciousness movement.[55] Still, it is clear that the Christian tradition in South Africa must also be one of struggle, one that intentionally seeks to identify with those on the periphery of society.

It is no secret that the fragmentation of the African happened on many fronts, chief among these his or her own culture. The refusal of some black Christians to be totally assimilated into Christianity clothed in Western cultures contributed to the formation of the African Initiated Churches, which are still frowned upon by African Christians who belong to confessional church traditions. From a very early age, the African Christian in this tradition has to learn to reconcile being African and Christian at the same time.[56] Once again, in this exercise we hear the indictment of Biko, which can be summarized as, "When will the African grow up?" In order to survive, the African had to learn to assume a persona in the country of his or her birth.

It was this obsession to survive that rendered the African Christian leader in the confessional church tradition dependent on the mother church. This Christian leader learns very quickly to give one particular sermon when one of the elders of the mother church comes to visit in the local church, and yet a totally different one when preaching in his or her local church. The perception that those Africans who are in the mainline church are better off than those who cling to an African expression of being church, has created huge cleavages between children of the same parents. It is important to deal with these issues as we probe the wholeness of the African and Africa. So how can black Christian people give witness to justice, reconciliation, and unity, not just with whites, but amongst themselves? One possible yardstick could be the Belhar Confession of the Uniting Reformed Church in Southern Africa of 1986.

The Belhar Confession[57] is a confession of the Uniting Reformed Church in Southern Africa (URCSA), a so-called coloured sister Church. It originated as a theological response against the biblical and theological legitimacy given to apartheid by the white Dutch Reformed Church in South Africa. The confession argues that apartheid is a sin and a heresy.[58] This confession was brought about by a confessional church, which fundamentally believes in the confessional inscribing and documenting of its faith.[59] While the stimulus for the confession was apartheid, many have failed to see its ongoing contemporary relevance and applicability to matters where the church still has a responsibility for aligning it with marginalized. It is true that cowardly acts against foreign blacks impelled Christian organizations to at least make statements to illustrate that they are opposed to such acts. The URCSA, for example, issued a statement on the matter, Xenophobic Attacks on Refugees. In this statement the URCSA reminded Christians that Christ himself was a refugee and therefore they should have compassion for refugees.[60]

Many evoke the Belhar Confession when talking about justice and reconciliation with whites, yet this fundamental confession is ignored when the country is dealing with the tension that between black South Africans and Africans from neighboring countries. I believe the reason for this silence is, as the SAMP report has established, an understanding that whites are presumed to be the benefactors, while blacks are presumed to be the beneficiaries. The is no doubt in my mind that black Christians still have a long way to go to ensure that we roll back the devastation caused by our very painful past. The Belhar Confession remains one essential tool in this project, in that it forces us to see the African stranger as the one who is on the margins of society. More importantly, we need to begin to look at Belhar as a tool for addressing more than segregation between black and white; it speaks volumes about the segregation that was engineered and has become entrenched between black people themselves.

While it is imperative that we remember what distinguishes Christians from those who profess not to have any religious convictions, we must nonetheless begin to confront the evils that continue to plague our societies. Rather than simply providing some kind of ambulance service to our communities, we need to strive to do much more, critically engaging the systems that create this mess, instead of nursing symptoms. For this engagement to happen, we need to realize that not only the government, but Christian communities—especially black Christian communities—must realize the severity of the matter and address it powerfully.

Notes

A version of this essay was published previously by the author as "Do Our Theological Methodologies Help Us to Deal with Situations of Violence in Black Communities, Specifically Afrophobia?" *Journal of Theology for Southern Africa* (November 2012), 138. Republished by permission.

1. Cf. S. Hassim, T. Kupe, et al., eds., *Go Home or Die Here: Violence, Xenophobia and the Reinvention of Difference in South Africa* (Johannesburg: Wits University Press, 2008).
2. See photos of these riots at the *Mail & Guardian* (Johannesburg) website: http://photos.mg.co.za/view_gallery.php?gid=224 (accessed January 19, 2010).
3. There was serious talk of closing down the church, as it posed health and safety risks to the occupants due to crowding and lack of adequate facilities. See "Central Methodist Church Could Face Closure," *Mail & Guardian*, 30 October 2009, http://www.mg.co.za/article/2009-10-30-central-methodist-church-could-face-closure (accessed January 19, 2010).
4. The South African Migration Project (SAMP) provides an in-depth account of xenophobia in present-day South Africa. It locates the origin of the May 2008 events in the 1994 democratic elections. It also details the degrees of intolerance against black foreigners

among the four racial groups of South Africa. It notes rather sadly that South Africa has become one of the most intolerant countries to foreigners, especially black foreigners. Jonathan Crush, ed., *The Perfect Storm: The Realities of Xenophobia in Contemporary South Africa*. (Cape Town: Institute for Democracy in South Africa, 2008). For a visual overview of the material and spiritual destruction caused by the events mentioned, see also, S. Hassim et al., *Go Home or Die Here*.

5. Crush, *The Perfect Storm*, 1–11.

6. As part of my community engagement, I volunteer at the Northern Theological Seminary based in Pretoria. This is a seminary of the Uniting Reformed Church in Southern Africa, and among other things my responsibilities include teaching reformed theology. The history of the Dutch Reformed Church family reveals the so-called black "daughter churches" to have been heavily dependent on the white Dutch Reformed Church. Not much of has changed in this current context, since the economy of South Africa remains largely white controlled. The Belhar Confession is also seen negatively by students whose local congregations continue to depend on the white DRC for survival, thus the confession is simplistically associated with black liberation theology and viewed as problematic in some circles in South Africa. One of my resolutions for popularizing the Belhar Confession is to allow it to play a bigger role in the liturgy.

7. Quoted in Andile Mngxitama, "We Are Not All Like That: The Monster Bares Its Fangs," posted at the website of the Abahlali baseMjondolo (Shack Dwellers) Movement, Durban, http://.abahlali.org/node/3645 (accessed September 29, 2009).

8. "Negritude" and its celebration of "negro" or black African consciousness, was popularized in the 1930s by the likes of Léopold Sédar Senghor (who became president of Senegal), Aimé Césaire, and Leon Damas. Its objective was to unite Africans across the globe, a move that was primarily seen as a formidable tool in challenging French political and intellectual hegemony.

9. B. Tatum, *"Why Are All the Black Kids Sitting Together in the Cafeteria?" and Other Conversations about Race* (New York: Basic Books, 2003), 3.

10. And given the way blacks' and whites' lives have been structured in many parts of he world—and in South Africa in particular—it is impossible for the one to live in the world of the other. A person who came close to doing so was a white man in the United States, John Howard Griffin. In the late 1950s, when racial segregation and discrimination were still legal in America, Griffin darkened his skin so that he could pass as a black man. He traveled by bus throughout the racially segregated states of Louisiana, Mississippi, Alabama, and Georgia and was confronted with the treatment usually reserved for blacks. He kept a diary of the experiences, later published as J. Howard Griffin, *Black Like Me* (New York: New American Library, 1960).

11. Tatum, *"Why Are All the Black Kids Sitting Together,"* 5.

12. Ibid.

13. Ibid., 6.

14. Ibid.

15. Carter Woodson, *The Mis-Education of the Negro* (New York: Classic House Books, 2008).

16. Malcolm X, "The Ballot or the Bullet," *All Time Greatest Speeches* (Audio mp3) vol. 2/11, 2008.

17. See Harold Cruse, *The Crisis of the Negro Intellectual: A Historical Analysis of the Failure of Black Leadership* (New York: Morrow, 1967).

18. Frantz Fanon, *Black Skin, White Mask* (New York: Grove Press, 2008), 2.

19. Woodson, *The Mis-Education of the Negro*, 86.

20. Cedric Herring. "Skin Deep: Race and Complexion in a Color-Blind Era," in Cedric Herring, Verna Keith, and Hayward Derrick Horton, eds., *Skin Deep: How Race and Complexion Matter in the Color-Blind Era* (Chicago: University of Illinois Press, 2004), 3.

21. Ibid.

22. E. Bonilla-Silva and D. Dietrich, "The Latin Americanization of U.S. Race Relations," in E. Glenn, ed., *Shades of Difference: Why Skin Color Matters* (Redwood City, CA: Stanford University Press, 2009), 44.

23. Mngxitama, "We Are Not All Like That."

24. The current democratic South Africa is a product of a negotiated settlement. In the simplest terms, leaders of the masses managed to secure the political governance of the country, while the economy of the country was left largely under white minority control. Perhaps some black leaders thought that once they secured control over the country politically, the economy would merely follow government dictates. But the economy is not a department in government; it is a powerful and primary factor in its own right.

25. Cf. Tim J. Wise, *Speaking Treason Fluently: Anti-Racist Reflections from an Angry White Male* (Brooklyn, NY: Soft Skull Press, 2008), 11.

26. S. Biko, *I Write What I Like: Selected Writings* (Chicago, IL: Chicago University Press, 2002), 19.

27. Ransford Danso and David A, McDonald, "Writing Xenophobia: Immigration and the Print Media in Post-Apartheid South Africa," *Africa Today* 48, No. 3 (Fall 2001): 115–37.

28. Biko, *I Write What I Like*, 29.

29. While this essay focuses on the foul treatment by South African blacks of blacks from other African countries, it does not suggest that white people in this country are more tolerant of black foreigners. There are not, as the SAMP 2008 report cited above, *Perfect Storm*, indicates (see especially the executive summary to the report, pp. 1–11). The intolerance whites display towards black foreigners is underpinned by anxiety that the presence of more blacks will cause the white populace to lose more of its privileges.

30. Karin von Hippel, "Old Concepts and New Challenges: African Nationalism in the Post-Cold War Era," in S. Akinrinade and A. Sesay, eds., *Africa in the Post-Cold War International System* (London and Washington: Pinter, 1998), 28.

31. Francis B. Nyamnjoh, *Insiders and Outsiders: Citizenship and Xenophobia in Contemporary Southern Africa* (Dakar: Codesria Books, 2006), 28.

32. Ibid.

33. Jessie Kabwila Kapasula, "Patriarchy and the Oppression of African Women in the 21st Century: A Conversation with Adichie and Dangarembga," paper read at the "Africa Speaks" forum, University of South Africa, July 17, 2009.

34. Biko, *I Write What I Like*, 36.

35. Frantz Fanon, *The Wretched of the Earth* (London: Penguin Books. 2001), 129.

36. Ibid., 128.

37. Bouillon, in Nyamnjoh, *Insiders and Outsiders*, 39.

38. Mngxitama, "We Are Not All Like That," http://.abahlali.org/node/3645 (accessed September 29, 2009).

39. Nyamnjoh, *Insiders and Outsiders*, 39.

40. Cf. L. Landau, "Echoing Exclusion: Xenophobia, Law, and the Future of South Africa's Demonic Society," paper presented to the seminar series of the School for Graduate studies of UNISA, September 9, 2009.

41. Nyamnjoh, *Insiders and Outsiders*, 39.

42. Ibid., 40.

43. Ibid., 5.

44. Mngxitama, "We Are Not All Like That."

45. Fanon, *The Wretched of the Earth*, 30.

46. Ibid.

47. Ezekiel Mphahlele, cited in T. Maluleke, "Urban Black Townships: A Challenge to Christian Mission," *Missionalia* 23, No. 2 (August 1995): 165–83.

48. Biko, *I Write What I Like*, 34.

49. Fanon, *The Wretched of the Earth*, 127.

50. Thabo M. Mbeki, "Approaches to Poverty Eradication and Economic Development VII: Transform the Second Economy," *ANC Today*, November 26, 2006.

51. Biko, *I Write What I Like*, 75.

52. Sebastian Mallaby, "The Reluctant Imperialist: Terrorism, Failed States and the Case for American Empire," *Foreign Affairs* 81, No.2 (March–April 2002): 2–7.

53. "Mother church" refers to the white mainline church from which the missional churches for blacks originated. These missional churches for blacks are called "daughter churches."

54. A. Boesak, *Black and Reformed: Apartheid, Liberation and the Calvinist Tradition* (Maryknoll, NY: Orbis Books, 1984).

55. See Rothney S. Tshaka, "African You Are On Your Own! The Need for African Reformed Christians to Seriously Engage their Africanity in their Reformed Theological Reflections," *Scriptura* 96, No. 3 (2007): 533–48. As we critique the short sightedness of black liberation theology for not extending liberation to the integration of African culture with the Christian faith, it is important to remember the volatile situation then. Yet because we are faced with new challenges, we must ask difficult and uncomfortable questions to see where we might have gone wrong and how to correct such problems in the future.

56. Ibid.

57. www.en.wikipedia.org/wiki/Belhar_Confession (accessed October 17, 2009).

58. D. J. Smit and G. D, Cloete, eds., *A Moment of Truth: The Confession of the Dutch Reformed Mission Church, 1982* (Grand Rapids, MI: Eerdmans, 1984).

59. The Belhar Confession is not the only statement brought about by people of faith in this country. South Africa has seen numerous Christian documents oppose the ideology of

apartheid. See especially, "The *Kairos* Document, Challenge to the Church: A Theological Comment on the Political Crisis in South Africa," *Journal of Theology for Southern Africa* 51 (June 1985): 165ff.

60. R. W. Nel and K. M. Makofane, "The Black African Other, Oikos and Inclusivity: Reflections on the Response of URCSA to SA's Xenophobic Crisis," *Theologia Viatorum* 33, No. 3 (2009): 374–99; see also, Rev. Daniel Kuys, press release: "Xenophobic Attacks on Refugees," for the General Synod of the Uniting Reformed Church in Southern Africa, May 20, 2008, found at www.ngkerk.org.za/documents/Xenophobia.pdf (accessed October 17, 2009.

IV. Theology and (Re)Vitalized Race Consciousness

Collisions between Racism and the Truth of the Cross

Leah Gaskin Fitchue
Ebony Joy Fitchue

Introduction

This essay wrestles with a deep-seated contradiction at the heart of the American experience and at the heart of white Christian thought and practice. This contradiction refers to the problem of racism, as manifested in white Americans and their (1) pathological obsession with the lynching of black people; (2) psychological dependency on white supremacist arguments as a means of relieving doubts as to their superiority (whether those doubts emanate from themselves or from non-whites); and (3) unwillingness to acknowledge the distortions engendered by racism within American life. This last remains true even when whites are confronted with powerful reminders, whether in the form of empirical evidence (social and psychological analysis and data) or in the form of doctrines and symbolism at the heart of the Christian gospel (and therefore central to American culture)—specifically the cross. In making this argument, this essay draws on two different types of scholarly resources: psychological theories of racism, as outlined by scholars such as Michael D'Andrea and Judy Daniels; and theo-historical analyses of racism, as found primarily in the work of James H. Cone.

In his challenging book, *The Cross and the Lynching Tree*, James H. Cone tackles what few scholars have dared to approach: the symbolic connection of the cross and the lynching tree. As he himself states, one is a universal symbol of Christian faith, the other the quintessential symbol of black oppression in America. While separated by two thousand years, they bear a similar identity in that both are related to death. The commonality, however, ends there. The death on the cross is uncontestably the most beautiful gift of selflessness in the history of humanity. In contrast, death by lynching is the most heinous act perpetrated by white people tragically obsessed with what they erroneously believe to be the entitlement afforded by their white skins. As Cone reminds us, courageously exploring the connection of these two symbols, "An unspeakable crime, [lynching] is a memory that most white Americans would prefer to forget."[1]

As two black women born and raised in America, we know something about the tension of memory and identity. The problem with memory and being black is that one is always challenged with just how much recollection about the lived experience of blackness in America one can entertain and remain sane. This is the critical problem every black person in America has to face every day, as he or she navigates the "two-ness" of black reality.

W. E. B. Du Bois introduced America to this "double-consciousness" concept in his classic work, *The Souls of Black Folk*. Du Bois describes the phenomenon as an ingenious survival response to the plight of black people living in a racist America,

> a world that yields him no true self-consciousness, but only lets him see himself through the revelation of the other world. It is a peculiar sensation, this double-consciousness, this sense of always looking at one's self through the eyes of others, of measuring one's soul by the tape of a world that looks on in amused contempt and pity. One ever feels his two-ness—an American, a Negro; two souls, two thoughts, two unreconciled strivings; two warring ideals in one dark body, whose dogged strength alone keeps it from being torn asunder.[2]

Regrettably, the contortions of slavery, slave codes, separate but equal, and other legal atrocities have effectively numbed the historical consciousness of generations of black people, who have suffered oppressive practices in the United States for nearly four hundred years. They have chosen silence over madness. There comes a time, however—if one surrenders to the prompting of the Holy Spirit—when the struggle to make sense of being a black Christian in white America reaches its limit, and one refuses to be contained in silence and darkness. Triumphantly denouncing the manipulated trickery of black internalized oppression, one plunges forth out of darkness in search of the light of truth.

Cone speaks to that emergence, and he rips aside the veil of hypocrisy, demanding that we, as black Christians, risk the inevitable pain of recall and give voice to the fact that the cross and "the lynching tree represented the worst in human beings and at the same time, 'an unquenchable ontological thirst' for life that refuses to let the worst determine our final meaning."[3] Cone throws down the gauntlet, challenging the fraudulent "two-ness" of a democracy that mouths creeds of equality, while treating non-white citizens as less than equal. In doing so, he urges white Christians to gainsay the myth of white superiority, the cost of which is a compromised democracy that affirms a contaminated vision of justice and violates its core principles of equality.

Cone had lived his "two-ness" surrounded by the myth of white skin superiority, beginning with his birth in the lynching state of Arkansas. It is important to note that during his youth, America was dealing with the "Negro problem." Gunnar Myrdal's landmark 1944 study, *American Dilemma: The Negro Problem and Modern Democracy*, captured the dichotomy between the values of liberty, equality, and civility set forth in the "American Creed," and the nation's inhuman treatment of its black citizens:[4] "[F]or here the 'Creed' operated in a 'double direction'—on the one hand forbidding inequitable treatment of any human being, while on the other requiring dehumanization of the black victims to justify the departure, in their case, from its proclaimed values." "Race prejudice" was needed "for defense on the part of the Americans against their own national Creed."[5]

This paper explores some of the challenges of the myth of white skin superiority as justification for a "two-ness" democracy and its relationship to the truth of the cross and the lynching tree. It also explores the historical and psychological impact of racism on blacks and whites alike, with examination of the latter informed by compelling psychological theories and analysis provided by Michael D'Andrea and Judy Daniels, and by other scholars researching the psychological harm done to racists by their own racist sentiments and behaviors.

A premise of the present essay is that Cone's juxtaposition of the cross and the lynching tree provides our racialized America an opportunity to confront its racism and thereby take appropriate steps to move beyond it. These issues pose difficult challenges for churches, theological schools, and other faith-based institutions, which must speak up if America is to be given a second chance to model both liberation and reconciliation for all of her people. Given that the black church was born in protest and called to liberate an oppressed people, it does not have the freedom to remain silent about Cone's conversation about the intersection of the cross and the lynching tree. Neither does the white church. While its origins may differ from the black church's, as theologian Walter Wink observes white and black churches have the same calling, which is "to practice a ministry of disclosing the spirituality of these Powers . . . that are not off at the edge of space somewhere, but are in our very midst as the *interiority* of earthly institutions, systems, and structures."[6] The role of the church in this journey cannot be understated, because only through confession, forgiveness, and redemption can we hope to find justice, acknowledging as Dr. Martin Luther King Jr. reminded us, that justice is impossible without love.[7] Further, the church is where we derive our faith and empower ourselves by living the meaning of the cross and, in the words of Cone, "snatch[ing] victory out of defeat, life out of death, and hope out of despair."[8]

Cone and the Truth of *The Cross and the Lynching Tree*

The thesis that it is impossible to live the myth of white skin superiority and simultaneously live the truth of the cross expresses a contradiction experienced by Cone and other blacks. It was a truth Cone had been carrying in his spirit since his first book *Black Theology and Black Power* (1969), which he wrote in an "effort to relate the gospel and the black experience—the experience of oppression as well as the struggle to find liberation and meaning."[9] Cone states,

> Consumed by a passion to express myself about the liberating power of the black religious experience, I continued to write and speak about this spiritual revolution erupting in the cultural and political contexts of the African American community. This message of liberation was "something like a burning fire shut up in my bones," to use the language of Jeremiah; I (was) weary with holding it in, and I (could not) (Jer. 20:9).[10]

By the time Cone wrote *The Cross and the Lynching Tree*, he was simply taking another step along what has been for him a tedious journey with American racism. Growing up in the segregated South in the 1940s and 1950s, he had an up-close-and-personal experience with lynching. Daily he learned about white supremacy and its terroristic violence. He learned that "white people were virtually free to do anything to blacks with impunity."[11] He heard black people talk about the horrors of the Ku Klux Klan, and he saw the crosses that served as the staggering symbol of the Klan's philosophy of white supremacy. Cone knew, even as a youth, that the atrocities his family and the black community experienced were unjust. Early in life, he learned that to know the truth and not be able to speak it is the gut-wrenching burden of living a double consciousness in a flawed "two-ness" democracy.

This is how the lie of white skin superiority seduces its victims into a covenant of co-dependency as one is made to deny the truth. The flaw of white skin superiority is that, each time it seduces its victim, it re-victimizes, having to recommit to the denial that white skin superiority is a lie. A lie requires high maintenance and constant reinforcement owing to the fear of exposure.

Slaves and free blacks in the South understood the unarticulated and suppressed fear of whites, who could not gaze into the eyes of blacks, where the truth could be read. Black men and women were lynched for defiantly looking back at whites and telegraphing their knowledge of the lie:

> Nothing was more detested by whites than the idea that blacks were equal to them. "You don't act in a way to make white persons feel that you don't know they were white", commented an Arkansas interviewee about Jim Crow. Any word or body movement that was perceived to be insufficiently deferential, like standing upright and looking a white person in the eye could get a black beaten or killed.[12]

Here we stand in the intersection of racism and the truth of the cross. The cross, as a symbol of liberation, redemption, and selfless love counters oppression and keeps hope alive in Christ Jesus, even in the midst of despair, deception, and delusion. As historian Alexander Saxton points out, nineteenth-century racial doctrines that had abetted the myth of white skin superiority began to be challenged during the first decade of the twentieth century, and "showed signs of crumbling under the impact of scientific criticism and political and economic changes throughout the United States."[13] However, a consequence of the nineteenth-century shift from "theological to biological thinking" proved disastrous for African Americans, in that the new sense that human beings belonged to the "biological universe" caused the "unsophisticated white man," as Myrdal says, "to arrive at the opinion that blacks were biologically inferior."[14]

A similar kind of interpretive lens is provided by another black scholar, Dwight Hopkins, who, in addressing white supremacy in *Down, Up, and Over: Slave Religion and Black Theology*, claims total condemnation by Jesus. According to Hopkins, it is not unusual for "white churches, religious institutions, and the broader society to make racial classifications that discriminate against the biological make-up and physical characteristics of black folk."[15] In so doing, these persons and institutions do not display any awareness that to act in this manner is counter to the very ethics of Jesus. The lie of white skin superiority, having been practiced from generation to generation, is so protracted that white people have managed, in the name of white supremacy, to impose a white skin color on Jesus in order to establish a normative relationship between themselves and Jesus, and a dissonant relationship between Jesus and those who are not white. Hopkins says, "Yet Jesus condemns color supremacy because the forced normativity of whiteness creates a false idol at the center of all humanity. . . . in North American society, race still matters, due to the wicked spirit of white supremacy."[16]

In his home church, Macedonia AME Church, Cone learned that black Christians loved and trusted their Jesus and could tolerate their lot because they were modeling how Jesus went through his experience of suffering. Cone references historian Lerone Bennett Jr.'s reflections on the pain of black suffering which, says Bennett, was "at the deepest level . . . what it was like to be crucified . . . and more: that there were some things in this world that are worth being crucified for."[17] The hymn "Jesus Keep Me Near the Cross" captures these feelings:

> There a precious fountain,
> Free to all, a healing stream,
> Flows from Calvary's mountain.
> In the cross, in the cross,
> Be my glory ever,
> Till my raptured soul shall find
> Rest beyond the river.[18]

For this reason Cone was able to write, "The more black people struggled against white supremacy, the more they found in the cross the spiritual power to resist the violence they often suffered."[19]

Truth of the Lynching Tree Without the Cross

Murder in the Public Square

> They murdered the Negro in cold blood in the jail doorway; then they dragged him to the principal business street and hung him to a telegraph-pole, afterwards riddling his lifeless body with revolver shots . . . . And there the Negro hung until daylight the next morning—an unspeakably grisly, dangling horror.[20]

What is it about white male mobs that motivated them not only to murder innocent victims, but to continue to mutilate the body after the victim died? In the incident described above by Ray Stannard Baker, after the Negro was dead, having been murdered in cold blood and without attention to his innocence or guilt, members of the mob emptied their guns in his body, then dragged their "prize" to the public square, where they lynched his corpse. What is it about white Americans that the deaths of blacks are not enough, but must be followed by complete eradication of their victims?

Frances Cress Welsing, in *The Isis Papers*, offers a perspective worthy of review. Welsing states that just as racism "controlled events in the twentieth century, the *solution* to the problem will regulate events in the twenty-first century and beyond as we enter the era of justice."[21] Changes that occur in the twenty-first century will be, according to Welsing, "non-white people's ever increasing understanding of the behavioral phenomenon of white supremacy as a global terroristic power system."[22] For Welsing, the presence of racism in America and the "prevention of white genetic annihilation on Earth" are inextricably related.

Too many white scholars employ a blaming-the-victim pathological bias in describing black behavior. Welsing, while acknowledging the "disturbing individual and group destructive pathological forms of behavior" on the part of blacks, does not blame the victims. Instead, she states that such behaviors "are the *direct* and *indirect* by-products of a behavioral power system fundamentally structured for white genetic survival, locally and globally", and can be located in the urban epidemics devastating the very future of today's urban black family and community.[23]

> Today, the white genetic survival imperative, instead of using chemicals in gas chambers, is using chemicals on the streets—crack, crank, cocaine, ecstasy, PCP, heroin, and methadone (all "designer chemicals"). Ultimately, these chemicals are produced by whites and made available to urban blacks, particularly black males—upon whom the future of black people is dependent. The core dynamic of white genetic survival eventually leads whites to a major act of genocide (destruction of the genes of non-white people) or toward *genocidal imperatives*.[24]

Distinguished Professor of Social Christian Ethics, Dr. Charles Brown of Payne Theological Seminary (Wilberforce, Ohio) suggests that the obsession of the white lynch mob to not only kill, but to destroy and extinguish—perpetrating additional violent acts on the dead body, either by castration, dousing the corpse with gas and setting it afire, or firing bullets into it—is directly tied to genocidal imperatives. Brown believes that such racist behavior is tied to an impulse fueled by deep psychological woundedness, and a personal core of inferiority displayed in vicious self-imposed superiority that seeks total extinction of the problematic group.[25]

This historical and generational pattern of white oppression of blacks is captured in Cornel West's "normative gaze," a white supremacy construct addressed in "A Genealogy of Modern Racism" in his book *Prophecy Deliverance!*, West examines the emergence of modern racism in the nineteenth century and what he calls a "neglected variable in past explanatory models,[26] . . . namely, the way in which the very structure of modern discourse *at its inception* produced forms of rationality, scientificity, and objectivity as well as aesthetic and cultural ideals which require the constitution of the idea of white supremacy."[27]

In setting the stage for his exploration, West reminds his readers that "the notion that black people are humans is a relatively new discovery in the modern West."[28] Further, says West, even today, "the idea of black equality in beauty, culture, and intellectual capacity remains problematic and controversial" in America. The normative gaze of white supremacy continues to delegitimize the humanity of blacks, and in doing so, it minimizes the plausibility and visibility of blacks as human.

Whether we accept the white genetic survival thesis of Welsing, or the normative gaze and invisibility of blacks as human described by West, the results are the same. Within the constitution of white supremacy and the DNA of modern discourse, blacks are doomed. What is most significant for this discussion of the myth of white skin superiority and the truth of the cross is that any attention to the dismantling of white supremacy and its components, according to West, must acknowledge the role of "powers within the structure of modern discourse." These are "[p]owers to produce and prohibit, develop and delimit, forms of rationality, scientificity, and objectivity which set perimeters and draw boundaries for the intelligibility, availability, and legitimacy of certain ideas."[29] Here the myth of white skin superiority and the truth of the cross collide head-on, as the equality of beauty, culture, and intelligence granted to blacks as the beloved children of God's creation appear for the most part to be invisible to white Christians. Instead, shrouded by "the scientific stance of observation coupled with the Greek notion of beauty, we have the deprecation of blacks and the rise of the assumption of white supremacy."[30]

Analysis by biblical studies scholar Randall Bailey suggests how radical such negative ideas were at one point in black history. Describing the ancient Israelites' esteem of African nations, he writes, "Their wisdom was highly regarded . . . [and] they were utilized as a standard of measure for Israel . . . [whose] texts viewed these nations and their leaders as having great value. If an Israelite wished to show approval of something . . . favorable comparison to Africans was one way of doing it."[31] Bailey offers a stunning reminder to blacks not to omit the recognized ancient church standard of excellence and splendor attributed to Africans in articulating contemporary and future parameters of black identity.

Systems Intermediate (Black Cyclical Reality)

To show the intensity of the brutality of lynching, Cone once told how the dastardly white male behavior manifested itself in the extinction of a family in 1918, when a white mob lynched an innocent black man and proceeded to lynch his pregnant wife. After she was "stripped, hung upside down by the ankles, soaked with gasoline and roasted to death . . . a white man opened up her swollen belly with a hunting knife,"[32] and her yet-to-be-born infant fell to the ground. After the fetus hit the ground, members of the mob stomped it to death as well.[33]

The need of whites for unrelenting ritual killing or other forms of genocidal destruction of blacks—even in the wake of physical death—led Cone to question if white supremacy would ever stop in this country. His remarks give us an occasion to revisit what we have observed as the cyclical pattern of black liberation, in which periods of more intense punishment and abuse would be inflicted on blacks following periods in which they had the opportunity to express greater personal freedom and advancement. We refer to this phenomenon as black cyclical reality.

The cyclical pattern of black liberation is not fortuitous, but it is evidence of the existence of what Neely Fuller calls "a universally operating 'system' of white supremacy and domination in which the majority of the world's white people participate."[34] A significant clue to the origin of black cyclical reality was anticipated by Carl Schurz, a liberal statesman and journalist, following his post-Emancipation Proclamation tour of the south in 1865 on behalf of President Johnson:

> [T]he negro exists for the special objects of raising cotton, rice, and sugar *for the whites*, and . . . it is illegitimate for him to indulge, like other people, in the pursuit of his own happiness in his own way. Although it is admitted that he has ceased to be the property of a master, it is not admitted that he has a right to become his own master . . . . It is, indeed, not probable that a general attempt will be made to restore slavery in its old form . . . but there are systems intermediate between slavery as it formerly existed, and free labor as it existed in the north, but more nearly related to the former than the latter, *the introduction of which will be attempted*.[35]

Schurz was on target in alerting his readers to the reality that there would be "systems intermediate" that would be legally implemented to meet the political and economic needs of the white ruling class. While not restoring slavery in its old form, these systems would result in the re-enslavement of blacks in America.

From the earliest days of America, "systems intermediate" and other varying patterns of oppression have resulted in cyclical periods of liberating, enslaving, and then "freeing" blacks. In 1787, the constitution of our fledgling democracy counted slaves as three-fifths of a person, denying them their humanity. Then the status of blacks as lower than the lowest white person was confirmed in the 1857 *Dred Scott* decision. The 1863 Emancipation Proclamation and the twelve chaotic years of Reconstruction that followed gave blacks their freedom, only to see Jim Crow laws (first enacted in 1876 and federally legitimized by the 1896 *Plessy v. Ferguson* decision) again set blacks apart by the notion of "separate but equal." Not until 1954 and *Brown v. Board of Education* were blacks again lifted to a semblance of equality, which was subsequently reinforced by the Civil Rights Act of 1964 and the Voting Rights Act of 1965.

Less than twenty years later, President Ronald Reagan's launch of the "war on drugs", (a euphemism for "war on blacks"), renewed the cyclical reality of black enslavement. The onerous Anti-Drug Abuse Act of 1986, with its harsh drug sentences, set blacks on a path of sanctioned criminalization and mass incarceration that continues to decimate families and communities. In 2012, African Americans find themselves fighting repeated efforts to suppress the black vote, which signals yet another attempt to deny them justice. It is important to note that the institutionalization of "systems intermediate," over generations and utilizing different kinds of enslavement strategies, achieves the same outcome today as lynching and other genocidal imperatives did in previous times. Today, vast numbers of blacks, especially males, are being targeted for extinction, as Welsing delineates:

> The chain of events begins with the denial of full scale employment and advancement to black males so that they cannot adequately support themselves, their wives and their children. . . . once this atmosphere is established drugs are placed *deliberately* in the black community. The drugs are then used to "street-treat" black male frustration . . . guns are then placed at the disposal of the same black male persons, supposedly to aid them in enforcing payment for drugs. More important, the strategy is for black males to kill and destroy one another and then carry the blame. (It must be realized that no black males manufacture the chemicals used for drugs, nor do any black males manufacture guns).[36]

Nowhere is the current day lynching and genocidal imperative more visible than in the prison industrial complex, which is disproportionately and dramatically incarcerating and warehousing black men and women. Black males are 6 percent of the United States population, yet they constitute 40 percent of the nation's prison population, and black women make up the fastest-growing segment of the prison population.[37] As prisoners, these persons receive virtually no rehabilitation services and, upon release, have limited or no resources to assist them with reentry to their families and communities in order to restart their lives in a productive manner.

This dehumanizing and punitive nightmare for African Americans is described in Michelle Alexander's *The New Jim Crow: Mass Incarceration in the Age of Colorblindness*, which emphasizes long-term effects: "Their prison records ostracize them from mainstream American life for the remainder of their lives. African American men become the permanent under caste, prison becomes the revolving door, and they are 'out of sight' and 'out of mind.'"[38] Genocidal imperatives are at work again, as white supremacy "powers" resident in systems and structures continue to make money on the backs of black men and women—no longer in the cotton fields, but in the prison mills.

Consequences of the Myth of White Superiority in the American Democratic Context

The Psychology of White Christian Racism

Having considered Welsing's genocidal imperative as foundational to the pattern of unjust behavior of whites against blacks, and the related physic crevices in which color inadequacy of whiteness resides, our attention turns now to the defense mechanism of denial, one factor of the psychology of white Christian racism and the myth of white skin superiority. Admittedly, denial would be expected from whites, who would disagree with Welsing's attention to genetic origin as the appropriate starting point for dismantling white supremacy. As Welsing argues, white supremacy notions compensate at points for white feelings of genetic and numerical inferiority, and require casting non-whites as genetic inferiors:

> The white personality, in the presence of color, can be stabilized only by keeping blacks and other non-whites in obviously inferior positions. . . . The color inadequacy of whiteness necessitates a social structure based on white supremacy. Only tokenism can be tolerated by such a motivational psychological state, wherein the evolution of the myth of the exceptional non-white is used, again, as a defense mechanism.[39]

The role of psychological illness in white racist behavior, highlighted by Welsing and others, is the subject of a study by Michael D'Andrea and Judy Daniels, *Exploring the Psychology of White Racism through Naturalistic Inquiry*. These authors, following research into the psychological factors that impact racist thoughts and behaviors in white Americans, conclude that whites also experience psychological illnesses related to how they internalize racist ideals, and that "white racism continues to have a toxic effect on the lives of millions of people in the United States."[40] In advocating the need for additional research on the psychological consequences of racism on white behavior, D'Andrea and Daniels further conclude, "One of the major factors contributing to the lack of attention that has been directed to this area is the broad-based sense of denial that many whites exhibit in response to this problem."[41]

This research, conducted over sixteen years, utilized more than twelve hundred observations of whites from varied geographical, professional, educational, economical, and religious backgrounds, and engaged participants in dialogue about race and race relations.[42] "Cognitive, affective, and behavioral reactions" were noted, and data collected from their findings resulted in five proposed "psychological dispositions" of racism exhibited by white Americans: 1) affective-impulsive disposition, 2) rational disposition, 3) liberal disposition, 4) principled disposition, and 5) principled activist disposition.[43]

Affective-impulsive disposition refers to hostile ways of looking at racial differences, and an inability to identify similarities and/or differences in comparison to individuals from another race. Persons exhibiting this disposition would arguably be among those inclined to participate in the horrors of lynching described earlier. Rational disposition applies to persons evidencing an inability to identify racial differences, yet, contradictorily, tending to embrace racial stereotypes and engage in "covert" forms of racism by not supporting legislation or policies, such as affirmative action, intended to aid the advancement of people of color. Liberal disposition is expressed in acceptance of racial differences and similarities, an ability to understand the complexity of racism by exuding a "cognitive maturity," and respect for human rights. Nevertheless, this disposition often tends towards inaction or an effective state of apathy or lack of empathy, aimed at avoiding negativity with regard to racial issues.[44] Principled disposition applies to those with an ability to comprehend how racism is sustained by white privilege through the historical, social, and political tenets that contribute to racism, who nonetheless fail to acknowledge their own shortcomings or to initiate more than minimal action when addressing observed racial injustices. Principled activist disposition, applicable to only one percent of all participants in the study, reflects a deeper understanding of racism, greater optimism for racial resolution, and a humanistic perspective that reflects willingness to act for social change.

For the purpose of this discussion and Cone's observations, it would appear that the principled activist disposition, which reflects what D'Andrea and Daniels call a "genuine nonracist ideology, would have an operative role."[45] "These people manifested a much greater understanding of the types of individual, institutional, and cultural changes that need to occur to successfully ameliorate this social pathology. This understanding was clearly apparent in the way these people were able to articulate the specific types of changes that our societal institutions need to undergo to foster racial justice in our nation."[46] Of the five psychological dispositions of racism outlined by D'Andrea and Daniels, it appears that only a minority of the participants in this study did not suffer from white denial and its associated dysfunctional behavior.

Sigmund Freud was one of the first psychiatrists to provide research on the function and impact of denial, "in which a person is faced with a fact that is too uncomfortable to accept and rejects it instead, insisting that it is not true despite what may be overwhelming evidence."[47] By its very nature, denial is a defense mechanism, a distortion of reality, a delusional projection to reshape reality in a way one desires to see it. James Perkinson's study, *White Theology*, counters white denial in calling for a "white theology of responsibility (agreeing with Cone) that a serious engagement with history and culture must be at the heart of any American projection of integrity or 'salvation.'"[48] White responsibility is the focus of pastor and anti-racism trainer, Joseph Barndt's *Understanding and Dismantling Racism*: "I believe that we who are white need to come to a new understanding about ourselves and about our racism, and we need to take responsibility for bringing racism to an end."[49] The good news from D'Andrea and Daniels, Perkinson, Barndt, and others is that there are white people who are committed to a "genuine nonracist ideology" and who are ready to be partners in Cone's conversation.

Justice Conversation for Community Solidarity

The search for truth and meaning and speaking truth to power are ongoing pursuits in *The Cross and the Lynching Tree*. Cone ponders the absence of motivation and courage in addressing white supremacy among clergy and theology professors. He sets that reticence against the hermeneutics of Ida B. Wells, a one-woman anti-lynching crusader, and Fannie Lou Hamer, a Mississippi sharecropper who was beaten without mercy because of her involvement in the struggle for freedom.[50]

It would appear that Cone, like these heroines, decided that his research and writing about lynching were worth some anguish. Admitting that *The Cross and the Lynching Tree* was the most "painful" book he has written, he adds it was also the most liberating. This is the kind of transcendent, life-giving breakthrough that he read about in Mircea Eliade's *The Sacred and the Profane: The Nature of Religion*: "Life is not possible without an opening toward the transcendent."[51] Cone goes on to say that once contact with the "transcendent is found, a new existence in the world becomes possible, a transcendent reality that lifts our spirits to a world far removed from the suffering of this one."[52] He gained transcendent wisdom from theologian Howard Thurman, who celebrated the preeminence of the spirit in human survival in *Jesus and the Disinherited*: "Wherever [Jesus's] spirit appears, the oppressed gather fresh courage; for he announced the good news that fear, hypocrisy, and hatred, the three hounds of hell that track the trail of the disinherited, need have no dominion over them."[53]

When West states that "the role of classical aesthetic and cultural norms in the emergence of the idea of white supremacy as an object of modern discourse cannot be underestimated,"[54] he gives us clear warning that any contemporary conversations about racism and injustice, or collisions between race and the cross, must first pause to establish an alternative normative gaze whereby blacks are valued as human, beautiful, cultured, and intelligent. Here is why Cone, the prophet and professor, hovers so close to the transcendent and fights so vigorously for an alternative to the status: "I concluded that an immanent presence of a transcendent revelation, confirming for blacks that they were more than what whites said about them, gave them an inner spiritual strength to cope with anything that came their way. I wrote because words were my weapons to resist, to affirm black humanity, and to defend it."[55]

Equipped with the teachings of Eliade, Thurman, and King, Cone realized why Martin Luther King Jr. advocated for an imperative of love as the only legitimate power that could counter injustice. In his 1967 Southern Christian Leadership Conference annual report, "Where Do We Go from Here?," King describes how the concepts of love and power have usually been contrasted as opposites that will not lead us where we want to go. Then he declares:

> Now we got to get this thing right. What is needed is a realization that power without love is reckless and abusive, and that love without power is sentimental and anemic. Power at its best is love implementing the demands of justice, and justice at its best is love correcting everything that stands against love. And this is what we must see as we move on.[56]

West shares a similar perspective, believing "any disease of the soul," such as nihilism, racism, or white supremacy, cannot "be overcome by arguments or analyses; it is tamed by love and care."[57]

We agree with Cone, King, and West that we must move on. In this second decade of the twenty-first century, as we continue our ongoing battle with white supremacy, we look back one hundred years to the color line that Du Bois called America's number one problem and ask, what will be different about the conversation this time?[58]

First, we must initiate a conversation with confessing, mature Christian men and women who are transcendently inspired to marry love and justice and be accountable beneficiaries of the liberating and energizing power that results. Those who join this conversation must give witness to the fact that blacks are members of the first human family and, therefore, embody the genetic wisdom and circuitry for both the origin and future of humankind. This bold truth must be the focus of the conversation and set the tone for open and honest dialogue about white supremacists' addiction to racism and oppression, which Welsing calls "a survival necessity for the white collective."[59]

Second, we must honor the divine charge of Ephesians 3:10 and "put on the full armor of God." Such armor is a requirement in dismantling a legally structured system of racial control, undergirded, according to Richard Snyder, by a spirit of punishment that seduces our society to wallow in the ethos of punishment.[60] Here the church becomes the teacher in modeling how "to let the oppressed go free"[61] through dismantling powers and principalities of white supremacy structures and systems— including an apathetic and silent church and seminary, an unbalanced economic hierarchy, and an unjust criminal justice system. We must robustly pursue restorative justice in place of the current common practice of retributive justice, and rethink redemptive grace and its influence on the punitive spirit of the age. As Snyder reminds us, "Redemptive grace in individualistic terms denies the fullness of what we are up against, and at the same time it denies the fullness of God's grace."[62]

Third, given the mental, physical, and spiritual burdens African Americans face owing to the contradictions of democracy, the distortions of white supremacy, and the lack of "true power to determine ultimately what happens to their individual and collective lives,"[63] there is a pressing need for a black-on-black, in-the-name-of-Jesus discourse to address the costs and residuals of internalized oppression and structural injustices.

Fourth, we must issue a call for radical restructuring and systemic overhaul of the nation's public education system, which is rapidly becoming a wasteland of mediocrity and a prison pipeline supported by high school dropout rate that hovers around 50 percent in some urban centers. An education system that uplifts and empowers students, that fosters strong parental involvement, and that is available to all regardless of color or class is the only hope for the twenty-first century's multi-ethnic and multilingual citizenry. Our students must be equipped to confront an unprecedented rate of change and the intellectual and technological requirements of America's new "oneness" democracy of true equality.

And finally, with respect for and in the spirit of the country's first African American president and First Lady, Barack and Michelle Obama, two of this world's most eloquent and exquisitely beautiful, cultured, and intelligent human beings, the call must go out to all Americans to imitate what Cone models: the "courage to confront the great sin and ongoing legacy of white supremacy with repentance and reparation in order to move beyond tragedy and experience the triumphant beauty of the divine."[64]

Let the conversation begin.

Notes

1. James H. Cone, *The Cross and the Lynching Tree* (Maryknoll, NY: Orbis Books, 2011), xiv.
2. W. E. B. Du Bois, *The Souls of Black Folk*, Henry L. Gates Jr. and Terri Hume Oliver, eds. (New York: Norton, 1999), 11.
3. Cone, *The Cross and the Lynching Tree*, 3.
4. Alexander Saxton, *The Rise and Fall of the White Republic: Class Politics and Mass Culture in Nineteenth-Century America* (London: Verso, 1990), 3.
5. Saxton, *The Rise and Fall of the White Republic*, 3–4.
6. Walter Wink, *Engaging the Powers: Discernment and Resistance in a World of Domination* (Minneapolis: Fortress, 1992), 164.
7. Greg Moses, *Revolution of Conscience: Martin Luther King, Jr., and the Philosophy of Nonviolence* (New York: Guilford, 1997), 186.
8. Cone, *The Cross and the Lynching Tree*, 150.
9. Cone, *The Cross and the Lynching Tree*, 154.
10. Ibid.
11. Cone, *The Cross and the Lynching Tree*, xv.
12. Cone, *The Cross and the Lynching Tree*, 128.
13. Saxton, *The Rise and Fall of the White Republic*, 3.
14. Ibid.
15. Dwight N. Hopkins, *Down, Up, and Over: Slave Religion and Black Theology* (Minneapolis: Fortress, 2000), 204.
16. Ibid., 204.
17. Cone, *The Cross and the Lynching Tree*, 22.

18. Fanny J. Crosby and William H. Doane, "Near the Cross," in *AMEC Hymnal* (Nashville, TN: African Methodist Episcopal Church, 2000), 321.

19. Ibid.

20. Ray Stannard Baker, "What is a Lynching? A Study of Mob Justice, South and North," at Digital History, http://www.digitalhistory.uh.edu/learning_history/lynching/baker1.cfm (accessed April 2012). Original source *McClure's Magazine* 24, No. 4 (Feb 1905), 422.

21. Frances Cress Welsing, *The Isis Papers: The Keys to the Colors* (New York: C. W. Publishing, 2004), I.

22. Ibid., i–ii.

23. Ibid., ii.

24. Ibid., iv.

25. Charles Brown, conversation with author.

26. Cornel West, *Prophesy Deliverance: An Afro-American Revolutionary Christianity* (Philadelphia: Westminster, 1982), 47.

27. Ibid.

28. Ibid.

29. Ibid., 49.

30. Ibid., 57–58.

31. Randall C. Bailey, "Beyond Identification: The Use of Africans in Old Testament Poetry and Narratives," in Cain Hope Felder, *Stony the Road We Trod: African American Biblical Interpretation* (Minneapolis: Fortress, 1991), 183.

32. Cone, *The Cross and the Lynching Tree*, 120.

33. "Lynchings & Hangings," Legends of America, http://legendsofamerica.com/ah-lynching8.html (accessed July 11, 2014).

34. Welsing, *The Isis Papers*, 3.

35. Dan Lacy, *The White Use of Blacks in America* (New York: Athenaeum, 1972), 77–78.

36. Welsing, *The Isis Papers*, v.

37. Michelle Alexander, "Study Guide to *The New Jim Crow: Mass Incarceration in the Age of Colorblindness*" (Samuel DeWitt Proctor Conference, Inc., 2011), 21.

38. Alexander, Study Guide to *The New Jim Crow*, 21.

39. Welsing, *The Isis Papers*, 9.

40. Michael D'Andrea and Judy Daniels, "Exploring the Psychology of White Racism through Naturalistic Inquiry," *Journal of Counseling & Development* 77, No. 1 (1999): 93–101 (PsycINFO, EBSCOhost).

41. Ibid., 93.

42. Ibid., 94.

43. Ibid., 95.

44. Ibid., 97.

45. West, *Prophesy*, 53–58.

46. D'Andrea, "Exploring the Psychology of White Racism," 100.

47. http://en.wikipedia.org/wiki/Denial (accessed July 11, 2014).

48. James W. Perkinson, *White Theology: Outing Supremacy in Modernity* (New York: Palgrave Macmillan, 2004), cover note.

49. Joseph R. Barndt, *Understanding and Dismantling Racism: The Twenty-First Century Challenge to White America* (Minneapolis: Fortress, 2007), 6.

50. Cone, *The Cross and the Lynching Tree*, 143–44.

51. Mircea Eliade, *The Sacred and the Profane: The Nature of Religion*, trans. Willard R. Trask. (New York: Harcourt Brace & World, 1959), 34.

52. Cone, *The Cross and the Lynching Tree*, 155.

53. Howard Thurman, *Jesus and the Disinherited* (New York: Abingdon-Cokesbury, 1949), cxiv.

54. West, *Prophesy*, 54.

55. Cone, *The Cross and the Lynching Tree*, xviii.

56. Martin Luther King, "Where Do We Go from Here?" delivered at the eleventh annual SCLC convention, Aug. 16, 1967, King Center, Stanford University, http://mlk-kpp01.stanford.edu/index.php/encyclopedia/documentsentry/where_do_we_go_from_here_delivered_at_the_11th_annual_sclc_convention/, 5 (accessed July 11, 2014).

57. Cornel West, *Race Matters* (Boston: Beacon, 1993), 29.

58. Du Bois, *The Souls of Black Folk*, 5.

59. Welsing, *The Isis Papers*, 44.

60. T. Richard Snyder, *The Protestant Ethic and the Spirit of Punishment* (Grand Rapids, MI: Eerdmans, 2000), 5.

61. Isaiah 58:6, NIV.

62. Snyder, *The Protestant Ethic*, 73.

63. Welsing, *The Isis Papers*, 154.

64. Cone, *The Cross and the Lynching Tree*, 166.

Pursuing American Racial Justice and a Politically and Theologically Informed Black Church Praxis

Forrest E. Harris Sr.

At the height of the struggle against South African apartheid, Archbishop Desmond Tutu stated, "*Liberation* is costly. It needs unity."[1] It is particularly empowering to join with scholars and church leaders around the world in London, the heart of colonial history, to rethink global strategies against systems of domination and oppression that permeate international communities. The topic, black church activism and contested multiculturalism in Africa, Europe, and North America, provides opportunities for reflecting on new forms of racism that are manifesting globally which are, as Donaldo Macedo and Panayota Gounari assert, "exacerbated by the commonsense discourse of neoliberalism and its theological embrace of the market as a panacea for all world problems."[2] Racism in the United States has reached outrageous levels of institutionalize hegemony that warrant serious investigation of its widespread impact on racial and gender identities at all levels of American life. Racism in North America has historical antecedents normalized in the political currency of race, class, and gender and in various modes of social arrangements of power. Our coming together is evidence of a collective social obligation we share to pursue justice activism, As such, it is not dissimilar from that of our ancestors who worked to dismantle what is now understood as "matrixes of dominance,"[3] new forms of systemic racism in an era assumed to be colorblind.

The limits of this essay will become obvious, as it invites but does not fully delineate comprehensive strategies for dialogue between the disciplines of theology, postcolonial theory, and race theory. What is trotted out here is a praxis commitment to frame a justice agenda at the intersection of race, class, and gender, which, as I propose, requires a revision of the black church under a new ecclesial paradigm of theological and political literacy. The challenge of a new ecclesial paradigm for black churches is problematic at several levels of political and theological complexity. This complexity at one level exposes the nature of imperialism in the globalization of racism, Western capitalism in sync with ecclesiology, and theology associated with North American Christianity. And at another level this complexity is manifest in a culture of privatization and public morality in American life, where matters of racial and gender justice are increasingly subject to the politics of denial joined by "Western Christianity's continual misunderstanding of the theological power of white and black identities."[4] Put succinctly, with few exceptions in the American context, I agree with scholars like Anthony Pinn and Willie James Jennings that "Christian theologians and intellectuals continue to theologize and theorize race and gender identities very poorly."[5] Race, class, and gender justice (the right ordering of relationships and identities for equitable reversals of oppression, poverty, and suffering) require new organizing centers of identity beyond what Henry A. Giroux calls a "neoliberalism that shapes how Americans understand notions of agency, identity, freedom and politics itself."[6] Giroux's observation is very much on point when he states, "[I]ncreasingly a concern with either the past or the future is replaced by uncertainty, and traditional human bonds rooted in compassion, justice, and respect for others are now replaced by a revitalized social Darwinism, played out nightly in the celebration of reality-based television, in which rabid self-interest becomes the organizing principle for a winner-take-all society."[7]

Under an ecclesial paradigm of liberation and justice, I propose that black church activism must take the form of new platforms or Christian logic for theological and political literacy. In order to do so, the old colonial legacies of theological insight must be abandoned for a new theological literacy that not only advocates for an egalitarian democracy, but substantively shifts the pedagogical aims and logic of North American Christianity and theology. While racial exclusion and discrimination in various forms have changed and evolved over time, the outcome remains largely the same as the America version of the God-human relationship, and creation infused in the ecclesial knowledge of black churches is not the theology capable of liberating the oppressed or, as Dubois's famous work puts it, "the souls of Black folk." The past three decades of black and womanist theological discourse has shown the inherent flaw in Western theological identity—what Frantz Fanon termed "the colonial wound" still lingering in the psychology, sociology, and theology of the "wretched of the earth."[8] Quoting Walter Mignol, Willie Jennings's insightful understanding of the lingering disfigurement and disease of the "colonial wound" speaks to the formative power of "blackness in the white imagination" and the hegemonic grasp and hold of whiteness in the black imagination, which perpetuates racism in the theological and conceptual world of race and gender in America.

Coloniality names the experiences and views of the world and history of these whom Fanon called "the wretched of the earth," those who have been, and continue to be, subjected to the standards of modernity. Willie Jennings rightly sees Fanon's "wretched of the earth" through the lens of colonial legacies' wounded existence. The colonial wound, physical and/or psychological, as Jennings notes, is "a consequence of racism, the hegemonic discourse that questions the humanity of all those who do not belong to the locus of enunciation (and the geo-politics of knowledge) of those who assign the standards of classification and assign themselves the right to classify." Jennings further outlines Fanon's analysis that obliviousness to histories and expression lying outside the local history of Western Christianity, as shown by secular Europeans and grounded in Greek and Latin Languages (and unfolded in the six vernacular imperial languages: Italian, Spanish, Portuguese, French, German, and English) "has been and continues to be a trademark of intellectual history and its ethical, political, and economic consequences."[9]

While the enduring legacy of structural racism and gender discrimination helps explain why poverty flourishes along the lines of race, class, and gender, the particular concern of this essay is possessing theological and political literacy about the nature and character of systemic racism and the central role it plays in the production and reproduction of supremacist values of politics and power, which at bottom seeks to define and control the expression of race and gender identities. While racism must be historically and materially defined and located, I maintain that racism is a continuous theological matter, for exposing and understanding its reoccurring platforms of entrenchment against not only change in structural social justice, but the denial of race and gender identities as political and economic considerations. What is inherent in the western Christian and theological imagination and makes for ineptness in responding to disturbing injustices and disparities of poverty along the lines of race and gender, is a continuing dilemma for black church activism. As bell hooks observes, "[E]ven though legal racial apartheid [or segregation] no longer is a norm in the United States, the habits of being cultivated to uphold and maintain blackness in the white imagination and institutionalized white supremacy still linger."[10]

Justice in a diverse and unequal society presents a complex problem for developing an activist agenda to counter twenty-first century realities of race, class, and gender oppression. The level of complexity and the continuing effects of past racial patterns of structural injustice are formidable, to say the least. But they are overwhelmingly demanding for black church activist agendas, particularly those without a fresh understanding of the political character of theology and the exercise of political life and involvement as a theological act. The story of race and gender is a story of place (geo-politics of space and knowledge), power (communal, political, and material), and privilege (access to education and control of communication). I propose here a theological and sociological framework for the formation of a social justice credo along the lines of the suggestions made by the late Manning Marable. In the book *Walk Together Children: Black and Womanist Theologies, Church, and Theological Education*, my article, "The Children Have Come to Birth: A Theological Response for Survival and Quality of Life," includes a revision of Marable's social justice credo, which outlines the basis for forming an agenda to combat systems of power and inequality, particularly in North America.[11] Before concluding this essay, more needs to be said about the contemporary political and economic climate black churches face in their effort to form new ecclesial paradigms with the underpinning and paradigmatic shifts of theological and political literacy. Ultimately, what theological and literacy means for black churches is broadening of their capacity to affirm race and gender identities that embody justice and liberation beyond the moral, spiritual, intellectual, environmental, and theological entrapments of Western ideological Christian logic and subjectivity, which limit the power of Christian faith in what Victor Anderson describes as the "blackness that whiteness created."[12] The durability of white supremacy over long stretches of United States history marks North American Christian logic with a deeply embedded moral flaw that recycles supremacist values within its religious imagination. Liberation has not been and is not today embodied in North American Christian logic; however, it continues to reinvent ways to tighten its hold on a religious imagination in conformity with notions of American essentialism, capitalism, and manifest destiny. Freedom and justice movements in America have resisted this logic with jeremiads taken from dissent and prophetic traditions of black Christianity. Yet "blackness in white imagination" persists as North American Christian logic, and it uncritically perpetuates capitalist logic that economically and politically undermines race and gender identities.

Because the imperialist character and socio-political tentacles of North American Christianity and capitalist logic mutate into complex social forms, the American crisis of systemic racism is a crisis that is part of a global, historical crisis not likely to resolve itself soon. David R. Roediger understands this persistent crisis as part of what cultural theorist Stuart Hall describes as "imperatives of [imperialist] habits" of empire control and dominance. Such persistence amidst challenge and changes, Roediger observes, is like Malcolm X's comparison of racism to various models of the Cadillac, which despite model configurations and design differences leave the essence of the Cadillac brand intact.[13] Roediger notes that although North American Christianity's complicity with capitalist logic of white supremacy has undergone centuries of model changes, there have been no substantive changes in the brand itself.[14] Why white supremacy has lurked, morphed, and survived is not the immediate concern of this essay. Our goal is to determine how such logic can be countered by a new ecclesial paradigm of theological and political literacy. Undeniably, as part and parcel of systems of power—particularly in African American history—racism is a system of economic and political domination that over many decades created and placed the black masses in a complex caste system of poverty. The reconstruction of New Orleans and the Gulf Coast after Hurricane Katrina is a case in point for understanding how over many years public and private institutions—schools, colleges, universities, employers, banks, housing, transportation system, and new media—are complicit with "matrixes of dominance" that perpetuate the cultural, economic, and political reproduction of race and gender poverty. If past patterns of structural racism and poverty provide any clue as to the ways these public resources have been deployed, "the reconstruction of New Orleans and the Gulf follows that same social order based on race, class, gender before Katrina."[15] As Cheryl Kirk-Duggan notes, it is important that in the aftermath of the devastation left by Hurricane Katrina, "we name, expose and ultimately transform systemic, human evil that contributes to disasters when race, class and gender result in those deemed 'other' are being scapegoated, often at the cost of their lives."[16]

Since the events of Hurricane Katrina, arguably the worst storm ever to hit the Gulf Coast, followed by the terrorist attack of September 11, 2001 and the unprecedented 2008 election of Barack Obama as president of the United States, systemic support for racism has broadened and deepened. Hurricane Katrina unearthed weaknesses, inequalities, and prejudice hidden in structural realities of class, gender, and racial poverty that remain formidable socio-political and economic barriers to equitable reconstruction. We are now in a period of frightening and disturbing change. Unbridled militarism combined with unfettered capitalism is part of a trend towards dehumanization that deeply affects minorities. The politics of the theological, Christian, and religious imagination in American Protestantism and Catholicism cannot be overlooked in the role they have and continue to play in making and persevering control over defining race and gender identities, which I argue is tied to the reproduction of supremacist values of power and privilege. Racism's social mode of production and reproduction grows out of profoundly complex economic, political, technological, and educational circumstances that

are tied to American theological identity and traditions. Black church activism against "matrixes of oppression" would be of little if it failed to consider
the influences of western theological traditions, Christian and religious narra-
tions upon nation-building, and the political sensibilities associated with race
and gender oppression. The role religion or theology has played in the making of "blackness" and "whiteness"—the latter in superior images of power
and privilege and the former in political powerlessness and inferiority—is
a matter for theological and ethical reflection. Of critical concern is what
role colonial theological interpretation or religion, particularly the values of
supremacist normativity and excessive forms of capitalist accumulation and
wealth for a few, played in shaping racial representation and nation-building.
In his classic book *The Protestant Era*, Paul Tillich unveils the idolatrous state
of American Christianity now seen in contemporary reproduction of racism
and capitalism as sanctioned by western theology and religion. Tillich's prophetic anticipation of the state of American religion is worth repeating here,
as it speaks to "a hermeneutic of idolatry and hypocrisy" at work in the current arrangements of theology, politics, and religion in America. Religion has
consecrated nationalism without transforming it. Religion has consecrated
democracy without judging it. "Religion has consecrated the bourgeois ideal
of family and property without judging it and has consecrated systems of
exploitation of men by men without transcending them; on the contrary, it
has used them for its own benefit."[17] It is now apparent that the Christian
movement in American is part of a global process of human commodifi-
cation and social fragmentation forcing racial and ethnic communities to
either reflect global networks of exchange and the politics of containment,
or remain socially and economically expendable. Activism against such an
idolatrous system of power must not only discover the knowledge needed for
theological and political literacy, but also create counter-narratives of theology and Christian logic for social change. The reconstruction of knowledge
is crucial for the kind of prophetic activism this essay proposes. Challenging
oppressive race, class, and gender relations requires reconstructing knowledge
to change damaging and dehumanizing systems of oppression.

In his provocative work *The Christian Imagination: Theology and the Origins of Race*, Willie James Jennings outlines the conceptual world of western
Christianity in which theologians have not in any substantive way dealt with
the "ramifications of colonialism for Christian identity and the identity of
theology."[18] Similar to Jennings's thesis is James Cone's theological critique
of white supremacy in his most recent work, *The Cross and the Lynching Tree*.
Cone posits that "the cultural and religious resources in the Black experience
could help all Americans cope with the legacy of white supremacy and also

deal more effectively with what is called 'the war on terror.'"[19] In Cone's view, racialized equality will not happen until serious questions left unaddressed by white theology are addressed. "How could whites confess and live the Christian faith and also impose three-and-a-half centuries of slavery and segregation upon black people? How could any theologian explain the meaning of Christian identity in America and fail to engage white supremacy, its primary negation?"[20] Similarly, Jennings raises this question from the perspective of the Christian-colonial way of imaging the world: "How is it possible for Christians and Christian communities to naturalize cultural fragmentation and operationalize racial vision from within the social logic and theological imagination of Christianity itself?"[21] Jennings and Cone make the fundamental claim that the "Christian social imagination is diseased and disfigured."[22] Jennings links this problem with "the grotesque nature of Christianity's social performance that imagines Christian identity floating above land, poverty, and place leaving these realities to the machinations of capitalistic calculations as commodity exchange of private property."[23] The point Jennings makes is that just as American Christianity has joined with the system of slavery, so has democracy joined with capitalism in an effort to bolster the power of whiteness, a "conceptual imperialism, quietly in operation through America's colonist and theological logic."[24]

The historic election of Barack Obama to the presidency of the United States presents a kairos moment to advance theological and political literacy on the matter of race, class, and gender oppression. What has emerged, however, is an "aversive racism" that denies white supremacy still exists, while at the same time unleashing a new racism in the form of social policy. This phenomenon gained momentum following Obama's victory in the primary election caucuses in the overwhelmingly white state of Iowa, and Obama's eventual presidential victory ushered in the belief that Martin Luther King's dream of a post-racial, colorblind society had arrived in America. Yet what emerged in Barack Obama's first term and the serious determined opposition against his re-election counters the premise of post-racial colorblind society. At best, the Obama phenomenon represents black genius finally reaching the high stage of leadership in America, even as "the Cadillac brand of white supremacy"[25] remains intact.

Barack Obama gives credit to the black church for his formative understanding of the core commitment of the Christian gospel to liberation and justice. As a member of the Trinity United Church of Christ, Obama heard the Reverend Jeremiah Wright inveigh against American racism in ways reminiscent of Malcolm X, Ida B. Wells, and Martin Luther King Jr. In the 2008 primary campaign, when Obama's association with Jeremiah Wright came under attack, Obama gave a speech in Philadelphia to separate himself from Wright's prophetic denunciation of American exceptionalism and view of American racism as being an endemic moral flaw. In the Philadelphia speech, Obama framed a constitutional defense against racism in support of a logic that joined American Christianity and constitutional principles. In Obama's estimation, Christian faith and the principles of American governance will ultimately be victorious against racism. But as David Roediger observes, Obama's view of North American Christian and constitutional logic serves to distort white supremacy, past and present. Roediger notes that Obama moves from casting race as "divisive," to calling it a diversion from "real" issues affecting American life, such as the environment, war, housing, jobs, and healthcare.[26] These are social justice matters of race and gender which North America Christian logic attempts to separate from white supremacist values. But as James Cone notes, "White supremacy was and is an American reality."[27]

The pervasiveness of this Christian logic is perhaps why some whites and blacks alike believe Obama's election affirms America's entry into a colorblind era in which racism no longer exists, however veiled. The colorblind paradigm allows for assimilation and forgetfulness that sanction and give license to forms of structural racism as basic components of America's political landscape and public policy. Behind the election of the first person of color as president of the United States is an eagerness to dehistorize racism, replacing it with evocations of pluralism and diversity that in reality further mask the reality of white supremacy. It is easy to imagine that if one were born in a particular place, with particular opportunities and enough money, educational, economic, social, political, and cultural support that race and gender might not matter—or at least might be rendered non-determinative. However, as Willie Jennings posits, "[I]f a post-racial future is possible that future requires an intense consideration of the formative power of whiteness [and its accompanying literature, art, and theology]."[28] White supremacy must be analyzed not simply as "substantiation of European hegemonic gestures but more precisely it must be examined in its identity-facilitating characteristics of power and privilege, and global deployment of [its version of truth and distribution of wealth]."[29] Analyzing white supremacy requires nothing less that theological literacy that deconstructs this evil and demonic power against the background of the dream of an egalitarian, multiracial democracy.

James Cone's *The Cross and the Lynching Tree* represents the kind of theological literacy and logic that locates what he captions the "crucified people of history," trapped between the dark theodicy of "black faith and brutalized bodies."[30] Cone asserts that until we can identify Christ with a "recrucified black body hanging from a lynching tree, there can be no genuine under-standing of Christian identity in America."[31] Cone's narrative opens elements of theological literacy that enable a clearer grasp of the machinations of death and the demonic at work in the world of racism, class, and gender oppres-sion. As a contemporary example of the lynching tree, Cone preferences Michelle Alexander's observation that mass incarceration is a new modern racial caste system, a version of lynching and control over black flesh. Alexan-der's research reveals that "in less than thirty years, the U.S. penal population exploded from around 300,000 to more than 2 million. . . . the United States now has the highest rate of incarceration in the world, dwarfing the rates of nearly every developed country, even surpassing highly repressive regimes like Russia, China, and Iran."[32] Unfortunately, the creation of this new racial caste system went unnoticed as western Christian identity perceptively took root in prosperity theology—prominent in some contemporary black churches—which in essence mimics the same materiality and commodifica-tion of racial existence in a system bell hooks describes as "white patriarchy capitalist supremacy."[33] This system, born of colonialism, articulates a theo-logical vision bent on eradicating peoples' way of life into perverted practices and processes of commoditized race, class, and gender identities. It is a vision informed by "colonialist logic of Christianity," wholly consumed by capitalist networks of global production and consumption.

It is curious that black churches today have become naïve about the fact that from the beginning colonial Christian reasoning sanctioned violence against black bodies, while infusing the religious imagination of black peo-ple with the necessity of assuring the salvation of their souls. Many black churches are uncritically complicit with a theological framework antitheti-cal to black people's experience and struggle for justice and liberation. The result is that these black churches take their place alongside traditional white churches where, historically, Christianity has been largely privatized within a cultural value system supporting white supremacy.

What forms should black church activism take against supremacist values of dominance, capitalist exploitation and oppression? First and foremost, it must be a theological and political task of activism to decolonize our minds and imaginations toward a new determination, a new social performance of race and gender identity that takes direction from theological frameworks of justice and liberation. The question facing the leadership of black churches is how to determine the strengths of its religious traditions, identities tied to the experience of black bodies. Prophetic traditions demanding alterna-tive justice and political consciousness, and literary traditions affirming cul-tures of black beauty and liberation can theologically inform and organize the effort to confront various forms of human oppression. These traditions show a history of theological and cultural resistance to complete transformation into whiteness. Unfortunately, black churches have accommodated the cultural systems and conditions of post-modernity that insist on a division of life into public and private, individualism and materialism comfortably compromising the prophetic voice once prominent in the faith of black religious leaders. When comfortably domesticated by individualism that promotes an understanding of the self as autonomous and absorbed in a culture of consumption, it is easy to abandon the prophetic tradition and theological vision that gave birth to the particular genius of leaders like Ella Baker, Martin Luther King Jr., and Malcolm X.

Today the global counter-cultural rumbling of discontent and protest against war, poverty, and economic exploitation is a sign that our time is ready for a new era of justice, wherein the identities of race, gender, and sexual minorities are accounted for in the complexities of our multicultural world. The essential theological task of black churches is to nurture an alternative consciousness of Christian social activism, civically responsible to social justice change. To see black churches being revitalized by an outpouring of neo-Pentecostalism, rather than concern for race, class, and gender is a tragic betrayal of the faith heritage and activist tradition that birthed black churches on America soil. It is a problem of theological literacy when black churches carry forward a theological pedagogy thwarted by colonial legacies of race and racism. Since its birth on American soil, black Christianity sought to make sense of a colonialist world in which constructed theological platforms and practices had limited import in effecting change in the world. How theologically do black churches reconcile what they see with what they believe is the basic pedagogical question for Christian activism? When prison industrial corporations warehouse black flesh for profit-making in the United States, and when Africans are dying at a monstrous rate through violence, hunger, and disease, how do these realities form and inform our theological pedagogy and identity?

Carefully attention to the realities of race and gender identities speaks to the need for black churches to construct a theological vision of life inclusive of religious worldviews that affirm liberation and justice. It is important to include religions and religious expression beyond a Christian worldview in order to reflect on the liberation and justice for black bodies touched colonialism's history of oppression. Learning to reread Christian theological narratives marked by the deep effects of disfigured and distorted American Christianity and its socio-psychic and social effects is a task that demands the church and the academy to be in dialogue with each other. I conclude with the insertion of the social justice credo, referred to earlier in this essay, as a possible precursor to the task of building black church activism to explore issues of contested multi-cultural in Europe, Africa, and North America in the search for a new human paradigm for full humanity and justice.

Social Justice Credo

We must strive for theological literacy that makes essential the God-human relationship in the world to reveal and sustain a movement of liberation.
This form of theological literacy deconstructs theological identities that turn God's creation into a culture of privatization, individualism, and wealth accumulation for a few. It is a theological literacy that nurtures the possibility of new identities resistant to racist and sexist oppressive practices, but is not bound by a narrow nationalist conception of identity. At the same time, these new identities draw on the experience of the concrete realities of suffering and liberation of marginalized people.

We must strive for quality education for all.
We must develop the civic capacity of the black community to build and maintain effective alliances among a broad cross- section of stakeholders who will work towards a collective goal for reform of public education. We should demand greater funding for our public schools, investment in black teacher development and teacher salaries, classroom construction, computers, and other materials which make learning possible. We should support anti-racist curricula and educational programs and reinforcing black history and culture.

We must strive for the emotional, physical, spiritual, and intellectual health of black people.
The quality of life, health, and health care involves more than the absence of disease. Black churches should establish educational programs of health awareness that include spiritual, emotional, intellectual, and physical health. More attention must be paid to the political education and literacy of black clergy in the area of public health and poverty. We must be committed to a society that allows for the healthy and positive development of children. We must demand quality education, health care, housing, and safety for every child.

We must be committed to a social policy agenda, which means investment in human beings. We must strive for a society in which all people have the resources to develop their fullest potential.

This can only occur when the basic needs of all people are met. At a minimum, these needs include: free and universal health care, childcare, quality education, lifelong access to retraining and vocational learning, and low-cost quality public housing. We must strive for a comprehensive national and global economic policy that places the interest of people above profits. We should replace minimum wage with a mandated living wage for the poor.

We must strive for justice in the legal system.
Michelle Alexander's work, *The New Jim Crow: Mass Incarceration in an Age of Color Blindness*, considers data from the United States prison-industrial complex, which has become a vast warehouse for millions of poor and unemployed blacks. Her analysis warrants mounting a movement against the systemic racism and calling for the abolition of the death penalty, the twentieth-first century version of a new caste system. Alexander notes that private prison companies are now listed on the New York Stock exchange as "prison profiteers." The prison-industrial complex employs millions of people directly and indirectly. We must build a movement for education, not incarceration. A movement for jobs, not jails. A movement that will end all forms of discrimination against people released from prison, discrimination that denies basic human rights to work, shelter, and food.

We must strive for gender justice and women's rights.
We must support economic equity and the abolition of gender discrimination. We must support strong measures to protect black women's lives from domestic violence, sexism, sexual abuse, and harassment in black churches and the wider society.

We must strive for an end to homophobia and discrimination against people of different sexual orientations.
We should oppose and reject any arguments that exclude or marginalize the contributions of people of different sexual orientations.

We must strive for liberation for all oppressed people throughout the world. We must strive for human and civil rights, justice action, and compensation for centuries of institutional racism.
The struggles of peoples of African descent are inextricably linked to the diverse struggles of oppressed peoples and nations across the globe.

And finally, we must commit ourselves to strive for egalitarian democracy globally.

Notes

1. See "Liberation is Costly," in *Singing the Living Tradition* (Boston: Unitarian Universalist Association, 1993), 593.

2. Donaldo Macedo and Panayota Gournari, *The Globalization of Racism* (Boulder, CO: Paradigm Publishers, 2006), 6.

3. This phrase is used several times in the sixth edition of *Race, Class and Gender: An Anthology*, ed. Margaret L. Anderson and Patricia Hill Collins, (Stamford, CT: Cengage, 2007), 5.

4. Willie Jennings, *The Christian Imagination: Theology and the Origin of Race* (New Haven, CT: Yale University Press, 2010), 65.

5. Ibid.

6. Macedo and Gournari, *The Globalization of Racism*, 72.

7. Ibid.

8. Jennings, *The Christian Imagination*, 115.

9. Ibid., 114, 115.

10. See *Displacing Whiteness: Essays in Social and Cultural Criticism*, ed. Ruth Frankenburg (Durham, NC: Duke University Press, 1997), 168.

11. Dwight N. Hopkins and Linda E. Thomas, *Walk Together Children: Black and Womanist Theologies, Church, and Theological Education* (Eugene, OR: Cascade Books), 2010.

12. Victor Anderson, *Beyond Ontological Blackness: An Essay on African American Religious and Cultural Criticism* (New York: Continuum Publishing, 1995), 16.

13. David R. Roediger, *How Race Survived U. S. History: From Settlement and Slavery to the Obama Phenomenon* (London: Verso, 2008), xiii.

14. Ibid.

15. Ibid, 3.

16. Cheryl Kirk-Duggan, *The Sky Is Crying: Race, Class, and Natural Disaster* (Nashville: Abingdon Press, 2006), xiv.

17. Paul Tillich, *The Protestant Era* (Chicago: University of Chicago Press, 1957), 185.

18. Jennings, *The Christian Imagination*, 125.

19. James Cone, *The Cross and the Lynching Tree* (Maryknoll, NY: Orbis Books, 2011), 34.

20. Ibid., 25.

21. Jennings, *The Christian Imagination*, 208.

22. Ibid., 229.

23. Ibid.

24. Ibid., 226.

25. Roediger, *How Race Survived U. S. History*, xiii.

26. Ibid., 225.

27. Cone, *The Cross and the Lynching Tree*, 65.

28. Ibid., 208.

29. Ibid., 291.

30. Ibid., 45.

31. Ibid., 45.

32. Michelle Alexander, *The New Jim Crow: Mass Incarceration in an Age of Colorblindness* (New York: New Press, 2010), 6.

33. See the essay by bell hooks, *Displacing Whiteness: Essays in Social and Cultural Criticism*, ed. Ruth Frankenburg (Durham, NC: Duke University Press, 1997), 165–79.

In Defense of "Christian Activism": The Case of Allan Boesak

Boitumelo Senokoane

Introduction

The aim of this essay is to contribute to the ongoing discussions about "Christian Activism."[1] I begin this discussion by looking at Allan Boesak, one of the many South African clergymen who have been activists and an outspoken opponent of the apartheid system. This essay reflects on the period when his status as a "minister of the word" in the Uniting Reformed Church in Southern Africa (URCSA) was withdrawn or forfeited because of his involvement with Congress of the People, a newly formed political party, of which he became National Executive member. The action by the URCSA General Synod Actuary and General Synod Support Ministry for Judicial Matters was suspicious, because Boesak was involved in party politics starting in the 1980s, and there was never any action taken against him. What compounded the strangeness of this situation was the fact that other ministers of the word from the Dutch Reformed Church in Africa, and now URCSA—specifically, Rev. Sam Buti (who was elected mayor of Alexander in the 1980s) and Rev. Piet Moatshe (who was a member of parliament representing the African National Congress)—were not subjects of disciplinary action on the part of the church. In essence, the stipulation against Boesak contradicts the history of the URCSA, which has always been seen as "in a position to tie together the way in which Scripture and culture function together in the task of theology."[2]

Boesak's penalty was even more suspicious because it could not be justified by Calvinistic theology or an accompanying African traditional worldview. In essence, the stipulation mocks the dogmatic logic of the URCSA:

Dogmatic refers to the attempt to clarify the distinctive content of the Christian faith for the church in order to enable the Christian community to be clear about what it believes in its witness to the world. It is also an investigation of the content of Christian theology for the practical purpose of considering how that content is to be most properly and effectively conveyed and communicated in each new social, linguistic, and cultural setting.[3]

Moreover, the current URCSA stance on politics implies that the church is restricted to a "certain human association," which I should label "inside the church wall." Boesak's excommunication implies that mixing religion and politics is "heresy." Schall explains this false claim of heresy and its complications, quoting Dale Vree: "What I am concerned about is the failure of current trends of politically oriented theology, which, as Dale Vree has argued, flow largely from Christian 'heresy,' not Christian Orthodoxy. This failure consists in an inability to account for the realities of politics and economics."[4]

The call to defend Christian activism cannot be limited to the Boesak case only; this essay intends to defend Christian Activism using doctrinal and African traditional grounding. However, Boesak will be used as an example of how crucial Christian activism is and to prove that it is effective in influencing ideology, policy, and the wider society. But it must be clear that in any attempt to defend "Christian activism" using doctrinal, theological, and moral arguments, interpretation becomes a critical element because it will impact on the final product called understanding. In this instance, understanding will help to clarify the whole argument—especially the life of Boesak. Thus, this essay will explore Allan Boesak's activist career, proving that Boesak's involvement as a Christian activist was influenced by his church's (Protestant reformed) doctrine and his African traditional worldview, which he labels as context. Generally, the essay seeks to argue that any decision by a Christian to be an activist and politician should be determined by doctrinal, theological, and moral interpretation.

Before proceeding, I should clarify what I mean by "Christian activism." Christian activism generally consists of intentional action to bring about social, political, economic, or environmental change. Such activism can take a wide range of forms, such as writing letters to newspapers or politicians, political campaigning, economic activism such as boycotts or preferentially patronizing business, rallies, street marches, strikes, both sit-ins and hunger strikes, and involvement in party politics, as that is where decisions about life and society are taken. However, some activists try to persuade people to change their behavior directly, rather than persuade governments to change laws. The following section intends to examine the topic of activism from a faith perspective.

Allan Boesak: Faith-Based Radical and Militant

Allan Boesak was born February 23, 1945, in Kakamas, Northern Cape. At an early age he developed his dual interests in religion and politics. He later studied theology at Bellville Theological Seminary and graduated in 1967. By his late teens, Boesak was voicing mounting displeasure with South Africa's apartheid structure. From 1970 to 1976, Boesak studied at the Kampen Theological Institute in Holland, where he completed his doctorate in ethics. He returned to South Africa after the 1976 Soweto uprising. Boesak exercised and molded his political activities through his church, the Dutch Reformed Mission.

In 1981, a mixture of reformed churches established ABRECSA (the Alliance of Black Reformed Christians in Southern Africa), and Boesak was designated as chairperson. The alliance's declaration reflected many of Boesak's beliefs. It discarded the use of religion as an artistic or racist ideology (as employed by the White Dutch Reformed Church, according to the alliance). The alliance rejected the notion of disconnecting religion from political activism. Boesak and the alliance believed that the struggle against apartheid symbolized a struggle for Christianity's integrity.

The impact and end product of Boesak's faith-based radicalism and militancy first received international attention in August of 1982, when the World Alliance of Reformed Churches (WARC) met in Canada. WARC represented about 150 churches of Calvinist tradition in seventy-six countries and boasting membership of over 50 million. During the meeting, Boesak submitted a motion recommending that WARC declare apartheid a heresy contrary to both the gospel and the reformed tradition. The alliance adopted the Declaration on Racism. This led to the suspension of the white church (DRC). Boesak was then elected as president of WARC and held the post until 1989.

In January of 1983 Boesak recommended that all groups opposed to the government's new constitution should unite. The government of Piet Willem Botha had proposed giving enlarged powers to the state president, while allowing inadequate representation in parliament to mixed-race people and Asians and total exclusion of South Africa's blacks, who constituted 73 percent of the population. Boesak opposed the constitution on moral grounds, since it excluded the majority of South Africans, entrenched apartheid and white domination, and accepted ethnicity as the guiding principle for politics in South Africa.

Following Boesak's suggestion, a steering committee established the United Democratic Front (UDF). In August of 1983, before some twenty thousand supporters, Boesak helped launch the UDF at Mitchells Plain out-side of Cape Town. By early 1986 the UDF, an umbrella organization for some seven hundred organizations, was the largest and most powerful legal oppo-sition force on the South African political landscape. Its membership, and especially its goals, approximated those of the then banned African National Congress (ANC). In 1985, Boesak organized a march on Polsmoor Prison in Cape Town, demanding the release of Nelson Mandela, who had been trans-ferred from Robben Island. Boesak was detained and interrogated, and his passport was confiscated. Subversion charges, however, were dropped. After the fall of apartheid in the early 1990s, Boesak remained active in the ANC.

The point being emphasized in this section is that activism is a doctrine or practice of direct, vigorous action especially in support of or in opposi-tion to one side of a controversial issue. Moreover, through the faith-based radicalism and militancy of Boesak, we see the contribution of religion to the struggle for social justice. Corwin Smidt and others argue for the link between religion and society, stating, "[R]eligion can contribute to the foun-dation of democratic society by shaping individual character and virtue."[5] Throughout the political activism of Boesak, we have witnesses the influence of his religious reformed affiliation and African worldview. Moreover, we have seen the impact and effect of Christian activism, as is argued in detail in the following section.

Protestant Reformed Doctrinal Influences on Boesak's Faith-Based Militancy

Boesak's involvement with politics was never coincidental or what he labels "accidental" in a recent book. I am saying this because Boesak is a reformed theologian, and no properly trained and conscious reformed theologian can escape being a politician—be it party politician or advocacy politician. Thus, Boesak is a product of his reformed community, a Calvinist to the core. I will show that Boesak was influenced by John Calvin, but I will concentrate mainly on Calvin's life and Calvinistic theology to show why it is that a properly trained reformed theologian will not escape politics because, "[f]or reformed people, all of life (including art, education, music, government and so forth) belong to God the creator."[6]

The life of Calvin in Geneva reveals him to have been a man with numer-ous political connections. He had contact with important political figures. For instance, he "went to Ferrara, Italy, in February 1536. There he was the guest of Renee de France, wife of Hercules d'Este and Duchess of Ferrara."[7] Moreover, his theology penetrated civil society. C. H. Irwin attests to this influence: "[S]oon after Calvin's coming to Geneva in 1536, he began the work of ecclesiastical organization and moral and social reform. . . . Such reforms, accepted and enforced by the civil authorities, soon began to excite opposition."[8] Later, Calvin's demeanor in the Geneva political arena showed how his theology was integrated into the political order of the day. In Calvin's system, church and state were closely interwoven. And while he maintained, as we have seen, the spiritual independence of the church in matters affecting doctrine and worship, he reserved a large place for the civil government.[9]

The writing of *The Institutes of the Christian Religion* outlines Christianity as both religious and political quite clearly, as the institutes were dedicated to Francis I. Irwin, quoting M, Guizot, states, "In order to understand the fundamental idea and true aim of Calvin's book, we must transport ourselves to the precise period when he originated and wrote it."[10] The prefatory address of Calvin's *Institutes*, dated Basel, August I, 1536, is addressed "To His Most Christian Majesty, the Most Mighty and illustrious Monarch, Francis, King of the French, His Sovereign; John Calvin prays peace and salvation in Christ."[11] Thus the theology of the *Institutes* is one that treats royal authority with respect. He praises the king to try to mollify him, but the *Institutes* nonetheless sent a very strong message that Calvin's theology dealt with political powers. It is a theology that had no option but to be political from its birth.

Dirkie Smit traces Calvin's strong political language even to the theologian's deathbed: "[C]haracteristics of Reformed ecclesiology are already captured and illustrated in the well-known incident on Calvin's death-bed, when he reportedly remembered that when he arrived at Geneva for the first time, there was 'only preaching, no reformation.' For him, reformation obviously referred to the continuous formation and reformation of the social form and life of the church and society, in accordance with the Word of God."[12] By exploring Calvin's life at Geneva, I am demonstrating how he lived as a fully conscious religious-political figure, and showing that reformed tradition as a theology comes from within the "womb" of politics. I do not wish to deny that if Christian doctrine is interpreted in a nontraditional way, some other political structure will follow. This indeed is what can and does happen. What I propose, rather, is that the traditional affirmations are the more fertile and correct ones, if we want to keep a sensible politics that will not promise to men and women something that no politics can deliver.[13]

Reformed tradition offers us the gift of sensible politics. Calvin clarifies that the church should be involved in aspects of life when he says, "Thus life, though abounding in all kinds of wretchedness, is justly classed among divine blessings which are not to be despised. Wherefore, if we do not recognize the kindness of God in it, we are chargeable with no little ingratitude towards him."[14] Calvin does not deny that life has its evils, however, he maintains that all spheres of life, even in the midst of wretchedness, are definitely suffused with divine blessings. Furthermore, he indicates that those who are ungrateful about life will be charged. But if we are convinced that life in its wretchedness is of God, this belief can be used to justify oppressive system. We should take into consideration the warning of Simon Maimela, who asked, "Can we really correlate Christ and Black life in such a way that it is possible for us to claim that Christ is the author of such a truncated and distorted existence?"[15] He asked this because "Blacks have a right to a life of dignity and justice."[16] Throughout Calvin's theology and Calvinism we see that both are concerned with proper diet, proper sexual relationships, proper financial management, proper working habits, proper rest, proper communities and neighborhoods, and proper worship of God—in short, everyday life.

In the reformed tradition, one can never divorce theology from a way of life, because reformed theology is a way of life. One of the sub-headings in Calvin's *Institutes* is "How to use the Present Life, and the Comforts of it." As I have mentioned, when Calvin wrote the *Institutes*, he was engaging with a political figure (Francis, King of France). This engagement shows that reformed theology was a political theology, a claim can only be understood within a framework, which is outlined by C. Gousmett: "The roots of radical Calvinism are found in the thought of Abraham Kuyper, who held that Calvinism solely or primarily as a theological system is to destroy its inherent genius; that is, the recognition that theology is not an end in itself but a servant of the social life of human kind."[17]

Once we consider Calvinism as a worldview, we have to understand what is meant by it. Mokgethi Motlhabi says this about any worldview:

> If for instance, our worldview includes a conception of a God who is concerned about how we live and treat one another in this life, and who will acquire an account of our conduct in the end, we will be naturally concerned to become what God expects us to be and to act accordingly. Our conceptions of the "will of God" will govern our lives and help to give them direction.[18]

Thus a worldview is a particular philosophy of life and a framework that we operate within. Boesak shares this conclusion when he equally declares in his book *Black and Reformed*, "We believe passionately with Abraham Kuyper that there is not a single inch of life that does not fall under the Lordship of Christ. All of life—personal and public, politics and economics, sports and arts, science and liturgy . . . ."[19] Boesak's understanding of religion and politics and other spheres indicates that the Christian should pursue a consistent relationship between life and the spiritual journey. Thus the Christian should set up constructive bridges between the spiritual life and its theology, and failure would contribute to what Gousmett[20] labels "dualism." He says that dualistic thinking interferes with social responsibility. Moreover, dualistic thinking denies that "the scripture speaks directly to political life."[21] Dualism is seen as a contradicting message because we find out about the political struggle of the Israelites in the scriptures. Dualistic thinking is also anti-Calvinist, as this perspective harshly separates holiness from secularism, and yet pastors and so-called laypeople alike are called to serve God in this world. All careers, including politics, are ministries under God. Therefore, all the careers Christians hold are sacred, and their workplaces are the contexts where they fulfill their spiritual calling. The spirit of priesthood in all believers is as important as the teaching of the sovereignty of God.

What should be emphasized is that Calvinism is active faith or faith at work. Gousmett shares the same sentiments: "Calvinism as part of the Protestant Reformation rejected the medieval ideal of faith as the contemplation of God, and instead posited the ideal of faith as obedience to God. Obedience in this context implies responsibility."[22] If, then, it is correct that we are a product of our communities, Boesak became involved with politics because he is a product of his reformed background, meaning that he was influenced by the stories and theology of his community.

African Traditional Influences on Boesak's Faith-Based Militancy

The previous section concentrated on the Protestant reformed doctrinal influences on Allan Boesak's faith and political militancy. This section will argue that Boesak's understanding of politics and religion was equally influenced by his African framework. How likely it is that one can be influenced by multiple worldviews? On this point, Charles Kammer argues, "Obviously we have a number of frameworks that come into play in various areas of our lives. When in the science laboratory, we may have one framework. When we are on the golf course, we have another. We do not hit the ball in order to study the effects of physical forces on its flight. Other frameworks may govern our political life, our family."[23] An important framework influencing Boesak's understanding of religion as political and politics as religious is the African traditional worldview, which he refers as "Black experience" in the foreword to his book *Farewell to Innocence*.

The connectivity between religion and politics in the African traditional worldview is outlined by H. J. Mugabe:

> In their understanding of salvation, many Africans are influenced in their mind-set by their African cultures and their understanding of scripture. For many of them, Christianity in its biblical representation appears to be significantly African. . . . For example, the biblical teaching on salvation does include rescue, healing, liberation and being delivered from physical danger.[24]

The African traditional view of God is of the God who is present. Emmanuel Larbi says this about African salvation which, in Akan terms, is referred to as "nkwagye": "It is made up of two words: nkwa and gye . . . . In short, nkwa means abundant life, that is, life in all its fullness."[25]

The holistic approach to life embraces all facets of being, physical, emotional, and spiritual. These things are inter-connected; one affects the other. The concept of wholeness refers to the idea that all properties of a given system in any field of study cannot be determined or explained by the sum of its component parts. Instead, the system as a whole determines how its parts behave. A holistic way of thinking tries to encompass and integrate multiple layers of meaning and experience, rather than defining human possibilities narrowly. Samuel Pang sheds light on the concept of "salvation as wholeness." Quoting Manas Buthelezi, Pang writes: "Buthelezi emphasizes, the African has a sense of the wholeness of life, and their religions are characterized by it, since there is no separate idea on life and religion in traditional society. In the concept of 'the wholeness of life,' the whole being of man, the living or dead, is a participant of the active presence of the Creator of life."[26] Thus the concept of wholeness brings two worlds together, the world of the living and the dead, a connection between the spiritual and the physical.

Larbi shares similar sentiments:

> In the foregoing considerations of the Akan concept of salvation, I have stated that salvation has to do with concrete realities, things one can identify with in the day-to-day life. It has to do with physical and immediate dangers that militate against individual or communal survival and enjoyment of nkwa, that is, life in all its fullness. It embodies ahonyade (good health, general prosperity and safety and security); it also embodies asomdwei (the state of being which radiates peace and tranquility). This is the general context within which salvation is perceived and appropriated. It is this worldview that Christianity encountered.[27]

Larbi's argument points to the advantages of a salvation that is concretized in the realities of life. But there is also a danger in divorcing the spiritual world from the material and physical world. John Mbiti discourages this divorce, including placing the spiritual world as the first condition to be saved and physical world as secondary:

> Often in the New Testament, individuals are physically saved first by Jesus and through the Acts of the Apostles. Only later does the spiritual dimension of their salvation surface and grow. But this need not be the order or sequence since God's grace is not confined to one method, and the experience of Paul on the road to Damascus is clear illustration of the reversal of this sequence. Indeed many African Christians came to the Christian message of salvation, which speaks first about physical welfare in their lives . . . . What is important here is to consider salvation in holistic terms. . . . Only when one is expressed at the expense of the other, a distortion of biblical salvation ensues and one part of man is virtually excluded and starved out.[28]

African worldviews are of particular significance in this regard, because human beings do not exist for their own sakes. It is therefore not by coincidence that we have a common understanding of human beings in relation to other human beings in the so-called "Bantu" languages across the African continent.

As it has already been pointed out, human beings are not simply women and men in general, who as such are members of humankind. Instead, we are concrete beings who exist in particular societies or nations.[29] Africans take their particular community very seriously, as is shown through the relationship between their God and themselves, their relationships with fellow human beings, and between themselves and the cosmos. The African worldview promotes the care and love of others. Thus, any worldview that does not entertain the "other" (community) is not African. It is foreign to Africa and does not belong. Love and care for the community includes attacking any system that impacts negatively on communal life, and Simon Maimela shows how to go about doing this:

> To confront the situation in which African humanity exists is to confront the situation which negates that which makes for the life of the community. This fundamental breach of fellowship with our neighbours and the refusal to care for them, which is also the breach of fellowship with God and the manifestation of our disobedience to the divine will, is the cause of the concrete sins which we

meet in concrete interhuman relationships: sins such as poverty, socio-economic injustice, political repression, hatred, racism, denial of human freedom and other forms of structural violence against our fellows which provoke conflicts and polarisation between people.[30]

Religion and life are intertwined. Religion is part of our life; so is politics. In fact, religion is our life, and politics is our life. And if religion is our life, and politics is our life, then without doubt, religion is politics and politics is religion.

Based upon this premise, then, it can be argued that URCSA misunderstood and misinterpreted religion in its stipulation that politics is evil and immoral territory. We must take care that unless we include religion our politics, we will be making them more dangerous, because the fear of doing evil will be eliminated. Moreover, failing to give our politics a religious dimension will be un-African and foreign to our traditional worldview that everything is joined together. Religion covers the inner as well as the outer life of people. As W. Miles suggests, "The claim that one can differentiate between authentic religious behaviour and para-theology rests on a controvertible proposition; namely, that one can separate religion from politics."[31] This idea is reiterated by Jose Casanova: "Religion cannot easily be encased in a strictly private individual sphere.... [There is an enduring] tension between religious private and public roles."[32] Even in cases where politicians having a great lust for power try to exploit religion for their own benefit, politics cannot be divorced from religion. The question is, can't we be religious and good citizens at the same time? I believe that if and when we are not politically stable, we will be disturbed in our spiritual life. Senokoane and Kritzinger warn against the privatization of Christianity:

> If we as Christians, who make up a statistical majority of 70% of South African society, do not commit ourselves to significant processes of people-centred development, anti-racism and church-re-unification, but continue in our lukewarm and comfortable private Christianities, we should not be surprised when South African society at large leaves us behind or even spits us out.[33]

In essence, politics are not as private as others would like to believe, because those who claim to be faithful and private find themselves holding baskets and collecting tithes and offerings. So the question should be: Between the politician and the faithful, who compromises faith most?

Moreover, in African traditional settings, "religion and life belong together. Far from being a department of life, religion was life."[34] Adu Boahen expresses similar sentiments: "African culture is intricately intertwined with religion."[35] What has to be clarified is that the African traditional religious system is also the basis for understanding the Christian spiritual experience within an African context and content. For example, Christian liberation theology "claims that political neutrality legitimates the suffering of the oppressed, the very people whom Jesus was sent to serve and save."[36] One can describe African religion as "this-worldly," a religion of salvation that promises wellbeing and wholeness here and now. It is a religion that affirms life and celebrates life in its fullness. These aspects account for the lively and celebratory mood that characterizes African worship in all its manifestations. Africans believe that life is a complex web of relationships that may either enhance and preserve life, or diminish and destroy it. The goal of religion is to maintain those relationships that protect and preserve life. For it is the harmony and stability provided in these relationships, both spiritual and material, that create the conditions for well-being and wholeness.

Conclusion

Since entering the post-apartheid era, South African Christianity has become more inward-looking than outward-looking, frequently emotional, but rarely practical and powerful. For this reason, today's activists in South Africa regard the once radical South African church sector as having retreated to the private sphere, out of touch with the social struggles of the people. Activists today rarely associate these churches with the kind of militant faith embodied by struggle leaders such as Allan Boesak. Generally, South African Christians have avoided power and conflict, preferring cordial relations with business and political leaders in our communities. Now, we are powerless and discarded or treated as a "voting segment" to be placated with a few phrases at election time. We are not seen as a source of wisdom and moral value.

Christian activism or faith-based radicalism and militancy in the context of social disintegration and national polarization demands a practical socio-political and economic engagement with the relevant arms of government and other political players, with the aim of working toward a socio-political contract which will give birth to peace and democratic space for all. For churches to resume that role will require retrieving some of the radical substance and spirit that animated Allan Boesak and other Christian leaders in the struggle against apartheid—and, even now, from the wildernesses of our South African complacency, where their voices can still be heard calling for justice.

Notes

1. This builds on some of my previous writings, including: B. B. (Tumi) Senokoane and
J. N. J. Kritzinger, "Tambach Remixed: Christians in South African Society," *HTS* 63, No.
4 (November 2007): 1713; and, B. B. (Tumi) Senokoane and R. S. Tshaka, "The Christian
Politician? An Investigation into the Theological Grounding for Christians' Participation
in Politics," a paper presented at the sixth biennial symposium on religion and politics, the
Henry Institute, Calvin College, April 28–30, 2011.

2. J. R. Franke, "Reforming Theology: Towards a Postmodern Reformed Dogmatics,"
Westminster Theological Journal 65, No. 1 (Spring, 2003): 29.

3. Ibid., 29, 4.

4. J. V. Schall, *Christianity and Politics* (Boston: S. T. Paul's Editions, 1981).

5. C. Smidt et al., *Pews, Prayers, and Participation: Religion and Civic Responsibility in
America* (Washington, DC: Georgetown University, 2008), 9–10.

6. C. Smidt, "Reformed Church in America," in *Pulpit and Politics: Clergy in American
Politics at the Advent of the Millennium*, ed. C. E. Smidt (Waco, TX: Baylor University Press,
2004), 72.

7. C. H. Irwin, *John Calvin: The Man and His Work*, 2nd ed. (London: Tract Society,
1909), 77.

8. Ibid., 89–90.

9. Ibid., 135.

10. Ibid., 23–24.

11. Ibid., 27.

12. D. Smit, "Challenges for Reformed Churches in Africa: A Contemporary Narrative,"
International Journal for the Study of the Christian Church 8, No. 4 (November 2008): 321.

13. Schall, *Christianity and Politics*, 4.

14. J. Calvin, *Institutes of Christian Religion*, tr. H. Beveridge (Grand Rapids, MI: Eerdmans, 1989), 27.

15. S. Maimela, *Proclaim Freedom to My People* (Braamfontein: Skotaville Publishers,
1987), 103.

16. Ibid., 104.

17. C. Gousmett, *Christianity and Politics: A Reformed Perspective* (Potchefstroom, South
Africa: Potchefstroom University, 1999), 1.

18. M. B. G. Motlhabi, "Ethics and Moral Decision Making," study guide for TIC302-
C, Department of Systematic Theology (University of South Africa, 2001), 81.

19. A. A. Boesak,(Maryknoll, NY: Orbis Books, 1984), 95.

20. Gousmett, *Christianity and Politics*, 57.

21. Ibid.

22. Ibid, 1.

23. C. L. Kammer, *Ethics and Liberation: An Introduction* (Maryknoll, NY: Orbis Books,
1988), 20.

24. H. J. Mugabe, "Salvation from an African Perspective," paper presented at Baptist
International Conference on Theological Education (Johannesburg, South Africa, August,
1993), 34.

25. E. K. Larbi, "The Nature of Continuity and Discontinuity of Ghananian Pentecostal Concept of Salvation in African Cosmology," at http://www. Pctii.org/cyberj/cyberrj10/larbi.html (accessed October 14, 2011).

26. http://yonshin.yonsei.ac.kr/data/%BD%C5%C7%Do%B3%ED%B4%DC50-5.pdf page 457.

27. Larbi, "The Nature of Continuity and Discontinuity," 7.

28. J. Mbiti, *Bible and Theology in African Christianity* (Nairobi: Oxford University Press, 1986), 166, 167.

29. S. Maimela, *Proclaim Freedom to My People* (Braamfontein: Skotaville Publishers, 1987), 111.

30. Ibid., 113–14.

31. W. F. S. Miles, "Political Para-Theology: Rethinking Religion, Politics and Democracy," *Third World Quarterly* 17, No. 3 (1996): 525.

32. J. Casanova, "Private and Public Religions," *Social Research* 59, No.1 (Spring 1992), 17–57.

33. Senokoane and Kritzinger, "Tambach Remixed," 1713.

34. M. Buthelezi, "Salvation as Wholeness," in *A Reader in African Christian Theology*, ed. J. Parrat (London: SPCK, 1987), 95-102.

35. A. Adu Boahen, *Africa Under Colonial Domination: 1880–1935* (New York: James Currey, 1990), 225.

36. Miles, "Political Para-Theology," 528.

Legitimacy: The Praxis of Consensing and Consenting in the Contested Post-Racial Democratic Discourse in South Africa

Vuyani Vellem

Introduction

This essay is concerned with the notion of legitimacy. In this work I am arguing that legitimacy is achieved via a two-pronged process that is validated through consensing and consenting. Both these prongs require mediation by symbols of the marginalized harnessed outside the contours of western traditional forms of ecclesiology to validate state legitimacy. In this work, I will be arguing that after the demise of apartheid there is a disjuncture between consenting and consensing in the quest for state legitimacy. It will be argued that there has been a disjuncture between the political procedures (legal) and the mystical (symbolic, normative), which has a bearing on progressive church activism in the contested post-racial democratic discourse in South Africa. I intend to argue that this state of affairs has been addressed by a black theology of liberation, which expanded the contours of traditional western forms of theology in South Africa in order to frame an alternative paradigm for the continued quest for a comprehensive justice for all.

Political change in South Africa, which coincided with changes in the world, changed the role that church leaders played before the demise of apartheid. The need for a critical assessment of the legitimacy of the current government and, therefore, the state, is urgent. This transformation to an all-encompassing democracy was led by comrades who were on the same side as the progressive ecclesial forces in the struggle against apartheid. The need for a critical assessment urgently needed for the praxis of the church, if it is to regain its social and political potency in the contested post-racial democratic order in South Africa. If Nelson Mandela inspired the formation of the National Religious Leadership Forum (NRLF), is it not fascinating that Thabo Mbeki became a parliamentary "lay preacher"[1] during his tenure as president of the Republic, and that Jacob Zuma[2] became a pastor?

Since the onset of African National Congress (ANC) rule in 1994, the relationship between the church and the state has been an intriguing phenomenon. For the past eighteen years of democracy, political activism by church leaders, among others, seen in the context of the observations we have made above about the presidents of the Republic, has been somehow muted, diffused, or dumbfounded. It would appear that an element of complacency has taken hold in the post-apartheid landscape, in which the assumed benefits of democracy have led to widespread abandonment of the prophetic charge in grassroots activism, such as that undertaken by the church before the demise of apartheid. Black liberation theology can no longer afford to leave the interpretation of democracy to "some," allegedly for the benefit of all. Black liberation theology is charged with continuing the battle of effecting a critical and challenging position on the political class in post-apartheid South Africa in order to bring to the fore the necessity of continued vigilance over what we regard as democracy.

This essay will attempt to accomplish the aforementioned task by examining the notion of legitimacy in terms of differentiating two prongs of this concept: namely, consenting and consensing.[3] These two concepts simply distinguish contract from covenant or legal frames from symbolic normative values. What follows thereafter is a concise exposition on some of the tenets of this thesis, mainly contrasting the language of ordinary people with the language of the powerful in our society. We conclude by examining the undemocratic nature of the neoliberal democracy in South Africa and its implications for Black liberation theology.

Consenting and Consensing: Two prongs of Legitimating

The notion of legitimacy requires that attention be given to consenting and consensing in public life. This requirement is imperative if black liberation theology is to participate in the discourses legitimizing the state after the demise of an illegitimate state of apartheid in South Africa. Luminaries[4] in South Africa have repeatedly stated that it was easy to engage the apartheid state because it was easy to identify the enemy. The argument adds that it is far more complex and challenging to engage theologically in the context of a legitimate state. The enemy or enemies are not so obvious, and the people in power are often one's former comrades and fellow travelers on the journey towards liberation and full legitimacy. In this paper, the notion of legitimacy is approached through the two prongs of consenting and consensing—particularly the latter, which renders the mythological normative and symbolical, indispensable for the legitimization of power. For example, if the Reconstruction and Development Programme (RDP) was a manifesto that the African National Congress sold to the South African public to obtain the people's consent to the ANC's assumption of power, then we need to remember the consensing prong to the consent that millions gave to the ANC's rule. The moral and ethical vision that was expressed in 1994 by the founding father of our democracy, former President Nelson Mandela, in his first speech in government, goes this way:

> Our definition of the freedom of an individual must be instructed by the fundamental objective to restore the human dignity of each and every South African. This requires that we speak not only of political freedoms . . . . My government's commitment to create a people-centred society of liberty binds us to the pursuit of the goals of freedom from want, freedom from hunger, freedom from deprivation, freedom from suppression and freedom from fear. These freedoms are fundamental to the guarantee of human dignity.[5]

In other words, what became known as the "Reconstruction and Development of the Soul" (RDP of the Soul), was a recognition by Nelson Mandela that formal consenting, formal democratic legitimacy, attained through legal processes of elections, democratic procedures, and institutions, was incomplete without a vision of consensing. The latter speaks to dignity—the symbolic and the mythical—cementing and validating the democratic contract that was ushered in after the demise of apartheid. Ultimately, the quotation above suggests that political freedoms are inadequate unless they are bonded to other freedoms that guarantee human dignity. This reminds us of the integrated and comprehensive vision of liberation and transformation that was outlined by black theology proponents in the 1970s and '80s. The movement that was black theology of liberation in South Africa argued for systemic and structural change, and also for a wholesale process of conscientization in order that the affirmation, dignity, and confidence of people at the grassroots was enhanced. The latter was seen as an important addition to the former, because without it, the hoped-for transformation would lack a degree of legitimacy because the powers-that-be would not be held to account. So, without much ado, let us give our consent and agree that the political space in South Africa is liberated.

The 2011 local elections in South Africa, hailed by many political commentators as testimony of political maturity, sealed one of the most important facts about our struggle for liberation in South Africa: namely, the achievement of political liberation. Excitement about our political liberation might have prompted the euphoria that even made us uncritically believe that our transition to democracy was a miracle![6] The danger of such a mythologized notion is that it suspends one of the central features of black liberation theology, the hermeneutic of suspicion. Hermeneutical or interpretive suspicion is often thought of in the context of engaging with biblical texts, but it can be argued that it is of equal importance in interpreting societal changes. It was important that there was an element of suspicion in the joyful pronouncements that a miracle had been unleashed in South Africa's movement to full democracy. Sadly, there was too little suspicion about this transformation, not enough healthy skepticism about the full implications of this new democratic dispensation. In the sheer excitement and perhaps relief of the moment, many of us bought into the narrative of the miracle. Black theologians, too, may have been so excited that some even forgot the scholarly and erudite debates characterized by various streams[7] of this school of thought which, when combined together, signify but one important lesson about the struggle for liberation and black liberation theology's contribution, namely a commitment to comprehensive liberation from organically integrated forms of oppression. Indeed, a cursory glance at the discourses of black liberation theology vividly brings out the elements of comprehensiveness, integratedness, clarity of interlocution, identification with the struggle, and planning of actions of faith (praxis), among others, as profound features of a school that was a departure from the Enlightenment project that ostensibly accompanied the hegemony of western theology and the colonial project of conquest.

The above-mentioned is important because it helps to frame the wider discourse on legitimacy in the context of consenting and consensing. The integrated nature of the comprehensive liberation for which black theologians argued was one that challenged the top-down paternalistic notions of knowledge and power that have been hallmarks of the western theological tradition arising from the Enlightenment. The praxis of faith was one that requires full participation by ordinary people and their lived experiences of struggle in the continued fight for liberation. This was a challenge of developing a shared praxis that worked with and not solely for the liberation of the many. The various strands of black liberation theology, while differing in emphasis and method, nonetheless remained committed to an agreed project of moving beyond a patrician mode of engagement to a participatory model of consensing.

The formal procedures and the constitution of our democratic dispensation have been adequately sanctioned by the will of the people—we must give consent! Nonetheless, if we were to follow on what Amartya Sen postulated some years ago, that political freedom—to reiterate Mandela's point—is not unrelated to the need to remove substantive "unfreedoms,"[8] then the democratic project in South Africa is incomplete. Freedoms must be linked to political freedom, but not constituted or composed by political freedom.

It is one thing to equate political liberation with the attainment of other substantive freedoms that might be linked to political freedom, but another to domesticate other substantive freedoms in the political sphere. One important work by a black theologian that has sharply raised the issue of political freedom, albeit from a different angle, is Allan Boesak's 2005 *Tenderness of Conscience*, which essentially challenges the sophistication of the exclusion of faith from the promises of democracy through a dangerous propensity by the government to equate every freedom we have struggled for with political liberation. His critique of this tendency is even sharper in his 2009 work, *Running with Horses*.[9] The emphasis upon political liberation is one that gives greater credence to the political class, and assumes a negotiated relationship with ordinary people by means of a form of legitimacy that is presumed in a democracy. But as I hope to show, this assumed relationship is not as straightforward or as transparent as one might wish. The emergence of political liberation in South Africa does not necessarily exhibit any commitment to consenting and consensing within the wider framework of legitimacy.

According to Kwame Gyekye, who distinguishes between formal and informal legitimacy, consenting and consensing need further clarification and distinction, and cannot be separated if full legitimacy is to be attained. Let us at this point draw extensively from Kwame Gyekye to delineate the contours of what I think is at the heart of this paper:

> The political institutions that were bequeathed to the African people by their colonial rulers, modeled, as they invariably were, on those colonial rulers, did not function properly. The democratic constitutions that were fashioned by the African peoples themselves suffered the same fate. This constitutional failure— the failure to rule in accordance with formally established procedures—may be explained in several ways. One explanation may be that the African people simply did not have the ability effectively to operate institutions of government that were entirely alien to them, institutions that had not taken root in—and so had not become part of—their political culture and, consequently, failed to elicit

cultural understanding and legitimacy, institutions to which they had no emotional, ideological, or intellectual attachments and whose nuances could not be fully appreciated: such institutions could easily be subverted. Another explanation might be that African people lacked certain moral or dispositional virtues or attitudes (such as patience, tolerance, moderation, incorruptibility) indispensable to the successful operation of those alien institutions. Yet another explanation might be that the political institutions—whether created by the colonial governments or by post-colonial African governments—would have worked well but for the disruptions of the constitutional process by the military.[10]

The first explanation for dysfunctional postcolonial constitutional projects concerns the ability of Africans to govern. We may recall the title of the book by Ronald Sureth Robert, *Fit to Govern*,[11] which attempted to be Thabo Mbeki's apologia on his fitness to govern. Robert says, "[T]he ideologically loaded notion of native 'fitness'"[12] is necessary for us to understand why Thabo Mbeki's administration was constantly put under scrutiny by the white political class of our country. Even though his project was a hopeless fiasco, Robert's alertness to the ideologically laden notion of native fitness is somehow tied to yet another, but different perspective by Xolela Mangcu,[13] who raises alarms about the racial naiveté that plagued if not distorted the heritage of black consciousness. We all remember that Mark Gevisser's *The Dream Deferred*[14] became more hegemonic in addressing the same question—the fitness of a native to govern—by pointing to detachment from the roots as a reason for the deferment of the dreams and promises of liberation.

This latter point takes us to another explanation by Kwame Gyeke, that failure becomes possible due to a lack of rootedness (or rootage, which resonates well with the theme of legitimacy). In other words, for consensing to flourish, formal democratic procedure must be rooted in the emotional, intellectual, cultural, and ideological understanding of a people. Alienation, therefore, is a failure to attain cultural legitimacy by democratic means and procedures that are adopted by postcolonial governments. At this juncture, it might be pertinent to employ the notion of an inferiority complex in association with black consciousness and thus to black liberation theology. Accordingly, the elitist failure expressed as detachment, if Sureth's point about fitness to govern is also taken into account, manifests in the preoccupation by the elites with their fitness. In the process, they lose their rootage in their own mythical and mystical heritage, one shared with their own people—the masses, in our particular case. In this regard Mahmood Mamdani's argument that South Africa is not different from the rest of Africa is an important critical insight.[15] Project South Africa as different has been one form of the sophistication of the inferiority complex that constantly alienates South Africa from its African roots. There has been an ongoing assumption that South Africa can be separated from the rest of the continent. With regard to the explanation of a lack of moral disposition to virtue, I guess I must be very careful! Nothing could confirm Kwame Gyekye's assertion more than the current levels of corruption in South Africa. Our creativity in this regard has even added new words to our lexicon: "tenderpreneurship," and most recently, "pastorpreneurship," both referring to a fast lane to wealth.[16]

To conclude this section, the main point here is to assert that legitimacy is two-pronged. While the legality of our democratic procedure validates the legitimacy of our political liberation, it will be a serious error for us to turn a blind eye to another prong of this phenomenon, namely, the symbolic, the cultural, and the mythical. Of course, Kwame Gyekye argues that traditional cultural values need to be integrated into the process of governance. South Africans will argue that this particular matter has been given attention in our constitution, as the concept of *ubuntu* was incorporated in the original drafting of this landmark document. Recognition of traditional institutions and customary laws inform our public discourse, so what is the problem, we may ask? We do not need to rearticulate or revise black theology's pertinence in public life. Black theology must seriously identify a project of formal democracy, which must be mediated through the symbols of the marginalized. And the process must be in line with a commitment to comprehensiveness, integratedness, clear interlocutions, and praxis for the legitimacy of the democratic project in South Africa.

To reiterate, black theology's public articulation of the vital importance of an ongoing project for liberation cannot be located solely in the singular gaze directed at political liberation. This process of marking the symbolic, the cultural and mythical, requires more than simply invoking *ubuntu*. This notion of the collective and the individual being intrinsically linked, which has become a hallmark of the communitarian spirit of African peoples, is important to be sure, but it can also function at the level of empty rhetoric if it is not supported by broader and more substantial practices that are in line with the ideas I am about to propose.

On Domocracy

The images that are coined by ordinary people can be thoroughly appealing. "Domocracy" is one of them. This term was used a few years ago during my graduate work after one caller, a woman, deliberately used the Afrikaans word *dom*, meaning dumb, to caricature our democracy.[17] Democracy is *dom*! I can still hear the frustration on that radio talk show. As employed in this essay, "democracy" is essentially a heuristic device used for dissonance and ambivalence. It is a residual term, meaning that the woman who coined it used her imagination to subvert the mainstream or conventional terms used to understand the notion of democracy. This is not necessarily a new phenomenon, and there are many examples of how ordinary people use their imagination to "consense" with power in their struggles for survival.

There is, however, concrete experience behind this satirical view of democracy and the creative imagination of ordinary people. The yearning for cleanliness in the city makes a comparison between apartheid and democracy possible and to pour scorn on the latter, because during apartheid, cities and townships were clean. The long queues at Noord Street (a taxi rank) for transport, the long queues and congestion at Park Station, the long queues in Makiwane Hospital (Eastern Cape), in Chris Hani Baragwaneth Hospital, the long queues of women waiting for their husbands who have gone to Jozi to search for work, queues for service delivery, rampant service delivery strikes—all render this formal democratic procedure cynical in the eyes of the poor and the marginalized. The list is endless. In punctuating this point, Mahmood Mamdani states:

> The other side of the politics of affirmative action was the struggle of the beneficiaries of the colonial order—mainly colons in the settler colonies and immigrant minorities (from India and Lebanon) in non-settler colonies—to defend racial privilege. The defense, too, took a historically specific form for the deracialization of the state, the language of that defense could no longer be racial. Racial privilege not only receded into civil society, but defended itself in the language of civil rights, of individual rights and institutional autonomy. To victims of racism the vocabulary of rights rang hollow, a lullaby for perpetuating racial privilege. Their demands were formulated in the language of nationalism and social justice. The result was a breach between the discourse on rights and the one on justice, with the language of the rights appearing as a fig leaf over the privilege and power appearing as the guarantor of social justice and redress.[18]

Domocracy, if we follow the logic of the sentiments above, is an expression of the hollow vocabulary of democracy perceived by the ordinary as a defense of racial privilege. Domocracy is the language used by the ordinary masses to express the lullaby of the perpetuation of racial privilege after the demise of apartheid. To the victims of racism in South Africa—standing in the long queues for everything, and now conscious of the death of Andries

Tatane in Ficksburg—democracy is hollow. We can only heed Ivan Petrella when he says,

> The development of new historical projects must begin by rejecting the main-stream definition of democracy as a political method for choosing leaders. In its present variants, this understanding of democracy completely severs the link between political democracy and the economic foundation of society, a link present even, as we saw, in Schumpter.[19]

Political liberation is not the only freedom for which the masses of South African struggled. The "unfreedoms" of the language and symbols used in the post-apartheid context need to be unveiled. This is the task of black liberation theology. The democracy deficit of the neoliberal ideology, and its synchronization with the demise of apartheid and the collapse of the Berlin Wall, undermine the political liberation that we all attained in South Africa. Scholars of globalization caution that we should not turn a blind eye to the positive aspects of this phenomenon. So, it is the hegemony of the neoliberal paradigm that must be unveiled? The pseudo-religious fervor of neoliberalism, the dethronement of life by profit (reification), the promises that cannot be guaranteed—to mention but a few—are symptoms that challenge black liberation theology to speak out vehemently against the link between our democratic project and neoliberalism. The way the macro-economic policy called Growth, Employment, and Redistribution (GEAR) was introduced in South Africa was simply undemocratic. The Bretton Woods institutions, which are the drivers of this ideology, are all undemocratic. Indeed, the justification and consensing of our democracy based on this ideological choice is *dom*—the lumpenproletariat roar!

Implications for Black Theology of Liberation

The notion of domocracy is a symbol, language, and syntax of the ills of democracy as we see it today in South Africa. Albie Sachs problematizes models of democracy and explains why liberal, social, and Africanization projects may not fit the South African context.[20] The most important point Sachs makes is that is that in South Africa, "we want freedom and we want bread."[21] He says:

> Democracy in South Africa will look at the rich and various experiences of western countries in overcoming the rich and varied forms of absolutism and tyranny

which western countries have thrown up over the centuries. It will pay special attention to the institutional mechanisms which have been created to guarantee human rights, as well as to ways and means of encouraging a rights culture in society as a whole. It will seek to ensure that in terms of language, symbols and personality it has a character that roots in Africa. The fact that religion plays a big role in South African life will find appropriate acknowledgement in the constitution, without creating a state religion or giving any religion preference over others.[22]

The language, symbols, and personality that are rooted in Africa, are indispensable for legitimizing the democratic project. Emmanuel Eze states:

> Any observation of successful political formation or governance, however, will show that the exercise of public power relies heavily on mythologies and symbols: the flag, the *patrie*, the Motherland, "the Party," "God," "freedom," "liberation," "progress," etc. Many of these notions invite, and often demand allegiance and assent from those subjected to them. Yet most of them are simply well-formed ancestral, social, religious, or mythological fantasies that succeed in achieving their effects quite often with little or no "reason." These fantasies frequently enable and persuade people to participate, to collaborate, and to "see reason" with each other and act together.[23]

The observations of Eze are applicable to the South African context. Black people are in danger of accepting symbols that effectively exclude and marginalize them from the substantive politics and economics of their nation. This is not a new phenomenon, as Hegel once declared that Africans are not fully conscious of themselves and as a result, are less human than Europeans.[24] The mythical "fantasies" of black people, while abused to legitimize yesterday's comrades, still leave many black people powerless in the current political environment. Many continue to be sidelined from the formal procedures of the democratic processes by an elite that seeks to prove its fitness and difference from other African states. Albie Sachs helps me articulate this point when he argues that our choice for constitutional democracy is ours because of our own struggle. Justice in South Africa is rooted in the imaginations and hearts of those who struggled against justice, so constitutional democracy must concretize and institutionalize those rights, symbols, and myths that were gained in the battle for liberation. It is therefore not the re-articulation of black liberation theology, but the articulation and institutionalization of the comprehensive vision of liberation in democratic South Africa that can legitimize our democratization processes.

Conclusion

Broadening the overall conceptualization of liberation, one that incorporates the symbolic, mythical, and cultural factors of African life, as outlined previously, can capture the imagination of all who struggled for justice against apartheid. It can be argued that engaging this broader understanding of liberation, beyond the obvious political process, gives rise to greater participation from ordinary black people in South Africa. As evidenced by the creation of the term "domocracy," the agency of an ordinary woman was harnessed to critique the obvious failings in the seemingly acceptable and representative democracy we have developed in South Africa.

Black theology is charged with committing itself to restating the vitality of a comprehensive vision of liberation. This broader conceptualization of liberation is necessary if our democracy is to attain a greater level of legitimacy with ordinary people. The movement towards greater levels of legitimacy can only be achieved if our democracy is infused with an enlarged sense of reciprocity, which can emerge from incorporating notions of consenting and consensing into the democratic process. Consenting and, particularly, consensing require the active participation and imaginative engagement of all those who have struggled for justice in South Africa, not just the elite political class. Consenting and consensing arises when we look beyond the process of political liberation and give renewed attention to the mythical, imaginative, cultural ways in which Africans have constructed their collective sense of identity and imagined equity and dignity for all people.

Notes

1. Former President Thabo Mbeki often used biblical texts in his speeches. Gerald West has even written an article entitled "Thabo Mbeki's Bible."

2. It is a fact that President Zuma, before he took office as president of the republic, appeared on television being robed as an associate pastor during the Polokwane Moment.

3. These two concepts are not mine; they are inspired by my reading of Emmanuel Eze's *African Philosophy* (Cambridge: Blackwell, 1998).

4. One example we can cite is Desmond Tutu, who at his birthday celebration in Cape Town in 2008 painstakingly alerted us to the "easiness" of the task of his generation in dealing with apartheid. It was easy to oppose apartheid, but the challenge for today, as he explained, is to be part of a nation-building exercise, while maintaining the critical distance between the Church and the State. Another attempt is Vellem's 2007 work, The Symbol of Liberation in South African Public Life: A Black Theological Perspective (PhD

dissertation, University of Pretoria, which examines liberation and its pertinence in public life after the demise of apartheid. He distinguishes, among others, the modes of articulating theology and the essence of the black theology of liberation.

5. Nelson Mandela (First Session, First Parliament), Sampie Terreblache, *A History of Inequality* (Pietermaritzburg: University of Natal Press, 2003), 442.

6. For many years after South Africa's 1994 elections, the negotiated settlement and the transition to democracy were couched in the mythical notion of a miracle. Indeed, the notion of South Africa being a miracle became current. One of the black theologians who criticized this notion as perhaps the exaggeration of a mythical metaphor, was Tinyiko Maluleke, who spoke out when the SACC was reviewing the first decade of democracy at Unisa in 2004.

7. One of the best analyses, by Ntintili, identifies three strands: the black solidarity strand, the non-racialist strand, and the black solidarity materiality strand. See Vuyani Prince Ntintili, Contending Notions of Liberation in Black Political Theology in South Africa: An Analysis and Evaluation, (PhD thesis, Drew University, Madison, New Jersey, 1992). Cf. Vuyani Vellem (2007), 65–68, for related debates.

8. Amartya Sen, *Development as Freedom*, (Oxford: Oxford University Press, 1999).

9. Allan Boesak, *Tenderness of Conscience: African Renascence and the Spirituality of Politics* (Stellenbosch: Sun Press, 2005); and Allan Boesak, *Running With Horses: Reflections of an Accidental Politician* (Cape Town: Joho Publishers, 2009).

10. Kwame Gyekye, *Tradition and Modernity: Philosophical Reflections on the African Experience* (New York: Oxford University Press, 1997), 114.

11. Ronald S. Robert, *Fit to Govern* (Johannesburg: STE Publishers, 2007).

12. Ibid., 27.

13. Xolela Mangcu, *To the Brink: The State of Democracy in South Africa* (Pietermaritzburg: University of Natal Press, 2008).

14. Mark Gevisser, *Thabo Mbeki: The Dream Deferred* (Jeppestown: Jonathan Ball Publishers, 2009).

15. Mahmood Mamdani, *Citizen and Subject: Contemporary Africa and the Legacy of Late Colonialism*, Princeton Studies in Culture/Power/History (Kampala: Fountain, 1996).

16. "Tenderpreneurship" refers to the pursuit of lucrative government contracts, and "pastorpreneurship" refers to the widespread resort to pastoral ministry as a pathway to wealth.

17. See Vuyani Vellem, "The Quest for *Ikhaya*: The Use of the African Concept of Home in Public Life" (master's dissertation, University of Cape Town, 2002), 137–56. The notion of domocracy was first used in this work. It sought to capture the spontaneous reaction of ordinary people to the advent of democracy in South Africa. The coinage is used in the same manner here to signify the subversive nature of language used by ordinary people.

18. Mamdani, *Citizen and Subject*, 20–21.

19. Ivan Petrella, *The Future of Liberation: An Argument and Manifesto* (Hampshire: Ashgate, 2004), 52.

20. Albie Sachs, *Human Rights in Africa* (Cape Town: Oxford University Press, 1992), 188–94.

21. Ibid., 190.

22. Ibid., 192.

23. E. Eze, *African Philosophy: An Anthology* (Cambridge: Blackwell, 1998), 317.

24. Ibid., 109.

In Search of a Transforming Public Theology: Drinking from the Wells of Black Theology

Nico Koopman

Introduction

It may not be pretentious to state that right through my life I was exposed to and engaged in what has, since 1974, been called public theology. North American theologian Max Stackhouse states that theologians like Ernst Troeltsch, Abraham Kuyper, Walter Rauschenbusch, Reinhold Niebuhr, Paul Tillich, Martin Luther King Jr., James Luther Adams, and Paul Ramsey contributed to the contemporary development of public theology, but that they did not use the concept or name it public theology.

This concept was used for the first time by the North American theologian Martin Marty in an article that analyzed the thought of Reinhold Niebuhr, *Reinhold Niebuhr: Public Theology and the American Experience.* Thereafter, various theologians started to use this term.[1] Today the notion of public theology is used worldwide. The formation of the Global Network for Public Theology in Princeton, New Jersey, in May 2007 bears witness to the growth of explicit public theological discourse on all continents of the world. Twenty-five research centers for public theology at institutions of higher education from all parts of the world collaborate within this network. The Beyers Naudé Centre for Public Theology at Stellenbosch University is a founding member of this network. In South Africa a growing number of theologians focus on public theological discourse explicitly, whilst others do public theological work without invoking the term. Some of them might even be skeptical of the concept, making room for it only in a qualified way.

During my childhood and youth I was exposed to the so-called informal public theological discourse of my parents, family, friends, local church communities, and local neighborhoods. In informal and sometimes in structured non-formal ways, these people reflected upon the contents of God's love for the world, and they continuously strove to discern what God's love meant for their daily problems and challenges, sorrows and plights, dreams and joys. These people lived with faith in the triune God of perfect love for the whole cosmos. And they reflected upon the meaning of that faith for all facets of their lives, from the intimately personal to the broadest public spheres of life.

They practiced public theology when they dealt with the public challenge of illness, suffering, and death. They would then pose the question what faith in the triune God of perfect love entails when you lose your grandma just when you had completed your teacher education program, and just when you had looked forward to repaying her in some small way for the sacrificial investments that she made in your life. What did this God have to say when you lost your husband in the first year of your marriage, and when you lost the son born of this marriage just when he had completed his training as an artisan, and just when he had embarked on a promising career.

These people from my childhood and youth practiced public theology when they dealt with the dehumanizing impact of the apartheid system on their daily lives. Then they reflected on the meaning of faith in a loving God when macro-apartheid measures determined their population group, areas of residence, and neighborhoods in which they were allowed to live, and what color people they could and could not marry, or with whom they could have a love relationship. What does faith in the God who loves the world so much mean, when various micro-apartheid measures dehumanize you—like the notice boards at beautiful Strand Beach, which read "Whites Only" and "No dogs allowed," respectively.

These people practiced transforming public theology when they reflected upon the meaning of faith in the triune God at the time Nelson Mandela was released. Such a theology was also in evidence when the nation faced the challenge of transformation, the challenge to transform and move from the old South Africa of "diverse and apart," to the new South Africa of "diverse and together." This was a movement from the "old of enmity," to the "new of friendship." This transformative movement from the old to the new incorporated changes in how we saw racism, classism, gender justice, age-ism, homophobia, eco-awareness, and xenophobia, to mention a few of the perennial ills that have confronted this nation. These people reflected upon the meaning of faith in the triune God when they realized that in a pluralis-tic, democratic society, the old ethos of uniformity at every cost and intoler-ance of alternative views does not suffice, and that new ways of dealing with plurality and ambiguity need to be explored. These people practiced a trans-forming public theology of hybridity when they realized that the meaning of God's love for this world cannot merely be described in theological language of vision and criticism, but that new ways to engage with public life from the perspective of faith in the triune God of love need to be formulated. New ways of engaging with a complex public in the context of democratization, Africanization, and globalization have to be found. To respond faithfully to the challenges of public life in this specific context we need a transforming public theology of hybridity.

My own involvement with public theology was nurtured by decades of drinking from the wells of black theology. These wells I discovered first of all in the ministry of Allan Boesak, including his weekly sermons in the chapel at the University of the Western Cape (UWC) in Bellville. I discovered this prophetic theology in his liturgies, hymns, prayers, and sermons in the Dutch Reformed Mission Church in Bellville (which, since 1994, has been the Uniting Reformed Church) and in his lectures in ethics at UWC. They could also be found in his cherished writings, and in his courageous local, national, and international political vision, initiative, leadership, speeches, protest actions, marches, and practices. My growing consciousness was nurtured by my reading of liberation theology, in my formal classes in black theology, and my exposure to lecturers like Jaap Durand, Dirk Smit, Daan Cloete, Hannes Adonis, Chris Loff, John de Gruchy, and again, Allan Boesak. These inspired and inspiring individuals exposed me to a liberating and black reformed theology.

To develop an adequate public theology in our contemporary context, I need to drink from the wells of black theology afresh. The water that black theology offers me to help develop a transforming public theology of hybridity can be described with reference to three central notions of black theology. First of these is the notion that God is involved in the affairs of this world, and that God reveals himself as the God that is in a special way the God of the most marginalized and vulnerable members of human and natural societies. The second indispensable notion that black theology offers to support a faithful transforming public theology of hybridity is the confession that neither classic nor contemporary empires rule us, but that Jesus Christ is Lord. The third notion that black theology offers to a transforming public theology of hybridity is the challenge to develop an ethic of hybridity in a society of complexity, plurality, and ambiguity. This third notion is not explicitly spelled out in black theological discourse, but I reckon it can legitimately be inferred from this discourse.

Public Theology and the God of the Most Vulnerable

The idea that God is in a special way the God of the destitute, the poor, and the wronged is a controversial formulation. It would, however, not be an exaggeration to say that the theme of God's special identification with suffering people runs like a golden thread through scripture. This theme is not referred to coincidentally. It cannot be ignored. Neither can it be countered with other evidence from scripture. Vast biblical evidence shows that this theme is at the heart of the Christian faith.

This confession of God's special identification with the marginalized received specific attention in the reformed tradition. The South African reformed theologian John de Gruchy[2] explains how this notion was prominent at the birth of the reformed tradition. De Gruchy shows that such was the case because many of the earliest reformed theologians and pastors, as well as congregations, were persecuted, and that much reformed theology was conceived in exile, in poverty, amidst adversity, and in the struggle against social and ecclesiastical tyranny.

According to De Gruchy, this theologizing from the perspective of the destitute faded as reformed Christians became part of the so-called middle and upper classes, where the dominant political power also resided. It regained prominence in reformed theology as a result of the challenge posed by liberation and black theology concerning God's preference for the poor. De Gruchy is of the opinion that liberation and black theology's real challenge to reformed theology, however, was to rediscover and to revalue the notion of the preferential option, which was central to the birth of reformed theology. This prophetic challenge was to express its commitment to the public square from the perspective and in the interest of victims of oppressive power.

De Gruchy[3] explains, with an appeal to Gustavo Gutierrez, that the notion of the preferential option for the poor and marginalized should not be interpreted in an exclusive manner, as if God chooses against some. This option for the poor indicates how God works in the world, from the particular to the universal. The option for the poor, therefore, also does not imply that even the poor are ends in themselves. In the redemption and liberation of the poor and wronged, God is working towards the liberation of all, including those we name as oppressors.

The emphasis of liberation and black theology on this notion means not only that the interest of the marginalized should be viewed as a matter of social ethics, but that it be seen as a theological question. How we respond to the destitute in society has to do with how we respond to God.

Public Theology and the Lordship of Jesus Christ

Allan Boesak's theology is characterized by the central role of the confession of the lordship of Jesus Christ. In his first major work,[4] and also in a more recent theological work,[5] Boesak affirms the notion that Jesus Christ is Lord of all areas of life. He spells out the implications of this confessional position for public life, in the first publication for public life in apartheid South Africa, and in the latest publication for the challenges of public life in the very young democratic South Africa.

Boesak draws insights from Paul Lehmann about the extensive reign and involvement of Christ in public life. For Lehmann, the essence of being Christian does not reside in church membership or even baptism, but in whether we acknowledge the lordship of Christ in all walks of life. It lies in whether we recognize His presence and redemptive actions in the historical processes in the world, and whether we see Him at work in the church and in the world to make human life human.[6]

According to Boesak, a black social ethic, or black theology which takes the situation of oppression and dehumanization of black people and all other oppressed people seriously will take heed of the comprehensive lordship of Jesus Christ. His lordship calls for participation in God's liberating and humanizing activities in the world. It pleads for participation in the dawning of comprehensive salvation, or what the African tradition, according to Boesak, calls wholeness of life. This wholeness is expressed in liberation from internal bondage and external enslavement, and from psychological, cultural, political, economic, and theological dependency and oppression.[7]

As a member of the student congregation that Boesak ministered to in the apartheid years, I remember how this notion of the lordship of Christ enabled us to overcome the theological dualisms to which some strands of so-called reformed preaching wanted us to adhere. One of these was that salvation is only a spiritual matter, it is only for the soul. A life of quality is for the hereafter. One day when you die there will be a pie in the sky, was the motto. We suddenly found clear theological articulation for the public theology we were taught at home when our struggling parents told us about a God who does not view us as inferior, although apartheid ideology does. They told us about a God that held out the promise that injustice will not win the day, although the might of the oppressive apartheid regime seems to be invincible. The latter was true because there is a throne in heaven, and we need not fear, although the earthly thrones pose continuous threats to all who will not submit.

Yes, this notion of the comprehensive lordship of Christ broadened our understanding of Christian salvation; it opened our eyes to see that God is at work in all walks of life. It challenged us to develop broader understanding of obedience, faithfulness, social ethics, public theology, and public witness. Political life, economic life, ecological life, life in civil society, participation in the formation of public opinion—all of these came to be included in a life of discipleship. Though there are important distinctions between discipleship and citizenship,[8] they did not stand in an antagonistic relationship any longer. And it was exciting to perform these re-definitions within the framework of reformed theology.

But this notion of the reign of Christ encouraged and comforted us. And the famous chorus He's got the whole world in his hands powerfully expressed this faith in the inclusive and comprehensive reign of Christ. Moreover, it confirmed that we were all in safe hands in the midst of so much danger and insecurity. In his book of almost three decades later, it is clear that Boesak's understanding of the public role of the church is determined to an even greater extent by the notion that Jesus Christ is Lord. During the apartheid years, it was important to see that not the apartheid regime, but Jesus Christ is lord. And now that former comrades in the struggle are in government, there is real temptation for this vision of the reign of Christ to become blurred, with absolute, uncritical loyalty bestowed on the new, democratically elected government. In his discussion of the position of the church towards South Africa's first democratically elected government, Boesak offers a detailed critique of the notion of critical solidarity with the government. His analysis is informed by the notion that Jesus Christ is lord. The following long quotation articulates the foundation and core features of a public theology in democratic South Africa.

[F]or Christians from the Calvinist tradition the Lordship of Jesus Christ remains central in our thinking and our doings in the world. There is not one inch of life that does not fall under the sovereignty of Christ. No matter how sovereign nation states or other political entities regard themselves to be, ultimate sovereignty belongs only to God. There is thus no way in which a government can determine the boundaries of the testimony of the church, or dictate the public actions of the church. For the church to speak publicly on behalf of the poor, the silent and the dejected, and for justice, peace and equity, is a biblical mandate the church dare not ignore or forget. We learned our commitment to justice and the poor not from Marx or Lenin, but from the Torah, the prophets and Jesus of Nazareth. We have inherited our passion not from political slogans and ideological philosophizing, but from the Psalms and the revolutionary songs of biblical women like Hannah and Mary, the mother of Jesus. The church of Jesus Christ is not just another non-governmental organization, however much the government would like to classify us as such. The church cannot be relegated to the sideline activism of volunteerism, charity and apolitical cheer-leadership, especially not at a time when critical engagement with our elected government is crucial in facing issues such as globalization, economic justice, HIV/AIDS and nation building, and the voice for public justice is so burningly necessary.[9]

According to Boesak, seen from a reformed perspective, the basis for public involvement is the lordship of Jesus Christ. This basic presupposition has important implications for doing theology in contemporary South Africa. As Boesak states:

> Highest loyalty is paid to God and not to earthly powers, not even to democrati-cally elected governments and former struggle comrades and their agendas.[10]
>   The church has a unique contribution to make to public life since it is a unique servant of the Lord of the universe.[11]
>   The Public Theology of the church is informed by the rich catholic and ecu-menical Judaeo-Christian tradition.[12]
>   The church does not accept a form of democratic centralism which implies that the masses of people, including churches, are marginalized within a democracy and that a select group of the political elite and intellectuals plan and execute the process of political transformation.[13]
>   The church is not a junior partner of government with the role of praise singer, but the church speaks out critically and cooperates with government on the formation of public opinion through inclusive public debate, and also the for-mulation and implementation of public policy on behalf of the silenced, most wronged and vulnerable in society.[14]
>   The primary solidarity of the church is not with governments, but with the poor, wronged and vulnerable.[15]

Public Theology and an Ethic of Hybridity

In black theological discourse, the view is continuously confirmed that the notion of blackness cannot be reduced to simply a color category, and that it cannot be used in an exclusive manner. For Boesak, the notion of black should not be reduced to a color category. The term refers to various black groups in South Africa. The experience of oppression and dehumanization of all black people is embodied in the word. To talk about black is to recog-nize your own agency and worth, and to become aware of what you suffer because of your blackness. But to do so is also to be aware of your power to change the situation. Blackness does not operate in isolation from other forms of identity. Black oppressed people can express true solidarity with all oppressed groups. They also have the power to love those who oppress them and to enhance their repentance and healing. In this sense, blackness refers to all forms of oppression and marginalization.[16] Against this background, one can infer that black theological discourse challenges us to develop categories that pave the way for inclusivity, whilst simultaneously giving priority to and addressing the plight of the most vulnerable and wronged in society.

I believe that the notion of hybridity offers a category that is inclusive and inviting, and that simultaneously facilitates and enhances the quest for actual dignity, justice, and freedom. Hybridity is used in contemporary social scientific discourses in the context of post-colonization and globalisation.[17] The word, which literally means mixture, has its origins in different plant species and different racial groups. It refers, for instance, to the mixing of races. In modern race discourse, these hybrid or mixed races were viewed as the most inferior races, particularly in various frameworks that prized notions of purity.

A more positive view of the concept of hybridity has developed in the last few decades. In racial discourse, the idea of a so-called pure race without any form of hybridity is increasingly rejected. In apartheid South Africa, the work of the historian Hans Heese, which traced the roots of some extremist white apartheid ideologists to the Khoi-San indigenous groups, amongst others, caused quite a stir, and paved the way for a revaluation of the notion of hybridity.[18]

Employment of the notion of hybridity in social scientific discourse that is of special interest. Hybridity challenges certainties and essentialisms. It resists monophony and promotes the idea of polyphony. It carries the notion of liminality, which refers to an in-between state during which old, certain, clearly defined identities are re-negotiated, and the door is opened for the new, the imaginative, and the surprising. Hybridity acknowledges complexity and ambiguity. Although there is criticism of the notion of hybridity—amongst others, that it is too theoretical and that it is employed in questionable ways, for example with regard to sexuality—I think nevertheless that it is worth exploring the constructive potential of the notion.

Hybridity, it seems to me, does not advance a type of mixing that dissolves the entities that mix, that brings forth a totally new uniform entity. Hybridity, rather, refers to a mingling, to an exposure to the other, dialogue with the other, interaction with the other, participation in the life of the other, hospitality to the other, and learning from the other. This exposure does not leave you unchanged. You have internalized something of the other.

Owing to participation in each other's lives, it becomes increasingly difficult to talk about yourself as merely coloured or South African. Participation in the lives of my black, white, and Indian brothers, and in the lives of my brothers and sisters from other countries, has not left me unchanged. This exposure affects me and now co-defines me. I am still a coloured, but I am also more than that. I am still South African, but at the same time I am more than that.

Through sharing in the lives of my Dutch Reformed brothers and sisters, my ecclesial identity has become more complex. I am still Uniting Reformed, but I am also more than that. And through exposure and hospitality to other confessional traditions, I have become something other, something richer than just a reformed Christian. I am still reformed, but I am simultaneously something more.

This "something more" applies to all the others with whom I mingle, commune, share, with whom I live in a relationship of interdependency, and in whose lives I participate. These others are of other genders, sexual orientations, socio-economic groupings, age groups, and also dis- or differently abled persons, as well as the natural environment. And where this proximity and mingling, sharing and solidarity grow, and a life of reparative healing and forgiveness takes shape.

I suggest some ways in which an ethic of hybridity can serve processes of inclusion, reconciliation, and justice. We might deal more constructively and faithfully with the challenges of reconciliation and justice in our societies if the following features of an ethic of hybridity guide and drive us. I suggest at least seven features of an ethic of hybridity in service of inclusion, reconciliation, and justice.

Plurality

There is a plurality of voices, opinions, and perspectives on challenges like reconciliation and justice. These voices are manifold and often contradictory. An ethic of hybridity accepts this plurality and deals constructively with it by exposure of views to each other, through dialogue and the search for consensus—or even through peaceful co-existence and continuous deliberation in the case of incommensurable positions.

Ambiguity

Ambiguity refers to the fact that the same phenomenon or reality can be described in different and even contradictory ways by different people and in different contexts. Ambiguity also refers to the shifting meanings of words, sentences, and concepts. Often we want to avoid ambiguity.[19] People who cannot live with ambiguity choose absolutism or relativism. Absolutism implies that only my interpretation, description, and solution is right.

Absolutism and paves the way for judgmentalism, fundamentalism, even some form of anti-intellectualism or irrationality—and also the stereotyping, stigmatization, demonization, and annihilation of the other. Relativism feeds an attitude of passivity, acedia, melancholy, pessimism, internal emigration, and nihilism.

In our reconciliation and justice discourses, we have seen that either one of these—absolutism and relativism—can be a popular option. Traveling the road of ambiguity calls for wisdom, courage, and patience. It also calls for the ability to communicate sophisticated positions in clear and intellectually accessible ways. Ambiguity should not be confused with lack of clarity and vagueness.[20]

Complexity

We need to investigate the lessons that South Africans can learn from the quests for reconciliation, justice, and transformation in other post-liberation contexts. For the purposes of this discussion, I am thinking of such contexts as the post-South African War period, the post-Second World War era in Germany, the post-civil rights struggle years in the United States, and many others. This broader focus will shed more light on our own struggle. Thorough historical and cross-national analyses of our own and other quests for reconciliation and justice will help us describe our own challenges in a more nuanced way. It will also help us find strength and hope in others who struggle hard to actualize unity and reconciliation, justice and peace. Moreover, the broader focus helps to develop the right emotional orientation and sensitivity for our local challenges. It might free us from both over-sensitivity and insensitivity, which are stumbling blocks on the road to peace.

Duality

To address the challenging questions regarding reconciliation and justice we also need to live with duality. I mean here the capacity to live with the notion of "both" and "and," and not only with the more famous "either/or." We need to say yes to more than one thing, even though it might look as if these things contradict each other.

Take the question of whether we should talk about the past. Should we still continue to talk about the past? Yes! Yes, because if we do not talk about the past, anger and pain, shame and guilt will keep on haunting us. Should we stop talking about the past? Yes, because if we do not stop talking about the past we might keep each other trapped in that past, and foreclose the wonderful prospect of journeying together energetically into the future.

Or take another question: Do we need to refer to each other in color categories? Yes, we need to do this for the sake of trying to achieve some reparation for wrongs that were committed along color lines for centuries. But we deal with the past on the condition that this is a fairly applied and interim arrangement, and that we do so only if we also address other categories of injustice, such as those pertaining to gender, class, disability, age, and the environment. Do we need to stop referring to each other in terms of color? Yes, we need to avoid racial categorization for the sake of working together to actualize the vision of a non-racial South Africa!

An ethic of hybridity teaches us to say yes simultaneously to contradictory questions.

Paradoxality

Church reformers like Martin Luther identified the paradoxical nature of human anthropology. We are simultaneously sinners and justified individuals. This paradox, this apparent but faux contradiction permeates human existence. Faithful servants of reconciliation and justice learn to live with the tension of paradoxality. A while ago, the first black or coloured rector of the Free State University wrote about his positive experiences at the rugby test match between South Africa and New Zealand in Bloemfontein. A Sotho person sang traditional Afrikaans folksongs. The mainly white spectators loudly supported the brilliant black Springbok prop forward. At an earlier soccer match he attended, the main hero of the mainly black spectators was a white player for the South African national soccer team.

After reading this account, I watched the next rugby test a week later at the reunion function of university residence Huis Visser, where I was warden. A few hundred former residents of Huis Visser watched the match in a tent on a big screen. They jointly sang South Africa's national anthem. They sang the non-Afrikaans part just as loudly and enthusiastically as the Afrikaans part. They knew all the non-Afrikaans words. I was energized by the realization that these men, some of whom are in their eighties, sang the new anthem of a new society on the same grounds where they sang the anthem of apartheid South Africa for many decades. One of them even shouted out, "We should have recorded this on video!"

With these hopeful experiences in my mind and heart, I attended the celebration of a friend's fiftieth birthday later that evening. While we stood in line for food, one of the guests told me that he cannot support the Springbok rugby team. He explained that at the test match in Bloemfontein (the one that filled Jansen and me with hope for reconciliation and justice), a few white supporters insulted coloured supporters who were wearing Springbok jerseys. They told these coloured people that they were wearing the jerseys that actually belong to white people.

Although living in the same country, and sharing the same rugby stadium, these South Africans represent seemingly contradictory experiences. To serve reconciliation and justice we need to hold on to both. We cannot recognize only one of the two. We need to say yes, there are good things happening in South Africa; otherwise we will become discouraged, melancholic, and apathetic and acedic and unfaithful to our God-given calling. And yet, we need to say yes, there are still bad things happening in South Africa; otherwise we will become unrealistic and naive, and we will be insensitive to the pain and anger in our society. We must live with this paradoxality.[21]

Proximity

An ethic of hybridity also advances the notion of proximity amongst people. The logic of the three articles of the Belhar Confession is that visible, concrete, experienced unity, where people develop sympathy, empathy, interpathy, and solidarity (article 1), stands in service of reconciliation (article 2) and justice (article 3). Reconciliation and justice grow where people do not live outside of hearing distance[22], but where we hear each other, see each other, feel each other, participate and share in each other's lives, in our joys and sorrows, in our guilt and shame, in our anger and pain.

Absurdity

The last feature of an ethic of hybridity has to do with a logic that seems to be absurd, ridiculous, and foolish. For reconciliation and justice to materialize, we need forgiveness. Forgiveness opens the door for recognition of guilt, contrition, remorse, and confession of guilt in the face of overwhelming and forgiving love, a confession of faith that accepts forgiveness, a confession of hope that says yes to a new life of sanctification and restitution. Following such logic, Archbishop Emeritus Desmond Tutu calls his famous book *No Future Without Forgiveness.*[23]

South Africans are continuously surprised by private and public experiences of this absurd love, this forgiving love. This love is embodied in the life and person of Nelson Mandela. This absurd, forgiving love was experienced during the hearings of the Truth and Reconciliation Commission.

Manifestations of this love granted South Africa the wonder of a transition to democracy without civil war. The sustainability of our peace is dependent upon our commitment not to cheapen this forgiveness. We live with the hope and expectation that the wonder of a love that forgives will open the gates to a responding love that repents and repairs, a love that heals the brokenness and that rights the wrongs.

Conclusion

To be a transforming public theology, the vision and aim, methodology and approaches, agenda and priorities, interlocutors and language of public theology need to be informed and transformed by the central convictions of God's bias for the wronged, the lordship of Jesus Christ, and an ethic of hybridity. To fulfill a transforming and humanizing role in contemporary society, public theology needs to stand where God stands—namely, with the wronged and against dehumanization, injustice, and oppression. To fulfill a transformative and liberating role in a world fraught with the pervasive spirit and structures of empire, the lordship of Christ is the central conviction of those engaged in public theology. And to address the complexities of contemporary society faithfully, public theology is in urgent need of an ethic of hybridity. Older black theologians articulated these notions eloquently and convincingly. The journey should continue with new generations of black theologians in the United States, Britain, Africa, and other parts of the world—especially with the growing number of exciting women's voices in our ranks![24]

Notes

1. See M. Stackhouse, "Public theology and Ethical Judgment," *Theology Today* 54 (1996): 165, 167.

2. J. De Gruchy, "Towards a Reformed Theology of Liberation? Can We Retrieve the Reformed Symbols in the Struggle for Justice?," in W. A. Boesak and P. J. A. Fourie, eds., *Vraagtekens oor Gereformeerdheid* (Belhar: LUS Publishers, 1998), 74–76.

3. J. De Gruchy, *Liberating Reformed Theology: A South African Contribution to an Ecumenical Debate* (Grand Rapids, MI: Eerdmans, 1991), 133–34.

4. Allan Boesak, *Farewell to Innocence: A Social-Ethical Study of Black Theology and Black Power* (Johannesburg: Ravan Press, 1977).

5. Allan Boesak, *The Tenderness of Conscience: African Renaissance and the Spirituality of Politics* (Stellenbosch: Sun Press, 2005).

6. Ibid., 73–74.

7. Ibid., 112–13.

8. Boesak rightly refers to the warning of Bishop Zulu that human action not be identified with divine action, or in line with the themes here, that all activities of a citizen not be described as activities of a disciple of Jesus Christ per se: "Black theologians, he [Bishop Zulu] warns, should guard against equating God being on the side of the oppressed with the oppressed being on the side of God, and equating human love with God's love." See Boesak, *Farewell*, 111.

9. Boesak, *Tenderness*, 166–67.

10. Ibid., 154–60.

11. Ibid., 166.

12. Ibid.

13. Ibid., 164–66.

14. Ibid., 162–63.

15. Ibid., 168–70.

16. See Boesak, *Farewell*, 27–29, 109–10. "Blackness does not in the first place designate colour of skin. It is a discovery, a state of mind, a conversion, an affirmation of being, which is power. It is an insight that has to do with wisdom and responsibility; for it is now incumbent upon black people to make South Africa a country in which both white and black may live in peace. 'We have seen enough of white racism,' writes Adam Small [South African poet], 'we have suffered enough from its meaning—we cannot want to be racist in our blackness.'" See Boesak, *Farewell*, 110.

17. Some helpful sources on the notion of hybridity are: R. Young, *Colonial Desire: Hibridity in Theory, Culture and Race* (London: Routledge, 1995); J. Nederveen Pieterse, *Globalization and Culture: Global Mélange* (Oxford: Rowman & Littlefield, 2004); Homi K. Bhabha, *The Location of Culture* (London: Routledge, 1994). I use the notion of hybridity heuristically. The idea of hybridity might open new imaginative possibilities in our reflections on themes like justice and reconciliation. I also use it rhetorically. It helps to make Christian convictions accessible to contemporary public life. Lastly, I use the concept existentially. Although all races are hybrid in nature, I belong to an ethnic group that is described as the most hybrid!

18. H. F. Heese, *Groep sonder grense: die rol en grense van die gemengde bevolking van die Kaap, 1652–1795* (Pretoria: Protea Boekhuis, 2005; first edition 1984).

19. For a discussion of our resistance to ambiguity, see Donald N. Levine, *The Flight from Ambiguity: Essays in Social and Cultural Theory* (Chicago: University of Chicago Press, 1985).

20. For one of the best discussions of the notions of plurality and ambiguity, see David Tracy, *Plurality and Ambiguity: Hermeneutics, Religion, Hope* (Chicago: University of Chicago Press, 1994).

21. Dirkie Smit recently demonstrated the complex and paradoxical nature of our contemporary zeitgeist. In a lecture on the future of systematic theology, he argued that our zeitgeist is simultaneously becoming both more secular and more religious, both anti-foundational and fundamental, both positive about globalization and negative about it. See D. Smit, "Quo Vadis, Sistematiese Teologie?," *Scriptura: International Journal of Bible, Religion and Theology in Southern Africa* 1 (2009): 42–53.

22. In the apartheid era, South African philosopher and public intellectual Willie Esterhuyse wrote a book to describe the distance, separation, and alienation amongst South Africans. See W. P. Esterhuyse, *Broers buite hoorafstand: skeiding van die kerklike weë* (Kaapstad: Tafelberg, 1989).

23. See D. Tutu, *No Future Without Forgiveness* (London: Rider, 1999). For a helpful explication of this logic, see D. Smit, Confession-Guilt-Truth—and Forgiveness in the Christian Tradition, in E. Conradie, ed., *Essays in Public Theology* (Stellenbosch: Sun Press, 2007).

24. For an example of a recent doctoral dissertation that strengthens the dialogue between black theology and public theology, see N. Tenai, "The Poor and the Public: A Critical Evaluation of Public Theology from a Black Theological Perspective" (Stellenbosch University, 2010).

V. Concluding Thoughts

Whither Transcendence? Framing the Contours of Transatlantic Black Unity in Contested Post-Racialized Times

William Ackah

Three landmark struggles for freedom can be said to define the main contours of black identity in the twentieth century: the struggle to end apartheid
in South Africa, the battle for civil rights in the United States, and the fight
to end European colonialism in Africa. These events and the actors that took
part in them proved to be an inspiration for peoples of African descent and
others all over the world, providing a sense of solidarity and identity for those
suffering discrimination and oppression based on "race." This paper seeks to
engage with selected theological discourses emanating from two of these
struggles, those for civil rights and against apartheid. The focus is to consider
the utility of both struggles in inspiring and articulating a black unity and
collective consciousness for contested post-racialized times.

The emergence of black theological discourses in the United States and
South Africa as concrete responses to the scourge of racism was a critical
intervention in re-orienting the dimensions of religious thought that had
largely been the domain of white theologians. One of the concerns of this
essay is to consider whether ideas developed by black religious thinkers in
eras of systematic racialized oppression still have utility in an era some have
described as post-racial. Does the past, the wisdom of ancestors living and
dead, provide us with insights that can guide the future for transatlantic black
alliances? To what extent do new times demand new questions and new tools
for analysis?

I seek to answer these questions by a close reading and critical examination
of two texts from two key thinkers written during the civil rights and anti-
apartheid struggles. The two are Howard Thurman's *The Luminous Darkness:
A Personal Interpretation of the Anatomy of Segregation and the Ground of Hope,*[1]
and the other is Allan Boesak's *Farewell to Innocence: A Socio-Ethical Study on*

Black Theology and Power.[2] The life and work of both Howard Thurman and
Allan Boesak have in different ways been subject to much scrutiny and analysis, and both men are key figures in the history of, respectively, American and
South African religious and cultural life—Thurman as an educator and spiritual leader, and Boesak as a theologian, church leader, and political activist. It
is not the intention of this work to delve into their respective backgrounds and
assess their lives and works wholesale. These individuals were chosen because
both have been able to articulate a faith-based understanding of black experiences under oppressive circumstances from local, national, and global perspectives. The texts in question address issues related to the black church and
black community in the context of a segregated/integrated dichotomy, the
issue of whiteness and white institutional power, and both articulate a vision
of the potential of a Christian-inspired praxis to provide a model of societal
practice to end injustice and herald the arrival of a better society.

I am conscious that in reaching into the past, the works that I have chosen
are the writings of men, and while this fact in some ways reflects cultural
limitations of that historical era, nevertheless, in assessing the utility of these
works, this gender dimension will not go unaddressed. Part of the determination as to the utility for the contested post-racialized era of texts bearing on
black theology is whether these works can withstand what Jacqueline Grant
has described as the self-test.[3] This would include the degree to which these
works can articulate the oppression experienced by black women and offer
strategies that liberate them from the constraints of patriarchy as well as racism. One of the themes this essay seeks to consider in thinking about links
and possible discontinuities between the liberationist thought and practice
during the civil rights and anti-apartheid struggles and struggles of black
peoples within contemporary post-movement contexts, is whether the ideas
of the past have continuing relevance cross-culturally and trans-nationally in
African and African diasporic settings. Of interest as well is whether earlier
black theological assessments address issues related to oppressive practice
allied to but not subsumed by "race," such as social divisions based on gender,
sexual orientation, disability, class.

This essay argues that the construction of a broad anti-oppressive framework for trans-national black church thought and ethics is crucial for forging new and ongoing linkages between people of African descent across the
globe. The essay begins here by examining how the selected writings by Thurman and Boesak address: (1) black identity as a foundation for unity; (2) how
ideologies and practices of whiteness factor into formulations of blackness;
and (3) Christian thought and practice as the basis for a new society.

The Contours of Blackness in Church and Community:
A Continuing Racialized Framework?

A feature that segregation in the United States and in apartheid-era South Africa shared was the denial of basic human dignity for black people. Both systems, in their legal framings, social customs, economic transactions, and theological justifications sought to marginalize black people and confer on them second-class status. Howard Thurman recounts a personal childhood experience that exemplifies this state: A young white girl pricked him with a pin and stated, "That did not hurt you—you can't feel." Reflecting on the encounter, Thurman writes, "In other words, I was not human, nor was I even a creature capable of feeling pain."[4]

So having experienced this denial of his own humanity, and having witnessed the indignities suffered by African Americans and peoples of color all over the world, how did Thurman regard the utilization of blackness as an identity and tool that could be used to eliminate oppression and improve the lives of African Americans and others? Thurman outlines a complex understanding of black identity and identification, recognizing the importance of these factors in sustaining and enhancing the lives of black people in the face of dehumanization by whites, but not regarding blackness as an ultimate source of liberation or salvation in its own right. Thurman outlines this analysis with a profound statement at the opening of his book: "I know that a man must be at home somewhere before he can feel at home everywhere. Always the sense of separateness that is an essential part of individual consciousness must be overcome even as it sustains and supports. This is the crucial paradox in the achievement of an integrated personality as well as an integrated society."[5] For Thurman, the achievement of the integrated society did not mean that African Americans had to give up their culture or forgo their sense of identity and collective belonging. He saw value in black institutions and the role that they played in the community:

> It [black institutions, churches, businesses] establishes identity and confers persona upon individuals. It makes for the feeling of being "at home." But most important, it exploits whatever there is of an ethnic idiom. And this is good, very good. Such grounding of personal dignity gives to individuals a sense of center which in turn serves as a foil for the threatening impact of the hostility and indifference of the larger community. With this kind of inner reinforcement, it is possible for the ego structure to withstand the shattering impact of the wider rejection.[6] [my brackets]

One can see in the above quotation that Thurman understood and valued the sense of self that black people gained from having their own institutions, and the cultural and ethical values that could be transmitted to the community through them. He also recognized the value of the symbols of ethnic identification internationally. He cites the example of Japan as a non-white nation confronting white western nations in the Second World War, Indians resisting the British, and African leaders speaking at the United Nations as all having an important impact upon black communities locally and globally. He saw in these diverse examples that the symbolic and actual viewing of the empowerment of people of color undermined the notion of white supremacy that was so prevalent in this era.[7]

While Thurman viewed this empowerment as positive, he was less predisposed to the idea of racialized pride or Black Power as an end itself. Although he does not devote many words to it or define it in clear terms, Thurman speaks of a "Black Chauvinism" that he finds compelling for its passion but ultimately flawed because he feels it is based on an idea that will only continue to fuel hostility between whites and blacks. Therefore, he regards black chauvinism as valiant but self-defeating, and insists that the way forward must involve blacks and whites as equal citizens living harmoniously. He states: "To forget this is the great betrayal of the future."[8]

In sum, Thurman articulates a nuanced view of black identity and black institutions in the face of segregation, He understands their value and importance, but does not regard the embracing of a black identity as the ultimate determinant in regards to ending segregation and bringing about a better future for African Americans and others.

I think there is great value in Thurman's position that has utility in the contested post-racial era. It is evident that black institutions such as the church are still the conduit of values and ways of being that uplift community, however, I also think that Thurman shows that notions of blackness as wholly positive should not go unquestioned. He articulates this with regard to relations between black and white, but I would argue that in these contested times the interrogation and analysis of identity must include intersections with other identities such as gender, class, and sexual orientation. In a transnational context such as that being considered here between blacks in the United States and South Africa, there is also a need to include analyses of ways racialized identities are unfolding locally and nationally in ever-changing political and economic climates within both countries. Is being black and poor in South Africa the same as being black and poor in the USA? The simple answer is that there are similarities and differences. A black transatlantic dialogue and alliance in the contemporary contested era needs to be able to accommodate the difference—even as it seeks unity—if it is not to be accused of being oppressive or insensitive to the needs of a particular black constituency. This is something to which the essay will return after a consideration of the ideas of Boesak in relation to black identity and the black community.

Boesak's position regarding the role of black identity and consciousness in the context of Christian community is that it should be embraced as an essential (though, in some ways, still pending) component of the liberation struggle. He writes, "Black Theology is the theological reflection of black Christians on the situation in which they live and on their struggle for liberation. Blacks ask: What does it mean to believe in Jesus Christ when one is black and living in a world controlled by white racists?"[9] For Boesak, the answer to this question is for black people to embrace a sense of black theological and societal self-determination. Doing so requires blacks to throw off the shackles of white Christian reasoning and find their own voice, which is the voice of liberation. Liberation in this instance means liberation from racism, poverty, and other forms of oppression that prevent blacks and other oppressed people from realizing their true humanity. Boesak's assertion of black identity is more forceful than that espoused by Thurman. For example, he affirms the idea of black self-affirmation and black self-love as a way of finding one's humanity. However, Boesak, like Thurman, is nuanced in his expression of what blackness means in relation to the wider society. He argues that the expression of black identity through black theological reflection is contextual, that is, it speaks to and supports the experience of black people in their struggles, but it is not exclusivist: "It has in common with all the struggles in the Third World, the search for identity, genuine humanity and a truly human life."[10] Furthermore, it is not explicitly color coded: "Blackness does not in the first place designate color of skin. It is a discovery, a state of mind, a conversion, an affirmation of being which is power."[11]

For Boesak this identification is a new way of thinking, but it is tied to and related to older forms—in particular, to African traditions. He argues that there should not be a distinction between African theology and black theology; instead, black people should reach into their past and look at their traditions that have been dismissed by white society to see what can be utilized for liberation and a positive future. He adds, "There is also a call for the church to go (back) to the roots of broken African community and tradition. It must examine why certain traditions were considered wholesome for the African community and whether these traditions can have a humanizing influence on contemporary society."[12] Boesak is not advocating an uncritical acceptance of African heritage, but rather acknowledging that it can be an important resource for an oppressed people trying to free themselves mentally and culturally from white domination.

Although black identity and black self-worth are critically important for Boesak, rather than embracing blackness as an end in itself, he argues for a Christ-centered ethic of liberation as the final arbiter. He fears that some forms of black theological discourse are in danger of making blackness a religion in its own right:

> Black Theology's situation is the situation of blackness. We have warned earlier
> that a contextual theology should remain critical and prophetic with regard to
> its own situational experience, because it is critical reflection under the Word of
> God. This means that the liberation praxis is finally judged not by the demands
> of the situation, but by the liberating gospel of Jesus Christ. The danger of a
> contextual theology being over-ruled by the situational experience and as a result
> succumbing to absolutistic claims is very real.[13]

Boesak, like Thurman, is wary of a notion of blackness as the sole basis for liberation and of the quest for a new humanity. He, too, looks for a broader ethic and religious platform on which to ground this sense of blackness, and he locates this platform in the word of God, where he identifies God as liberator.

I think Boesak's focus on blackness as expressed through liberation-oriented theological reflections is important and does have value for the contemporary moment. It can be argued that although the formal mechanisms of apartheid have been dismantled, economic and social disadvantage are still the reality for the vast majority of black South Africans, thereby making liberation a persistently crucial issue. If one widens the perspective to look at African and African diasporic communities across the globe, generally they are still amongst the poorest, the sickest, and the most exploited people on earth. Even when taking into account diverse contexts of African experiences across time and space, this continued lack of equality in comparison with other groups is still stark. Boesak's *Farewell to Innocence* certainly speaks to this reality.

In the work of both Boesak and Thurman, one sees an admiration for blackness as a tool of empowerment and unification for oppressed peoples. They both, however, stop short of regarding blackness as the ultimate means by which oppression for African peoples and others will be ended. Black identity is a partial lens through which the vision of a better society may be realized, but it is not the sole vantage point. This is a very useful way of conceptualizing black identity, in that it opens up space for multiple forms of identity to emerge and be expressed. It enables us to get closer to passing the self-test[14] and resonates with what Cornel West describes as a prophetic framework for conceptualizing black identity that is based on moral reasoning, rather than solely on racialized ideals of black authenticity. What he articulates is important and worth quoting here as a basis for transatlantic dialogue and unity:

> The undermining and dismantling of the framework of racial reasoning—especially the basic notions of black authenticity, closed-ranks mentality, and black cultural conservatism—lead toward a new framework of black thought and practice. This new framework should be a prophetic one of moral reasoning with its fundamental ideas of a mature black identity, coalition strategy, and black cultural democracy.[15]

Having explored the dimensions of blackness in the two texts by Boesak and Thurman, our attention now turns to whiteness.

In Relation to Whiteness

If blackness is not the ultimate vehicle for the creation of a new society, is whiteness the ultimate impediment to its realization? How should blacks relate to whites in the contemporary era? Thurman and Boesak are both insightful when addressing these questions as they relate to segregation and apartheid.

In his analysis, Thurman articulates a view of whiteness under segregation as a world of its own, a system of thought and practice that impinged heavily on black life, but which regarded itself as operating above and beyond moral injunctions stemming from black culture. In turn, whiteness (with all of its supremacist and exclusionary connotations) was viewed by African Americans in the southern United States as outside, and counter to, acceptable societal norms and values, as Thurman outlines when talking about his childhood experience:

> [I]t never occurred to me, nor was I taught either at home or in church, to regard white persons as falling within the scope of the magnetic field of my morality. To all white persons, the category of exception applied .... They were in a world apart, in another universe of discourse. To lie to them or to deceive them had no moral relevancy; no category of guilt was involved in my behavior. There was fear of their power over my life.[16]

From this quote one can discern that whiteness under segregation was both real and surreal. It was real in terms of the strictures it could impose upon black lives, but unreal in the sense that it could not be touched or challenged. Thurman further outlines this sense of the real and surreal with regard to processes whereby whites framed laws to restrict black access to services and amenities, while ensuring whites had ready access to these same things. Hence even as they framed laws supposedly based on principles that were meant to serve all, whites were acting above and beyond the law. Thurman recalls that as a black person growing up in the segregated South, he was restricted in what he could do and where he could go by processes established by whites, although whites could freely enter black spaces (including churches) with impunity, flouting the very conventions that they established.[17]

The sense that whites under segregation had flexibility but were amoral is a recurring theme in the text. They would use laws to punish, restrict, manage, and dehumanize African Americans, but they were not subject to the law when it pertained to their relations with black people. The laws of segregation were for the protection and maintenance of whiteness as a system of power and privilege:

> What the law means is set forth in the behavior and actions of the sheriff and policeman. More often than not, such officers are also white. This means that the creators of the law are white, the interpreters of the law are white, and the enforcers of the law are white. There is little respect for the "majesty of the law" or confidence in the fairness and equality of the law . . . . The felt helplessness of the Negro before the law is notorious.[18]

The contradictoriness of a whiteness that operated outside the scope of moral and ethical decency, whilst framing blacks within such a code, was also very much in evidence within the life of the church. Thurman makes the point that white Christians have made it a key goal to convert as many people of all races as possible to the faith, but at the same time they are tacit in their approval of an evil that goes against the core principles of Christianity:

> To be specific: because a man is a Christian is no indication to me what his attitude may be toward me in any given circumstance . . . . It is to be understood that the curious distortion or corruption of the doctrine of grace supports a social attitude that is completely foreign to the mood and the spirit of the doctrine itself. Consequently, it is entirely possible that I, for instance, can work for the redemption of the souls of people, help them in their need in many critical ways, while at the same time keep them out of my neighborhood, out of my school

and out of my local church. And all of this with no apparent conflict in values or disturbance of conscience.[19]

What Thurman outlines here is of critical importance. Whiteness has still not been sufficiently held to account for the atrocities of apartheid or segregation. There has been little or no compensation—and very limited justice—for African Americans and black South Africans for the indignities and injustice that they suffered and continue to suffer as a result of these crimes against black humanity. In the contested post-racial era, an opposing set of ideas is once again gaining currency. In this interpretation, the victims of apartheid and segregation are asked to take responsibility and accountability for their own plight, as if the atrocities of the recent past have no bearing on the present.[20] This is an intolerable state of affairs and must be unmasked for what it is: whiteness operating above and beyond the laws of morality.

In explaining the title of his book *Farewell to Innocence*, Boesak reveals that it is a farewell for both whites and blacks. With regard to whites, it is a farewell to what he regards as a sham or pseudo innocence, whereby whites refuse to acknowledge and take responsibility for their actions in sustaining and perpetuating injustice against blacks, while still claiming to live the virtuous Christian life. For Boesak, whites need to jettison these vestiges of falsehood if genuine reconciliation in the society is to be achieved:

> It is a farewell to innocence for white people. In order to maintain the status quo, it is necessary for whites to believe, and keep on believing, that they are innocent. They are innocent because they "just happen to have the superior position in the world," or, in some mysterious way they have been placed in a position of leadership (guardianship) over blacks by nature, by virtue of their "superior" culture, or by God.[21]

Here and in his broader attack in the text on Afrikaner Christian nationalism, Boesak indicates whites have hypocritically used the guise of Christianity to maintain their privileges and power in South Africa's majority-black society.[22] For Boesak, though, whiteness is not some mystical entity that exists outside the parameters of society in the way that Thurman's articulation of whiteness might imply. Boesak is keen to identify whiteness as a system of power and privilege. Although not condemning white people in general, Boesak is clear about the extent to which the white power structure oppressing blacks is a problem: "The 'white power structure' far from being just a term, represents a reality blacks encounter every day. It represents the economic, political, cultural, religious and psychological forces which confine the realities of black experience. Concretely for black South Africans the white power structure is manifested in apartheid."[23] In spite of the atrocities committed by the white power structure, Boesak does not advocate hatred of whites; rather, he argues that genuine reconciliation will only be possible when justice has been realized. A key aspect of this justice is recognition of the humanity of black people, something that the white power structure, in theory and practice, has systematically sought to deny black South Africans.

Boesak, like Thurman, highlights an important ongoing aspect of black struggle that has utility for the contested post-racial era: mainly, that a closer interrogation of white privilege and white power structures is required. White institutions that have benefited and continue to benefit from the gross exploitation of black people need to be held to account. This reckoning—the crux of the hope of a better society—needs to occur if genuine justice and reconciliation is to be achieved, and is.

The Basis for a Better Society

For both Thurman and Boesak, the basis of a better society comes from renewal of spirituality. For Boesak, this renewal is premised upon liberation, whereas for Thurman, the search for the human in oneself and in the other is what ultimately brings about transformation. For both men, liberation and transformation take them beyond the bounds of "race." Thurman puts the matter this way:

> The burden of being black and the burden of being white is so heavy that it is rare in our society to experience oneself as a human being . . . . Precisely what does it mean to experience oneself as a human being? In the first place, it means that the individual must have a sense of kinship to life that transcends and goes beyond the immediate kinship of family or the organic kinship that binds him ethnically or "racially" or nationally. He has to feel that he belongs to his total environment.[24]

For Thurman, the sense of what it means to be human and to relate to others as fully human is triggered by the imagination and a desire to reach beyond oneself. He believes that religion provides the basis for this pursuit, but he laments the fact that the Christian Church, in failing to live up to its ethic of love and its commitment to the brotherhood and sisterhood of all believers, has failed to deliver the better society. Thurman still feels, however, that the positive effects of spirituality that contribute to the better society, even if not evident in churches, are nonetheless being felt within the wider community: "There is a spirit abroad in life of which the Judaeo-Christian ethic is but one expression. It is the spirit that makes for wholeness and for community."[25]

Thurman goes on to cite examples of situations in which he sees this spirit working to bring about positive changes in society, including in the courts, in non-violent protests, and in ecumenical gatherings where social divisions based on sex, race, and other social differences are transcended. Thurman's vision is quite an ethereal view of the better society as it could be everywhere and nowhere, making it impossible to verify or disprove empirically.

Boesak's quest for a new society focuses on liberation, but in the final chapter of *Farewell to Innocence* he asks himself and other black theologians what is meant by liberation. If one is seeking to be free from racist oppression and to live in a new society, can that society be genuinely new if racism is no longer evident, but other forms of oppressive practice, such as sexism and poverty are still in existence? Boesak argues that this is situation is unacceptable: "Black Theology, as an integral part of the theology of liberation realizes this and in its ethic seeks solidarity (true solidarity!) with oppressed people all over the world. In this way it will become clear that racism is but one incidental dimension of oppression against which the total struggle should be waged."[26]

For Boesak it is incumbent upon the church to be engaged in bringing about a new society by engaging in socio-political affairs and working on behalf of the oppressed as a group. He states that while his vision for a new society based on justice and equal relations between black and white may be considered utopian, the black vision of freedom throughout history has been a utopian one. In his final thoughts he tries to capture the essence of this vision: "Black Theology sincerely believes that it is possible to re-capture what was sacred in the African community long before white people came— solidarity, respect for life, humanity and community. It must be possible not only to recapture it, but to enhance it and bring it to full fruition in contemporary society."[27]

Boesak offers a compelling vision for contemporary society, one based on solidarity, humanity, and community free from racism and other exploitative oppressive practices. But whether such a society is based upon an appeal to the past on its own, or, as Thurman suggests, a spiritual awakening of our human potential, I am not convinced that we will arrive there. Nevertheless, the work of these two luminaries of black transatlantic religious and political thought does provide a way of thinking about how black transatlantic faith-based alliances that can be formed and hopefully maintained in the pursuit of the better society.

The Basis for Black Trans-National Alliances

Drawing on the work of Thurman and Boesak, here I want to go farther and lift up the methodological importance of transnational constructions as a means of forming new, non-oppressive formations of black solidarities across boundaries of race, gender, sexuality, and nationality. By constructions I mean the making or forging of black solidarities as unfolding identities and experiences that are made and continually re-made by ideas, circumstances, and interpretations of local, national, and transnational experiences. In overcoming localism, such transnational constructions potentially lead toward ending the "isms," phobias, and exploitative practices that have cast such a negative shadow over the lives of so many across Africa and the African diaspora over the last five hundred years. "Construction" connotes building, and in the case of black theology, the black aspect should not be viewed as static and fixed, or as amorphous and springing from nowhere and going nowhere. Rather, it should be seen as a point of departure for a process of constructive dialogue and exchange of ideas. The construction of racialized identities that have been the foundations for black social, political, and religious projects (such as Garveyism, pan-Africanism, black consciousness, and black theology) occurred primarily as a response to the dehumanizing practices engendered by white supremacy. To a degree, these philosophies and ideological constructions have been successful. Formal apartheid has ended, formal segregation is over, and Africa is free from colonial rule. However it is also apparent that the constructors of these racialized projects were primarily men who, relative to the vast majority of African peoples, were members of elites. And their maleness, elite circumstances, and experiences influenced the constructions of black political and religious discourses in the twentieth century and left some elements of the black experience—notably women—largely marginalized. In this chapter it is not possible to unravel all the implications behind the framing of these constructions, but only to suggest that in the twenty-first century, we can learn from the past and construct social, political, economic, and religious racialized projects that are more sensitive to our times, less absolutist in nature, and less oppressive to minorities both within and outside the umbrella of the black experience.[28]

Conclusion

Tuesday, July 10, 2012, in London I had the privilege of seeing two master craftsmen come together to perform a musical masterpiece. Winton Marsalis and

Jacub Addy, with their musicians from, respectively, the Lincoln Centre Jazz Orchestra and Adudia, transfixed the audience with a piece entitled "Congo Square." The work, first performed in 2006, combines continental African voices and drums with African American inspired jazz to produce a remarkable fusion of African continental and African diasporic sound. It was twenty-first century pan-Africanism in action. The piece Congo was named after a place in New Orleans where slaves and free Africans were able to perform their music at the height of the enslavement period, with the performance by Marsalis and Addy evoking a past where the sound and sense of Africa came together for slaves within the hostile environment of the antebellum slave South. Marsalis and Addy, however, were not engaged in a natural process. The twenty-first century Congo Square had to be constructed. Addy and Marsalis had to think, work, and critically engage with each other's tradition, style, and artistry in order to forge a transatlantic partnership and produce the spectacular.[29]

The lesson from the modern "Congo Square" is that rather than imposing an overarching idea of unity, what is needed within the contested post-racialized era will have to emanate from a constructive dialogue and engagement between separate groups as has been attempted here using the work of Thurman and Boesak. Within such a process, each party will need to recognize the local particularity of its articulation, and also that it is born out of localized experiences that have echoes and resonances that potentially reach across national and international boundaries. Nevertheless, in order to speak with a genuine transnational voice, local black contexts have to share with each other in a spirit of humility, realizing that no one expression speaks for all, forging and fashioning ways of speaking and listening that can feed into other cultural points of reference while engaging in mutual sharing and understanding that creates something new. Hopefully, as this pursuit of transcendent unity reaches various quarters, black churches will bring much to inform that unity, looking to the prophetic traditions that have informed so much of what has been best within black church praxis.

Notes

1. Howard Thurman, *The Luminous Darkness: A Personal Interpretation of the Anatomy of Segregation and the Ground of Hope* (New York: Harper and Row, 1965).

2. Allan Boesak, *Farewell to Innocence: A Socio-Ethical Study on Black Theology and Power* (Maryknoll, NY: Orbis Books, 1976).

3. Jacquelyn Grant, "Black Theology and the Black Woman," in Cornel West and Eddie S. Glaude Jr., eds., *African American Thought: An Anthology* (Louisville: Westminster John Knox Press, 2003), 841.

4. Thurman, *The Luminous Darkness*, 8.

5. Ibid., x.

6. Ibid., 30.

7. Ibid., 53–54.

8. Ibid., 58.

9. Boesak, *Farewell to Innocence*, 1.

10. Ibid., 15.

11. Ibid., 139.

12. Ibid., 141.

13. Ibid., 143.

14. Grant, "Black Theology and the Black Woman," 841.

15. Cornel West, *Race Matters* (New York: Vintage, 1994), 43.

16. Thurman, *The Luminous Darkness*, 3.

17. Ibid., 11–12.

18. Ibid., 80.

19. Ibid., 60.

20. R. D. G. Kelley, "Building a Progressive Movement in 2012," *Souls: A Critical Journal of Black Politics, Culture and Society* 14., No. 2 (2012): 10–18.

21. Boesak, *Farewell to Innocence*, 4.

22. Ibid., 111–16.

23. Ibid., 57.

24. Thurman, *The Luminous* Darkness, 94.

25. Ibid., 112.

26. Boesak, *Farewell to* Innocence, 151.

27. Ibid., 152.

28. W. Ackah, "Back to Black, or Diversity in the Diaspora? Re-imagining Pan-African Christian Identity in the Twenty-First Century," *Black Theology: An International Journal* 8, No. 3 (2010): 341–56.

29. A. Addy, *Guardian*, July 6, 2012 http://www.theguardian.com/music/2012/jul/06/wynton-marsalis-yacub-addy (accessed January 14, 2013).

Contextuality of Black Experience and Contributions to a Wider Debate

Anthony G. Reddie

The questions pertaining to social justice, blackness, and the promises of transcendence that have been addressed by my colleague William Ackah are specific contextual questions that have their resonances in nation states such as South Africa and the United States of America. In contexts where racialized oppression has sadly been part of the socio-political landscape, the issues explored in the previous essay have been more than necessary. In this brief piece, I want to build on the crucial insights provided by Ackah and seek to place the discussion of the contextuality of black experience into a broader framework—specifically, placing this discourse within the conceptual paradigms offered us by the study of contextual theology.

Throughout this book we have witnessed various authors seeking to problematize the contested ways in which human experience and the wider contexts in which lives are lived are juxtaposed with the trans-historical nature of Christianity. Given the role this religious framework has played transatlantic chattel slavery and colonialism—the subterranean paradigms that resonate to the scholarly activism of both Allan Boesak and Howard Thurman—the global phenomenon that is Christianity has always posed a number of challenging dilemmas for African peoples.

Juxtaposing the context-bound realities of human experience with the trans-historical nature of religion is not a new struggle for African peoples. This struggle takes on even greater import in light of the challenges presented by socially constructed notions of race that abound within such discourse. This dialectic of immanence versus transcendence is not new. In the late 1970s, Lawrence Jones, wrote this about the black experience in America: "The Black religious community has not had the luxury of dichotomizing faith and work, or religion and life, or the sacred and the secular. There is surely one beam of light it has to cast. The interface between time and eternity has always defined an area of tension in the Black religious community, the hopes of which have been directed at both."[1]

The challenges presented by faith and context (in which material cultures are incubated) are not new. The first major debates concerning this relationship emerged in the middle of the last century. The classic work on Christ and culture was written by H. Richard Niebuhr in the early 1950s.[2] Niebuhr offers a number of models for illustrating how the phenomenon of Christ at the center of Christianity engages with broader cultures within specific environments in which faith in Christ is located. Niebuhr's work was an attempt to create all-embracing taxonomies for detailing the locus of authority for how the religious life was to be lived within differing socio-political contexts. Niebuhr's formulations of Christ with, against, above, within, and transcending culture, and as a corollary context, have given rise in more recent times to the pioneering work of the likes of Stephen Bevans[3] and Robert Schreiter.[4] These writers have shown the extent to which the universal phenomenon that is Christianity is always tempered by its local expression in any particular space, place, and time.

This book provides a particular perspective on the broader hinterland of contextual realities—particularly those that pertain to contested notions of race and identity alongside religious faith and practice. While this work addresses issues as they pertain to the nexus of faith and context, it should not be seen as being overly concerned with the more specific question of how the Christian faith engages with the materiality of cultures. Debates on material cultures call for a more specific concern. The issue of how the Christian faith engages with the cultures in which the church is located has generated a great deal of academic thought. The academic study of Christianity and its relationship to culture, and how the latter can inform and impact on the practice of the former, is called "inculturation."[5] Questions pertaining to the nexus of Christianity and the cultures in which the faith is incubated, particularly as they relate to questions of worship and religious practice, are specific questions for liturgists and specialist scholars in the area of inculturation.[6]

Perhaps the most important voice in the contemporary discourse looking critically at the relationship between Christianity and context is Stephen Bevans. Bevans is a Euro-American, Roman Catholic scholar who has done a great deal of work assessing differing models of contextual theology, illustrating the relationship between religious faith and the cultures and settings in which that faith is located.[7] What Bevans terms "contextual theology" is in many respects simply a description of what has existed within the Christian faith from its earliest days—an ongoing, dynamic relationship between the faith as it has been developed across history, and the interpretation and expression of that faith in a specific socio-cultural environment. The localized expression of faith represents the very heart of contextual theology. Bevans describes the concept thus: "First of all, contextual theology understands the nature of theology in a new way. . . . Theology that is contextual realizes that culture, history, contemporary thought forms, and so forth are to be considered along with scripture and tradition as valid sources for theological expression."[8]

Of the different models of contextual theology Bevans outlines, the one that most reflects the central concerns of this book is the praxis model, an approach that emphasizes faithful action for social change.[9] In outlining the praxis model of contextual theology, Bevans highlights the means by which the various theological models identified within this typology express an element of identity politics. Whether in terms of feminist theology, queer theology, Dalit theology, or—most pertinent to this text—[10] black liberation theology, each model of theological expression utilizes the subjective experiences of subjugated people within a specific historical context as the point of departure in detailing the faith-based activism that subsequently gains expression in that particular socio-political milieu.[11] Angie Pears's work on contextual theology offers a helpful précis of the varying genres or approaches to situated, identity-based forms of theological reflection, including those frameworks whose modus operandi is confronting the stultifying effects of race-based thinking and action. In this respect, black liberation theology can be seen as a particularized form of contextual theology.[12]

In a number of the essays in this book, one can deduce that black liberation theology (black theology for short) is an important substratum. Black theology is not only a form of contextual theology, it is also a theology of liberation. Black theology like other theologies of liberation, emerges from specific locations and reflects the concrete experiences of particular groups of people who have been marginalized and oppressed for a number of reasons. All theologies of liberation[13] (indeed all theologies per se) are contextual. By this, I mean that the nature of any theological enterprise is influenced by and responds to the critical issues and experiences of the people in a particular time and space in their relationship to God. It is important to note, however, that while all theologies are contextual, some theologies of liberation, such as black theology, are not always contextual or liberative in character.

Indeed, a number of essays in this text have addressed the oppressive nature of Afrikaans theology, the white theology of the Dutch Reformed Church, which was distinctly oppressive for non-white people in South Africa. There is no doubting the contextual character of this theology, reflecting as it did the environmental and cultural milieu of the Boers and the broader white communities of South Africa. But by no stretch of the imagination could this theological perspective be described as liberative, or as an authentic theology of liberation. It is my contention that this book is offering something more incisive than merely a form of contextual theology. While not all contributors in this work would want to identify themselves or their work with the nomenclature of black theology, I have no doubt that the notion of liberative change remains at the heart of all the pieces in this work. Theologies of liberation do not merely reflect the contextual character of a particular cultural context, rather they seek to re-imagine and transform by means of a commitment to liberative praxis[14]. In using this term, I am speaking of the reflective faith-based activism that is committed to actualizing the liberative gospel of Jesus Christ and the "upside down" values of the Kingdom of God.[15]

It is this important distinction that brings me to a critical impasse with regard to Bevans's otherwise very fine work. Bevans's work lacks historical resonance regarding contested notions of reality, a deficiency that is rather alarming in what is often seen as a definitive work on contextual theology. In attempting to create a systematic framework, detailing differing taxonomies for the relationship of the Christian faith with the context in which it is rooted, Bevans has ignored the messiness of the context itself, which shapes the very nature of the contextual theological enterprise.

What the current volume demonstrates is that simply outlining differing models of contextual theology at the level of analytical discourse is inadequate when placed within the crises of historical projects. In the contexts in which Howard Thurman and Allan Boesak exercised their prophetic ministries, we see a critical dialectic at play that is essentially concerned with the relationship between power and epistemology. Knowledge and notions of truth are linked intractably with social and political hegemony and those possessing the ability to impose an idea of truth upon another—or indeed to deny the truth of the other. It is interesting to note that the question of which model of contextual theology is best arrives quite late in Bevans's thinking (appearing on pages 139–40 in a book consisting of 180 or so pages) and then without any conclusive declaration. This book, however, offers critical insight into the specific, concrete challenges posed to contextual theology, in that it seeks to identify with various forms of situation-specific theologies in order to shed light on the ways in which faith has interacted with the historical experiences, narratives, and cultures that have impacted on and shaped the lives of black people in specific contexts.

In more recent times, black and womanist[16] theologians have written at length on the nature and the theo-political importance and substance of the black body. While a good deal of early black theology concentrated on the damage racist and anti-black rhetoric and racialized teachings had exerted on the black mind, giving rise to significant levels of self-hatred,[17] later black scholars have focused on the theological significance of the visible black body. Of particular note is the work of Anthony Pinn[18] and Shawn Copeland.[19]

If one considers the violence unleashed on such innocent figures as Emmett Till in the United States in 1955, or on Stephen Lawrence in Britain in 1993—both, apparently, for the crime of simply being black—one is reminded of the continued political charge of being a human being in a black body. The challenge for any contextual theology that arises from black experience is the necessity of engaging with the deeply political and subversive reality of affirming black embodiment, cognizant that the very acknowledgment and celebration of blackness can remain unacceptable—often in terms of marketing and subsequent profit margins.[20]

The import of this text is that it adds to the repository of knowledge regarding the efficacy of contextual theology, but does so with a critical specificity that cannot be ignored. As Ackah demonstrates when outlining the searing prophetic scholarly activism of Thurman and Boesak, both theologians are constructing challenging ripostes to what are undeniably racist and myopic forms of religious truth. The truth of their assertions about the aberrant nature of white supremacy cannot be denied. One may disagree with their challenges to the warped religio-political conception of white normality achieved at the expense of blackness, but one surely cannot miss the epistemological challenge that lies in their theological articulation and its resultant praxis (they are asserting the falsehood of particular forms of white supremacist models of contextual theology, be they located on the continent of Africa south of the Limpopo River, or in the Deep South of the United States.

The work on black embodiment by black and womanist scholars—particularly within the context of contextual theological analysis—is crucial because it locates the possibilities of redemption and transcendence within the bounded realities of the immanent world in which black lives (indeed all lives) are lived. While there is no doubting that all people are in the business of creating theological frameworks that affirm their sense of what it means to be a human being, the fact that one's notion of contextual theology emerges from within the corpus of black bodies and within black historical experiences and cultures is of great importance. As Emmanuel Eze has shown, in the Enlightenment, the so-called age of reason, one still finds conceptualizations of black people predicated on the notion that they represent lower forms of humanity and so are incapable of the kinds of creative transformations that are considered the preserve of white Europeans.[21]

The present volume builds on the legacy bequeathed us by such thinkers by arguing that some models of contextual theology are diametrically opposed to some others. Dwight Hopkins, drawing on the work of James

Cone, the founding father of black theology, makes it clear that notions of liberation as understood within the economy of God are not compatible with all conceptualizations of God: "For Cone, Jesus is not for everybody in an abstract universal theological anthropology. Jesus is for the oppressed, whose true human identities arise in their struggle for Liberation."[22] Hopkins's work outlines many of the theological and methodological debates rehearsed under the rubric of contextual theology. For example, what are the dangers of collapsing and limiting the transcendent elements of religious faith within the narrow purview of contextual realities? As many of the essays in this volume demonstrate, it is difficult to combine social activism with religious convictions in ways that do not sacrifice faith on the altar of politics.

I would like to suggest, in a modest fashion, that perhaps the gift of this text is that it seeks to provide rich contextual specificity to the larger debates that have abounded within contextual theology over the past half-century or so. In so doing, it offers a challenge to the more generic, systemic treatment of the subject provided by such luminaries as Bevans. This work falls within the broader arena of contextual theology, but it does more than simply outline the analytical framework for what constitutes the methodological and epistemological articulation for an authentic expression of this discipline. Instead, the thrust of this work lies in the praxiological challenge of seeking to live holistically, as black people, in worlds not fashioned by ourselves, but by others with power, and to do so faithfully for the God and the religious traditions of which we are a part. This is not a new challenge, but as argued by the work in this text, it is a one that confronts black people within the differing contexts of South Africa and the United States of America.

Notes

1. Lawrence N. Jones, "Hope for Mankind: Insights from Black Religious History in the United States," *Journal of Religious Thought* 34, No. 2 (Fall–Winter 1978): 59.

2. See H. Richard Niebuhr, *Christ and Culture*, 50th anniversary ed. (San Francisco: Harper Collins, 2002).

3. See Stephen B. Bevans, *Models of Contextual Theology* (Maryknoll, NY: Orbis Books, 2002).

4. See Robert Schreiter, *Constructing Local Theologies* (Maryknoll, NY: Orbis Books, 1985).

5. See Gerald A. Arbuckle, *Earthing, the Gospel: An Inculturation Handbook for Pastoral Workers* (Eugene, OR: Wipf and Stock, 2002).

6. An excellent text in this regard is Michael N. Jagessar and Stephen Burns, *Christian Worship: Postcolonial Perspectives* (Sheffield: Equinox, 2011).

7. See Bevans, *Models of Contextual Theology.*

8. Ibid, 3–4

9. Ibid., 70–87.

10. One of the best texts that outlines the various types of contextual theology (as opposed to models or methods) is Angie Pears, *Doing Contextual Theology* (London: Routledge, 2009).

11. Bevans, *Models of Contextual Theology*, 70–87.

12. Pears, *Doing Contextual Theology*, 110–17.

13. The nomenclature of theologies of liberation refers to a group of socio-political theologies that seek to re-interpret the central meaning of the God event within history— particularly in terms of the life, death, and resurrection of Jesus the Christ. They provide a politicized, radical, and socially transformative understanding of the Christian faith in light of the lived realities and experiences of the poor, the marginalized, and the oppressed. For further details on the wider family of theologies of liberation, see Marcella Althaus-Reid, Ivan Patrella, and Luis Carlos Susin (eds.), *Another Possible World* (London: SCM, 2007).

14. Emmanuel Lartey provides a helpful analytical synthesis of theologies of liberation that articulates the central tenets of contextual theology alongside a commitment to practical theological engagement with the lived realities and experiences of people in a particular time and space. See Emmanuel Lartey, "Practical Theology as a Theological Form," in James Woodward and Stephen Pattison, eds., *The Blackwell Reader in Pastoral and Practical Theology* (Oxford: Blackwell, 2000), 128–34.

15. The centrality of this concept to theologies of liberation, particularly black theology, is addressed in Anthony G. Reddie, *SCM Core Text: Black Theology* (London: SCM Press, 2012), 1–26.

16. Womanist theology is the theological articulation of God as understood through the experiences of black (predominantly African American) women. It seeks to address the tripartite jeopardy of being black, female, and poor in the wealthiest nation in the world. Significant womanist theological texts include Jacquelyn Grant, *White Women's Christ and Black Women's Jesus* (Atlanta: Scholars Press, 1989); Delores Williams, *Sisters in the Wilderness: The Challenge of Womanist God-Talk* (Maryknoll, NY: Orbis Press, 1993); Kelly Brown Douglas, *The Black Christ* (Maryknoll, NY: Orbis Books, 1994); Emile Townes, *Womanist Justice, Womanist Hope* (Atlanta: Scholars Press, 1993); Renita J. Weems, *Just a Sister Away: A Womanist Vision of Women's Relationships in the Bible* (Philadelphia: Innisfree Press, 1988); Katie G. Cannon, *Black Womanist Ethics* (Atlanta: Scholars Press, 1988); Stacey Floyd-Thomas, ed., *Deeper Shade of Purple: Womanism in Religion and Society* (New York: New York University Press, 2006); and Monica A. Coleman, *Making a Way Out of No Way: A Womanist Theology* (Minneapolis: Fortress Press, 2008).

17. Vincent Harding, "Black Power and the American Christ," in Gayraud S. Wilmore and James H. Cone, eds., *Black Theology: A Documentary History, 1966–1979* (Maryknoll, NY: Orbis Books, 1979), 35–42. See also James H. Cone, *Black Theology and Black Power* (1969; Maryknoll, NY: Orbis Books, 1997), 5–30, and Walter Rodney, *The Groundings with My Brothers* (1969; London: Bogle-L-Ouverture Publications, 1990).

18. See Anthony B. Pinn, *Terror and Triumph: The Nature of Black Religion* (Minneapolis: Fortress Press, 2003); Anthony B. Pinn and Dwight N. Hopkins, eds., *Loving The Body: Black Religious Studies and the Erotic* (New York: Palgrave Macmillan, 2004); Anthony B. Pinn, "Sweaty Bodies in a Circle: Thoughts on the Subtle Dimensions of Black Religion as Protest," *Black Theology: An International Journal* 4, No. 1 (2006): 11–26; and Anthony B. Pinn, *Embodiment and the New Shape of Black Theological Thought* (New York: New York University Press, 2010).

19. See M. Shawn Copeland, *Enfleshing Freedom: Body, Race and Being* (Minneapolis: Fortress Press, 2010).

20. It is interesting to note the arguments that have been made by white editors of popular white-owned magazines dedicated to fashion and beauty, and that when such media place a black face on the cover, doing so often lowers sales of that particular issue. This issue has particular piquancy when applied to the cutthroat arena of high fashion. See http://bitchmagazine.org/article/when-tyra-met-naomi for an interesting insight into this issue. Note also the controversy that has arisen from George Lucas claiming that he was forced to self-finance *Red Tails*, the story of the Tuskegee Airmen, as Hollywood did not want to fund a film that featured an all-black cast. See http://www.huffingtonpost.com/2012/01/10/george-lucas-hollywood-di_n_1197227.html.

21. See Emmanuel C. Eze, ed., *Race and the Enlightenment* (Oxford: Wiley-Blackwell, 2008).

22. Dwight N. Hopkins, *Being Human: Race, Culture and Religion* (Minneapolis: Fortress Press, 2005), 36.

Contributors

William Ackah, PhD, is a lecturer in the Department of Geography, Environment and Development Studies and program director of BSc Community Development and Public Policy, Birkbeck, University of London. He is also a co-convener of the Transatlantic Roundtable on Religion and Race.

Allan Boesak, PhD, is Desmond Tutu Chair of Peace, Global Studies and Reconciliation at Christian Theological Seminary and Butler University in Indianapolis, Indiana.

Ebony Joy Fitchue, LSW, is a doctoral student in the School of Psychology, Howard University, in Washington, DC.

Leah Gaskin Fitchue, EdD, is president of Payne Theological Seminary in Wilberforce, Ohio.

Walter Earl Fluker, PhD, is Martin Luther King Jr. Professor of Ethical Leadership and the senior editor and director of the Howard Thurman Papers Project at Boston University.

Forrest E. Harris Sr., PhD, is president of American Baptist College in Nashville, Tennessee, and director of the Kelly Miller Smith Institute on Black Church Studies at Vanderbilt University, also in Nashville.

Nico Koopman, ThD, is a professor of systematic theology, the director of the Beyers Naudé Centre for Public Theology, and dean of the School of Theology, Stellenbosch University, in Stellenbosch, South Africa.

AnneMarie Mingo, PhD, is a post-doctoral scholar in African American studies at Pennsylvania State University in State College, Pennsylvania.

Reggie Nel, ThD, is an associate professor and head of missiology in the Department of Christian Spirituality, Church History and Missiology at the University of South Africa in Pretoria.

Chabo Freddy Pilusa is chief executive officer of FNP Communications, former president of the South African Youth Council, and former president of the Anglican Student Federation in South Africa.

Anthony G. Reddie, PhD, is a visiting fellow at Aston University in Birmingham, England, and editor of *Black Theology: An International Journal*.

Rev. Boitumelo Senokoane is a lecturer in the Department of Philosophy and Systematic Theology at the University of South Africa in Pretoria.

R. Drew Smith, PhD, is a professor of urban ministry at Pittsburgh Theological Seminary, a research fellow at the University of South Africa in Pretoria, and a co-convener of the Transatlantic Roundtable on Religion and Race.

Rothney S. Tshaka, ThD, is chair of Philosophy and Systematic Theology at University of South Africa in Pretoria, and is a co-convener of the Transatlantic Roundtable on Religion and Race.

Luci Vaden is a doctoral student in history at the University of South Carolina in Columbia.

Vuyani Vellem, PhD, is director of the Centre for Public Theology and senior lecturer in the Department of Dogmatics and Christian Ethics at the University of Pretoria School of Theology in South Africa.

Rev. Cobus van Wyngaard is a research assistant in the Department of Philosophy, Practical and Systematic Theology at the University of South Africa in Pretoria.

Index

CPSIA information can be obtained
at www.ICGtesting.com
Printed in the USA
BVHW08s1000120618
518452BV00001B/3/P